MW01170199

VIRAL SOVEREIGNTY AND TECHNOLOGY TRANSFER

In the global infectious-disease research community, there has long been uncertainty about the conditions under which biological resources may be studied or transferred out of countries. This work examines the reasons for that uncertainty and shows how global biomedical research has been shaped by international disputes over access to biological resources. Bringing together government leaders, World Health Organization officials, and experts in virology, wildlife biology, clinical ethics, technology transfer, and international law, the book identifies the critical problems – and implications of these problems – posed by negotiating for access and sharing benefits, and proposes solutions to ensure that biomedical advances are not threatened by global politics. Written in accessible, nontechnical language, this work should be read by anyone who sees global health and biomedical research as a priority for international lawmakers.

Sam Halabi is the Manley O. Hudson Professor of Law at the University of Missouri. He is also a scholar at the O'Neill Institute for National and Global Health Law and affiliated faculty at the Center for Global Health Science and Security at Georgetown University. His previous books include *Global Management of Infectious Disease after Ebola*, *Intellectual Property and the New International Economic Order*, and *Food and Drug Regulation in an Era of Globalized Markets*. He is also the co-chair (with Gian Luca Burci) of the Ethical, Legal, and Social Implications Committee of the Global Virome Project. Professor Halabi was the 1999 First Place Prize recipient of the Elie Wiesel Foundation for Humanity Essay in Ethics prize.

Rebecca Katz is a Professor and Director of the Center for Global Health Science and Security at Georgetown University. Prior to coming to Georgetown, she spent ten years at The George Washington University as faculty in the Milken Institute School of Public Health. Her research is focused on global health security, public health preparedness, and health diplomacy. Since 2007, much of her work has been on the domestic and global implementation of the International Health Regulations. From 2004 to 2019, Dr Katz was also a consultant to the Department of State, working on issues related to the Biological Weapons Convention, pandemic influenza, and disease surveillance.

Viral Sovereignty and Technology Transfer

THE CHANGING GLOBAL SYSTEM FOR SHARING PATHOGENS FOR PUBLIC HEALTH RESEARCH

Edited by

SAM HALABI

University of Missouri-Columbia School of Law

REBECCA KATZ

Georgetown University Center for Global Health Science and Security

CAMBRIDGE
UNIVERSITY PRESS

CAMBRIDGE
UNIVERSITY PRESS

University Printing House, Cambridge CB2 8BS, United Kingdom

One Liberty Plaza, 20th Floor, New York, NY 10006, USA

477 Williamstown Road, Port Melbourne, VIC 3207, Australia

314–321, 3rd Floor, Plot 3, Splendor Forum, Jasola District Centre, New Delhi – 110025, India

79 Anson Road, #06–04/06, Singapore 079906

Cambridge University Press is part of the University of Cambridge.

It furthers the University's mission by disseminating knowledge in the pursuit of education, learning, and research at the highest international levels of excellence.

www.cambridge.org
Information on this title: www.cambridge.org/9781108484725
DOI: 10.1017/9781108676076

© Cambridge University Press 2020

This publication is in copyright. Subject to statutory exception and to the provisions of relevant collective licensing agreements, no reproduction of any part may take place without the written permission of Cambridge University Press.

First published 2020

A catalogue record for this publication is available from the British Library.

ISBN 978-1-108-48472-5 Hardback

Cambridge University Press has no responsibility for the persistence or accuracy of URLs for external or third-party internet websites referred to in this publication and does not guarantee that any content on such websites is, or will remain, accurate or appropriate.

Contents

PART II   HEALTH SECURITY, RESEARCH ETHICS,
          AND HUMAN RIGHTS IMPLICATIONS

PART III   SOLUTIONS: STANDARD MATERIAL TRANSFER
           AGREEMENTS, REPOSITORIES, AND SPECIALIZED
           INTERNATIONAL INSTRUMENTS

Maps

Tables

Contributors

Lauren Barna, MPH, US Department of Health and Human Services (HHS), Assistant Secretary for Preparedness and Response (ASPR), is the former Deputy Director of the Division of International Health Security in HHS/ASPR. In this role, Lauren helped lead partnerships, develop policy, and manage cooperative agreements to strengthen public health and medical preparedness and response at the domestic/international interface. While with HHS/ASPR, Lauren supported the policy response to numerous public health incidents spanning this domestic/international interface including the Ebola outbreaks in West Africa (2014/2015) and Democratic Republic of the Congo (2018/2019), MERS-CoV outbreaks, Zika Virus Disease (ZVD) epidemic in the Americas, and the Fukushima earthquake and nuclear incident. Lauren also played an active role in the response to the 2009 H1N1 influenza pandemic, helping support the international deployment of H1N1 vaccine via the World Health Organization (WHO).

Benjamin Berkman, JD, MPH, NIH, is a faculty member in the National Institutes of Health (NIH) Department of Bioethics where he is the head of the section on the ethics of genetics and emerging technologies. He has a joint appointment in the National Human Genome Research Institute (NHGRI), where he serves as the Deputy Director of the NHGRI Bioethics Core. He was formerly the Deputy Director of the O'Neill Institute for National and Global Health Law at Georgetown Law (2007–2009), where he continues to serve as an adjunct professor. Mr Berkman received a Bachelor's Degree in the History of Science and Medicine at Harvard University (1999). He subsequently earned a Juris Doctor and a Master's in Public Health from the University of Michigan (2005). As a faculty member in the Department of Bioethics, Mr Berkman's research interests span a wide range of topics. His current work focuses on the legal and ethical issues associated with genomic research, genetic information privacy, and clinical adoption of new genetic and reproductive technologies.

Brian Bird, Director, Ebola Operations, University California-Davis, is a virologist at the University of California Davis One Health Institute, where he leads the

"Ebola Host Project" seeking to find the animal origins of Ebola virus in West Africa (Sierra Leone, Guinea, and Liberia) as part of the USAID-PREDICT project. During his PhD training and later while employed at the US Centers for Disease Control and Prevention (CDC), he made fundamental discoveries in the molecular mechanisms of disease pathogenesis, diagnostics, and animal models for a variety of high consequence viral hemorrhagic fevers (VHF) including Ebola, Marburg, Lassa fever, Junin, Rift Valley fever, and Kyasanur forest disease viruses. This basic research led to the commercialization of recombinant vaccine candidates for Rift Valley fever virus for which multiple patents have been awarded. He was previously a US Peace Corps volunteer stationed in Kazakhstan, and later during multiple deployments in a wide variety of countries (Kenya, Uganda, Democratic Republic of Congo, South Africa, Sierra Leone, Liberia, and Tanzania) for outbreak investigations, ecological studies, technology transfer trainings, or frontline clinical diagnostic activities. During the 2014–2016 Ebola outbreak in West Africa his combined expertise as a laboratory and field scientist were utilized in the CDC Emergency Operations Center and as the lead of CDC field-diagnostic activities in Sierra Leone.

Sherry Brett-Major, JD, MS, Principal, Brett-Major Law, founded Brett-Major Law with a focus on advancing initiatives that bring innovative products to meet global needs. In addition to her current practice in intellectual property and small business matters, she has leveraged her legal, biology, chemistry, and environmental engineering expertise in policy forums ranging from environmental issues of US interagency taskforces to global development issues in health at the World Intellectual Property Organization (WIPO). Ms Brett-Major has lectured on intellectual property issues in tropical medicine and emerging and reemerging infectious diseases both in the classroom and for research groups. Most recently, Ms Brett-Major's academic interests center on how different types of law converge upon the intellectual property interests of communities and researchers. She is a graduate of the Columbus School of Law at the Catholic University of America in Washington, DC. Ms Brett-Major also holds a MS in Environmental Engineering from The Johns Hopkins University, and a BS in Biology from Old Dominion University. She is licensed to practice law in Maryland, the District of Columbia, and before the US Patent and Trademark Office (USPTO).

Gian Luca Burci, Adjunct Professor of International Law, Graduate Institute of International and Development Studies, Geneva, Switzerland; Former Legal Counsel, World Health Organization. He worked in the Legal Office of the World Health Organization from 1998 to 2016 and served as its Legal Counsel from 2005 to 2016. Professor Burci previously served as Legal Officer at the International Atomic Energy Agency in Vienna (1988–1989) and in the Office of the Legal Counsel of the United Nations in New York for nearly a decade. At the Graduate Institute he directs the joint LLM in Global Health Law and

International Institutions programme in partnership with Georgetown University. He holds a postgraduate degree in law from the Università degli Studi di Genova, Italy. His areas of expertise are the law and practice of international organizations, international immunities, global health law and governance as well as global health security. Professor Burci is the coauthor of the main reference book in English on the WHO and coeditor of the Elgar *Research Handbook on Global Health Law*.

Ruvani Chandrasekera, US Department of Health and Human Services, Assistant Secretary for Preparedness and Response, serves as a public health analyst in the Division of International Health Security (DIHS) in the Office of the Assistant Secretary for Preparedness and Response at the US Department of Health and Human Services. Within DIHS, she works on global health security policy issues pertaining to response coordination and provision and acceptance of international assistance during public health emergencies. Specifically, for the past three years, Ruvani has been leading ASPR efforts both domestically and internationally to improve the timely collection and sharing of samples related to non-influenza pathogens that have the potential to cause a public health emergency of international concern. She has worked extensively with international partners including serving as the Secretariat for the Global Health Security Initiative's Sample Sharing Task Group. Prior to joining ASPR, Ruvani spent several years managing a portfolio of global infectious disease surveillance projects for the Global Emerging Infections Surveillance (GEIS) section at the Department of Defense's Armed Forces Health Surveillance Branch (AFHSB).

Sam Halabi is the Manley O. Hudson Professor of Law at the University of Missouri-Columbia and a scholar at the O'Neill Institute for National and Global Health Law at Georgetown University. During the 2017–18 academic year, he served as the Fulbright Canada Research Chair in Health Law, Policy, and Ethics at the University of Ottawa, Ontario. Professor Halabi is a scholar of national and global health law with a specialization in health services and pharmaceutical business organizations. He is the author of *Intellectual Property and the New International Economic Order: Oligopoly, Regulation, and Wealth Redistribution in the Global Knowledge Economy* (Cambridge University Press 2018) as well as edited volumes on infectious disease and food and drug law. Professor Halabi has served as an advisor to the World Health Organization and the National Foundation for the US Centers for Disease Control and Prevention as well as publishing widely on healthcare system design, biomedical innovation, and vaccine safety. Before earning his JD from Harvard Law School, Professor Halabi was awarded a British Marshall scholarship to study in the United Kingdom where he earned an MPhil in International Relations from the University of Oxford (St. Antony's College). He holds a BA and a BS from Kansas State University.

Anne Huvos, JD, DESS, Manager, World Health Organization PIP Framework Secretariat, Geneva, Switzerland, joined World Health Organization headquarters in 2006, when she began working on the formal and informal processes and negotiations that would lead to adoption of the Pandemic Influenza Preparedness (PIP) Framework. She has been leading the PIP Framework Secretariat since the framework's adoption by the World Health Assembly in 2011. Under her leadership, implementation of the framework has demonstrated its value as a model for strengthening public health security through an innovative partnership with public, private, and nongovernmental sectors. The PIP Framework has been instrumental in strengthening global pandemic influenza preparedness and response capacities in countries where they are weak, and establishing agreements to provide to WHO access to critical pandemic response supplies, in real time, at the time of a pandemic.

Dr Rebecca Katz is a professor and Director of the Center for Global Health Science and Security at Georgetown University. Prior to coming to Georgetown, she spent ten years at The George Washington University as faculty in the Milken Institute School of Public Health. Her research is focused on global health security, public health preparedness, and health diplomacy. Since 2007, much of her work has been on the domestic and global implementation of the International Health Regulations. From 2004 to 2019, Dr Katz was a consultant to the Department of State, working on issues related to the Biological Weapons Convention, pandemic influenza, and disease surveillance. Dr Katz received her undergraduate degree from Swarthmore College, an MPH from Yale University, and a PhD from Princeton University.

Benjamin Krohmal, JD, is Clinical Ethicist and Head of Ethics Law and Policy at the John J. Lynch, MD Center for Ethics, Washington Hospital Center. Krohmal conducts scholarly research in bioethics and serves as a clinical ethics consultant and chair of the hospital's Ethics Policy Subcommittee. Before joining MedStar, Krohmal spent nearly a decade as a senior attorney at a multinational firm, where he specialized in anti-corruption compliance and enforcement and settled the largest international corruption case in the healthcare industry. His scholarship addresses topics including physician aid in dying, surrogate decision-making, "dual use" research, international research ethics, and just access to healthcare. Krohmal completed a fellowship in the Bioethics Department at the National Institutes of Health, graduated from Boston College Law School (Cum Laude and Order of the Coif) and received a BA in biology and philosophy from the University of Virginia (Highest Honors and Phi Beta Kappa). Krohmal is barred in Washington, DC, and in New York.

Dr Theodore Kuschak serves as the Director of Networks and Resilience Development at the National Microbiology Laboratory (NML) within the Public

Health Agency of Canada (PHAC). His office hosts the secretariats for the Canadian Public Health Laboratory Network (CPHLN) and the Global Health Security Initiative's (GHSI) Global Health Security Action Group Laboratory Network. Within the NML, he works on global health security issues pertaining to laboratory preparedness and response coordination during public health emergencies. He is also frequently engaged in the development of laboratory and other types of networks in Canada and in the international community. For the past six years Theodore has been part of the Global Health Security Initiative's Sample Sharing Task Group's efforts to improve the timely international collection and sharing of samples related to non-influenza pathogens that have the potential to cause a public health emergency of international concern.

Dr Maria Julia Marinissen served as the Director of the Division of International Health Security in the Office of the Assistant Secretary for Preparedness and Response, at the US Department of Health and Human Services. She led ASPR engagement in global health security partnerships including serving as the US Liaison to the Global Health Security Initiative, Chair of the GHSI Medical Countermeasures Task Force and the North America Health Security Working Group. She also led the interagency collaboration for the development and implementation of national and international health security frameworks for response coordination and mutual assistance during public health emergencies including analyzing and addressing the legal, regulatory, and logistics barriers to mobilize laboratory samples, medical countermeasures, and personnel across borders. Her team managed the International Health Regulations (IHR) 2005 National Focal Point in the United States as well as the evaluation and monitoring of IHR implementation nationally in addition to managing capacity building programs in collaboration with partners in the Americas, Africa, and Southeast Asia. Prior to her work in policy, Maria Julia was a Senior Research Associate at NIH and a "Ramon y Cajal" Investigator at the Universidad Autonoma de Madrid.

Joshua Teperowski Monrad is a student at Yale University and an affiliated undergraduate researcher at the Center for Health Science and Security at Georgetown University. At Yale, his studies have focused on epidemic preparedness and his senior thesis examined the ethics, politics, and economics of immunization programs for nonroutine vaccines. As part of his undergraduate education, he has studied health economics at Oxford University, epidemiology and health policy at the Yale School of Public Health, and public health entrepreneurship at the Yale School of Management. Prior to doing research with the Center for Global Health Science and Security, he has published research on gender biases in pediatric pain assessment and written about public health issues for several newspapers in Denmark, the UK, and the US. He has previously worked in healthcare consulting, the pharmaceutical sector, and on a nongovernmental campaign to combat antibiotic resistance.

Claudia Nannini, PhD, is Legal Officer at the World Health Organization, where she has served since 2014. She earned her PhD in International Law and Legal Studies from the University of Milan. She has served as a Visiting Fellow at the Max Planck Institute for Comparative Public Law and International Law. She is a member of the Ecole de Formation du Barreau in France and the Court of Appeal of Florence, Italy.

Dr Michael R. Mowatt is Director, Technology Transfer and Intellectual Property Office, National Institute of Allergy and Infectious Diseases, National Institutes of Health, US Department of Health and Human Services. Since 2001 Dr Mowatt has directed the technology transfer program at the National Institute of Allergy and Infectious Diseases (NIAID). His staff support the mission of NIAID by facilitating discovery and promoting the development and commercialization of NIAID's biomedical innovations for the betterment of public health. Commercial successes based on NIAID innovations include vaccines for viral hepatitis, monoclonal antibodies against respiratory syncytial virus, veterinary vaccines that employ recombinant poxviruses, and diagnostic tests for gastrointestinal parasites and viruses. In addition to managing NIAID's intellectual property portfolio of 400 patent families, more than 30 percent of which have been licensed to commercial partners, the office negotiates and manages transactional agreements such as Cooperative Research and Development Agreements (CRADAs) and Material Transfer Agreements (MTAs), which underpin the success of NIAID's research and R&D programs. He and his staff have negotiated a wide variety of agreements with NIAID partners that include universities, nongovernmental organizations, other US government agencies, and philanthropic organizations such as the Bill and Melinda Gates Foundation, as well as commercial concerns ranging from large pharmaceutical companies with bureaucracies that rival that of the US government to small biotechnology companies and everything in between.

Dr Alexandra Phelan is a member of the Center for Global Health Science and Security and a Faculty Research Instructor in the Department of Microbiology and Immunology at Georgetown University. She advises on legal and policy issues related to infectious diseases, with a particular focus on emerging and reemerging infectious disease outbreaks and international law. Dr Phelan has worked as a consultant for the World Health Organization, the World Bank, and Gavi: the vaccine alliance, and has advised on matters including international law and pathogen sharing, human rights law and Zika, intellectual property law, and contract law. She is admitted to practice to the Supreme Court of Victoria and High Court of Australia in 2010. She holds a Master of Laws, specializing in international law, from the Australian National University, and a Bachelor of Biomedical Science/Bachelor of Laws (Honours) double degree from Monash University. She also holds a Diploma of Languages (Mandarin Chinese). Ms Phelan is a General Sir John Monash Scholar and was recognized as an Associate Fellow of the Royal

Commonwealth Society in 2015 for her human rights advocacy during the 2013–2015 Ebola outbreak.

Dr Mukul Ranjan is Senior Advisor for Innovation and Technology Transfer, Technology Transfer and Intellectual Property Office, National Institute of Allergy and Infectious Diseases, National Institutes of Health, US Department of Health and Human Services. Dr Ranjan has been with the NIH since 1990, first as a research scientist and since 1997 as a technology transfer professional. He has worked in several different institutes within NIH in both capacities. In addition to technology transfer, Dr Ranjan has extensive knowledge of intellectual property and US patent laws, issues, and procedures, and is a member of the US Patent Bar. He has worked at the US Patent and Trademark Office as a Biotechnology Patent Examiner dealing with receptors and cytokines. Dr Ranjan has a special interest in alleviating the global disease burden due to infectious disease and is keenly interested in international collaborations and development issues. He has attended and spoken at a number of international symposia on technology transfer in the developing world, including the US–Egypt "Investment in Biotechnology" workshop (Cairo, Egypt) and the US–India Technology Managers Symposia in 2001 and 2002 (Delhi, India), the US Licensing Executives Society, 2005 Annual Meeting on "Emerging Strategies and Structures in Global Health," the AUTM 2006 Annual Meeting where he chaired a panel on "Drugs and Vaccines for Global Health: Challenges and Strategies," the NIH/Nordic meeting, 2006 (Helsinki, Finland), World Vaccines Congress 2016 and 2017, Georgia's Innovation and Technology Agency, Tbilisi, Georgia 2016, and Universidad Andrés Bello, Santiago Chile, 2018. He has also lectured on Patent Law and international technology transfer to students from the Foundation for the Advancement of Education on the Sciences classes.

Dr Michelle Rourke is a Commonwealth Scientific and Industrial Research Organisation (CSIRO) Synthetic Biology Future Science Fellow at Griffith University Law School in Brisbane, Australia. Her research focuses on the global regulation of access to genetic resources for the Australian synthetic biology community. Her PhD examined how international access and benefit-sharing laws under the United Nations' Convention on Biological Diversity and its Nagoya Protocol impact access to physical virus samples and associated information, including genetic sequence data. Dr. Rourke is a member of the Global Virome Project's Ethical, Legal, and Social Implications Working Group and a non-resident Affiliate of the Center for Global Health Science and Security at Georgetown University.

Steven Solomon is Principal Legal Officer at the World Health Organization in Geneva, Switzerland. Prior to joining WHO, Steven served as deputy legal counselor at the United States Mission to United Nations Organizations in Geneva, negotiating a wide variety of human rights and humanitarian law instruments. He was an attorney with the State Department for several years before that, a leading participant in negotiations related to antipersonnel landmines, the protection of cultural property during armed conflict, and the International Criminal Court.

John Simpson, Professor, is Medical Director Emergency Preparedness, Resilience and Response (EPRR) at Public Health England (PHE), and formerly Director EPRR for PHE. He was for two years Medical Director of UK-Med. Formerly a consultant regional epidemiologist, he has expertise in chemical/ biological deliberate release. He is a WHO advisor on emergency planning and bioterrorism preparedness and is part of WHO Collaborating Centres on mass gatherings, extreme events, and chemical incidents.

Haley K. Sullivan, BS, Duke-Margolis Center for Health Policy, is a former post-baccalaureate fellow in the NIH Department of Bioethics. Ms Sullivan received a Bachelor's Degree in Neuroscience from Duke University. Her undergraduate research in neuroimmunology examined how infections early in life alter the structure and function of the brain's immune cells. At the NIH, she worked on a number of topics in clinical research ethics, including the ethics of genomic research and reproductive technologies. Ms Sullivan is currently a research assistant at the Duke-Margolis Center for Health Policy.

Preface

This is a book about how the regulation of biomedical research has been shaped by global trends in "access and benefit sharing," a phrase used specially to describe the distribution and redistribution of global wealth in the form of countries' biological and genetic endowments. Its contributors are national and global experts on the changing ways that biological samples are accessed, genetic sequence data obtained, pathogens transferred, and research benefits, including intellectual property rights, shared. For most of the twentieth century, inquiries into the nature of access to biological resources and the distribution of research benefits were rare and peripheral. Scientists largely based in Europe and North America enjoyed relatively easy access to biological samples in the form of fieldwork undertaken directly in foreign countries and/or conveyance from colleagues and affiliates abroad. Less commonly, scientists based in Europe or North America might work through an "annexed site," the physical presence of an institution, university, or laboratory operating under a foreign license. The "benefits" of research were coextensive with the scientific endeavor itself – more knowledge was produced, informing the next steps of the research process. The distinction between knowledge that resulted in consumer or patient products and knowledge that did not was blurry or nonexistent.

As the twentieth century neared its end, two long-running trends in international law converged on the field of global biological research: 1) growing concern for biodiversity losses in primarily tropical, low- or middle-income countries, and 2) increasing regard for biological resources as part of the "technology transfer" debates undertaken through the United Nations over the course of the 1960s and 1970s. In 1972, the UN held the first of many global conferences, on the Human Environment, at Stockholm, Sweden.[1] In the decade after the 1972 conference, scientists and nongovernmental organizations had elevated the issue of biodiversity as an urgent environmental issue.[2] While ecosystem collapse was identified as a potential problem in multiple regions, the threats to rainforests in the Amazon

---

[1] Roger Coate, *Civil Society as a Force for Peace*, 9(2) INT'L. J. PEACE STUDIES 57–86 (2004).
[2] D. H. Janzen, *The Future of Tropical Ecology*, 17 ANNUAL REVIEW OF ECOLOGY AND SYSTEMATICS 305 (1986); National Research Council (US); M. J. Novacek, *Engaging the Public in Biodiversity Issues*,

basin dramatically illustrated the rapid loss of known, unknown, and potentially crucial biological resources.[3] In 1987, the governing council of the United Nations Environment Programme resolved to create a working group to explore the possibility of developing a legally binding treaty to protect biological resources.[4] In 1991, formal multilateral negotiations began on a Convention for Biological Diversity.

These preparatory meetings resulted in the 1992 UN Conference on Environmental and Development (or "Earth Summit") held in June 1992 in Rio De Janeiro, the outcomes of which included the Convention on Biological Diversity (CBD), the UN Framework Convention on Climate Change, and the UN Convention to Combat Desertification. The CBD traced a direct line to the 1962 United Nations General Assembly's Declaration on Permanent Sovereignty over Natural Resources, which asserted that it was the inalienable right of each state to handle natural resources as they saw fit and that any profits resulting from the use of these resources should be shared "between investors and the recipient state."[5]

Article 15 of the CBD required "fair and equitable sharing of benefits arising out of the utilization of genetic resources," a phrase that gave rise to a great deal of uncertainty even as it shaped national "bioprospecting" laws.[6] Article 16 committed countries participating in the treaty (now nearly all countries in the world) to "take legislative, administrative or policy measures ... in particular those that are developing countries, which provide genetic resources *are provided access to and transfer of technology which makes use of those resources*, on mutually agreed terms, including technology protected by patents and other intellectual property rights ..."[7] The Convention on Biological Diversity (and the negotiations leading to it) thus paved the way for the transfer of biological resources to take place through formal mechanisms, often contracts for foreign investment or material transfer agreements, regulated by governments, rather than through informal sharing through scientific networks.[8]

In 1964, developing countries formed the United Nations Conference on Trade and Development (UNCTAD) in order to pursue trade-related development policies.[9] UNCTAD aimed to "maximize the trade, investment and development opportunities

in THE LIGHT OF EVOLUTION: VOLUME II: BIODIVERSITY AND EXTINCTION (J. C. Avise, S. P. Hubbell, F. J. Ayala eds.) (2008). Available from: www.ncbi.nlm.nih.gov/books/NBK214874/.
3 Michael J. Heckenberger, J. Christian Russell, Joshua R. Toney & Morgan J. Schmidt, *The Legacy of Cultural Landscapes in the Brazilian Amazon: Implications for Biodiversity*, 362 PHILOSOPHICAL TRANSACTIONS: BIOLOGICAL SCIS. 197, 197 (2007).
4 UNEP Resolution 14/26, adopted in 1987.
5 Permanent Sovereignty over Natural Resources, G.A. Res. 1803, U.N. GAOR, 17th Sess. Supp. No. 17. U.N. Soc. A/5127, 15 (1962); Stockholm Declaration, G.A. Res. 2998, U.N. Doc. A/CONF/48/14 (Dec. 15, 1972).
6 Thomas Kursar, *What Are the Implications of the Nagoya Protocol for Research on Biodiversity?*, 61(4) BIOSCIENCE 256–57 (2011).
7 Bonn Guidelines Paragraph 43 (emphasis added).
8 Sam Foster Halabi, *Multipolarity, Intellectual Property, and the Internationalization of Public Health Law*, 35 MICH. J. INT'L. L. 715 (2014).
9 JOHN TOYE, UNCTAD AT 50: A SHORT HISTORY 3 (2014).

of developing countries and assist them in their efforts to integrate into the world economy on an equitable basis."[10] Shortly after its formation, UNCTAD began to focus on technology transfer as a part of this mission.[11]

In general, technology may be transferred through patent licensing, joint ventures, research cooperation, technology servicing, foreign direct investment, technology sharing agreements, and training.[12] The CBD quickly provided a pathway for global biological research and technology transfer to become closer partners. Informed by CBD principles (although before the text was finalized), US pharmaceutical firm Merck entered into an agreement with the government of Costa Rica, under which the National Biodiversity Institute (INBio), a nonprofit scientific organization created by the government of Costa Rica, would provide 10,000 samples of plants, animals, and soil to Merck. Merck enjoyed the exclusive rights to study these samples for two years, and retained the patent rights on drugs developed using the samples. In return, Merck agreed to pay INBio $1 million as well as to transfer $130,000 worth of laboratory equipment.[13] The agreement also specified royalties to be paid to the Costa Rican government's Ministry of Natural Resources.[14] Many countries adopted "bioprospecting" legislation that tied permission for biological research to technology transfer including the involvement of local scientists and the sharing of resulting benefits or intellectual property rights.[15]

These developments quickly impacted research specific to animal and human health. The 1980s and early 1990s witnessed the emergence of new infectious diseases like HIV as well as the resurgence of older diseases like cholera. In 1995, shortly after the finalization of the CBD, the World Health Assembly, the governing body of the World Health Organization, instructed WHO's Director General to revisit the International Health Regulations (1969) – which only covered cholera, plague, and yellow fever – because they neglected "the emergence of new infectious agents" and failed to provide for an adequate response of those that were covered.[16] The World Health Assembly attributed these failures to the erosion of barriers

[10] DN DWIVELDI, INTERNATIONAL ECONOMICS: THEORY AND PRACTICE 464 (2013).
[11] UNCTAD, SECOND SESSION OF THE UNITED NATIONS CONFERENCE ON TRADE AND DEVELOPMENT, SECOND SESSION(UNCTAD II). 31 JANUARY–29 MARCH 1968. NEW DELHI (INDIA) 272 available at http://unctad.org/en/Docs/td97vol1_en.pdf; PETER DRAHOS, GLOBAL GOVERNANCE OF KNOWLEDGE: PATENT OFFICES AND THEIR CLIENTS xiv (2010).
[12] HIROKO YAMANE, INTERPRETING TRIPS: GLOBALIZATION OF INTELLECTUAL PROPERTY RIGHTS AND ACCESS TO MEDICINES 52 (2011).
[13] MD Coughlin Jr., *Using the Merck-INBio agreement to clarify the Convention on Biological Diversity*, 31(2)COLUMBIA JOURNAL OF TRANSNATIONAL LAW 337–75 (1993), available at www.ciesin.org /docs/oo8–129/oo8–129.html.
[14] *Id.*
[15] Agreement on Trade-Related Aspects of Intellectual Property Rights art. 8, Apr. 15, 1994, Marrakesh Agreement Establishing the World Trade Organization, Annex 1C, 1869 U.N.T.S. 299 [hereinafter TRIPS].
[16] World Health Organization. Revision Process of the International Health Regulations. Available at: www.who.int/ihr/revisionprocess/revision/en/index.html

between goods and people.[17] The IHR revision process overlapped with negotiations over technology transfer in the global free trade regime.[18] In 2003, the outbreak of SARS facilitated the 2005 revisions.[19]

The IHR (2005) was expanded to encompass the detection and prevention of all infectious diseases.[20] Their scope was broadened "to include any event that would constitute a public health emergency of international concern."[21]

> The Regulations now encompass public health risks whatever their origin or source (Article 1.1), including: (1) naturally occurring infectious diseases, whether of known or unknown etiological origin; (2) the potential international spread of non-communicable diseases caused by chemical or radiological agents in products moving in international commerce; and (3) suspected intentional or accidental releases of biological, chemical, or radiological substances.[22]

Acknowledging the importance of communication and cooperation to successful detection and prevention of communicable diseases, States Parties are obligated to "develop the means to detect, report, and respond to public health emergencies ... [and] establish a National IHR Focal Point (NFP)[23] for communication to and from WHO ..."[24]

While the IHR (2005) did not directly address research furthering their purpose (e.g. research into animal and human health), the concepts of "communication" and "cooperation" inevitably implicated that research. On the one hand, the spirit of the IHR encouraged open discovery and sharing of research into diseases, diagnostics, therapeutics, and vaccines that might touch and concern IHR components like detection, surveillance, communication, and response. However, some of the most significant pathogens specifically named in Annex 2 of the IHR (e.g. Ebola, influenza, SARS) necessarily involved research using genetic resources covered by the

---

[17] Rebecca Katz & Julie Fischer, *The Revised International Health Regulations: A Framework for Global Pandemic Response*, 3 GLOBAL HEALTH GOVERNANCE, 1, 2 (2010), available at http://blogs.shu.edu /ghg/files/2011/11/Katz-and-Fischer_The-Revised-International-Health-Regulations_Spring-2010.pdf. The threat of the Ebola virus and the emerging HIV/AIDS crisis (among other viruses) were major factors the global community considered when advocating revisions to the existing IHR. *Id.*

[18] David Fidler, The Revision of the IHR, ASIL INSIGHTS (April 2004) available at www.asil.org /insigh132.cfm

[19] Katz & Fischer, *supra* note 17, at 2.

[20] The stated purpose is to "prevent, protect against, control and provide a public health response to the international spread of disease in ways that are commensurate with and restricted to public health risks, and which avoid unnecessary interference with international traffic and trade." *International Health Regulations (2005)*, WORLD HEALTH ORGANIZATION 1 (2005).

[21] Katz & Fischer, *supra* note 17, at 2.

[22] Fidler, *supra* note 18.

[23] The NFP is a "national centre, established or designated by each State Party [and] must be accessible at all times for IHR (2005)-related communications with WHO." *International Health Regulations (2005): Toolkit for Implementation in National Legislation*, WORLD HEALTH ORGANIZATION 1, 7 (2009), available at www.who.int/ihr/NFP_Toolkit.pdf. As of July 2009, 99 percent of all States have established an NFP.

[24] Katz & Fischer, *supra* note 17, at 4.

CBD including Article 15 on access and benefit sharing and Article 16 on technology transfer.

In late 2006, the latent tension between sharing data relevant for outbreak response and asserting ownership over pathogens became manifest. Indonesia withheld samples of a highly infectious avian influenza strain from the World Health Organization on the basis that while free sharing of biological resources was expected, sharing of resulting products, especially influenza vaccines, was not.[25] Citing the CBD as a primary legal basis for their decision, the government interpreted the IHR (2005) to apply only to sharing of public health information, not biological materials.

In 2010, the Conference of the Parties to the CBD adopted the voluntary, but binding, Nagoya Protocol on Access to Genetic Resources and the Fair and Equitable Sharing of Benefits Arising from their Utilization (Nagoya Protocol) which requires researchers (whether commercial or nonprofit) interested in genetic resources to develop plans to obtain the consent of the states where those resources originate and to share benefits associated with their utilization (access and benefit sharing). The treaty became effective in 2014 and has propelled discussions in the research and public health communities about meanings and best practices with respect to the objectives of the scientific research process, the equitable considerations of the CBD and Nagoya Protocol, and, of course, public health needs. If a country's genetic resources are crucial to developing diagnostics, therapeutics, and vaccines against a public health threat, what conditions, if any, may it impose on access to those resources? How can negotiations over access and benefit sharing be reduced in time and expense for both emergency and nonemergency situations?

It is these questions this book aims to answer. Writing as members of the Global Virome Project's Ethical, Legal, and Social Implications Working Group and as scholars of international public health law and policy, we convened, with the support of the O'Neill Institute for National and Global Health Law at Georgetown University and the National Institute for Allergy and Infectious Diseases of the US National Institutes of Health, national, regional, and international leaders on the complex intersection between sovereign control over resources, technology transfer, and the needs of public health researchers. The result is, we believe, the first sustained scholarly contribution to this topic, and one we hope will guide researchers, policymakers, legislators, and regulators.

---

[25] David Fidler, *Influenza Virus Samples, International Law, and Global Health Diplomacy*, 14(1) EMERG INFECT DIS. 88–94 (2008).

Acknowledgments

As a book dedicated to fundamental changes in the structure and orientation of international public health research collaborations, especially as understood with reference to potentially pandemic diseases, it would not have been possible without a global audience of scholars, students, and researchers who contributed both time and expertise to the final volume. Barbara Mulach and Patricia Strickler-Dinglasan at the National Institute for Allergy and Infectious Diseases of the US National Institutes of Health worked closely with us as we sought support through NIH's Scientific Conferences program. We thank them for the time they took to do so as well as NIAID itself for ultimately supporting the conference, *The Changing Relevance of Material Transfer Agreements for Infectious Disease Research*. Katie Gottschalk, Mehgan Gallagher, Brigid Rayder, and Emily Wilkinson at the O'Neill Institute for National and Global Health Law at Georgetown University provided invaluable support to us as we organized the conference and we thank the O'Neill Institute for cosponsoring the meeting.

We presented the work at various stages at the Wiet Life Sciences Conference at the Loyola University, Chicago, the Global Health Security Conference in Sydney, Australia, and the American Society for Law, Medicine, and Ethics' Health Law Professors Conference. Thanks go to Matt Boyce, Yaniv Heled, Susan Kim, John Monahan, and Ana Santos Rutschman Josh Sarnoff and Andrew Torrance for helpful comments and suggestions during those presentations. Aurelia Attal-Juncqua, Amanda Mollett, and Jim Sanders provided excellent research assistance.

We thank Matt Gallaway and Cameron Daddis at Cambridge University Press for shepherding the project through the publication process and three anonymous reviewers for providing helpful comments. Finally, we thank our spouses and children for their patience and support throughout the publication process.

Introduction

Viral Sovereignty, Technology Transfer, and the Changing Global System for Sharing Pathogens for Public Health Research

Sam Halabi and Rebecca Katz

The free flow of biological resources, including pathogens, and the knowledge generated by those studying them, have generated some of the most important diagnostics, therapeutics, and vaccines that have saved billions of lives worldwide. The World Health Organization (WHO)'s Global Influenza Surveillance and Response System, GISRS (formerly Global Influenza Surveillance Network), which connects influenza samples from all over the world to reference laboratories, researchers, and vaccine manufacturers, has generated seasonal and pandemic flu vaccines that have saved hundreds of thousands of lives.[1] GISRS has performed this globally critical function since 1957.[2] Indeed, it is not HIV/AIDS nor noncommunicable diseases like cancer, diabetes or heart disease that have threatened large populations in developing countries – it is primarily influenza and other vaccine-preventable diseases.[3] The development of some vaccines, notably influenza, depends on biological resources in low- and middle-income countries being made available to researchers, organizations, governments, and pharmaceutical firms in the major industrialized countries.[4]

---

[1] CDC, *CDC Study: Flu Vaccine Saved 40,000 Lives During 9 Year Period*. Available at: www.cdc.gov/flu/news/flu-vaccine-saved-lives.htm.

[2] Jerome H. Reichman, Paul Uhlir, and Tom Dedeurwaerdere, GOVERNING DIGITALLY INTEGRATED GENETIC RESOURCES, DATA, AND LITERATURE: GLOBAL INTELLECTUAL PROPERTY STRATEGIES FOR A REDESIGNED MICROBIAL RESEARCH COMMONS, 44 (2016).

[3] Christopher Ingraham, *In 2013, Measles Killed More Kids Than Car Accidents or AIDS*, WASH. POST (Feb. 25, 2015) available at www.washingtonpost.com/blogs/wonkblog/wp/2015/02/25/in-2013-measles-killed-more-kids-than-car-accidents-or-aids/. ("Measles killed 82,100 children under age 5 in 2013, ranking the disease at No. 7 on the list of the top causes of child death, according to recent statistics from the Global Burden of Disease study published in the Lancet. Lower respiratory infections like pneumonia were the number one killer, followed by malaria, diarrhea, nutritional deficiencies, congenital defects and meningitis. More small children died from measles in 2013 than died from drowning, road injuries or aids.")

[4] Eileen Kane, *Achieving Clinical Equality in an Influenza Pandemic: Patent Realities*, 39 SETON HALL L. REV. 1137, 1143 (2009). ("The most significant pharmaceutical interventions that could be available in a viral pandemic are drawn from two distinct approaches: the administration of vaccines, which present a whole or partial virus to a potential host in order to generate an immune response that will be

In many ways, the importance of this volume is illustrated by the threat influenza pandemics pose, and the structures the world has put in place to prepare for them. Seasonal and pandemic influenza vaccines are possible in significant part because developing countries share influenza samples with GISRS, even though their populations have not historically received a proportionate benefit of resulting vaccines or other medical countermeasures.[5] Yet influenza pandemics have typically originated in low- or middle-income states like China, Indonesia, Mexico, and Vietnam. These states must therefore be willing to share disease samples and biological material relevant to risk assessment, risk management, disease research, and vaccine development.[6] Access to viruses is crucial to the development of vaccines and other forms of treatment and the WHO's system allows countries to effectively "coordinate surveillance efforts" for influenza outbreaks.[7] Through the GISRS, national influenza centers (NIC) submit local virus samples to the WHO for monitoring and research.[8] NICs also provide epidemiological information accessible to all participating laboratories and, in turn, may share samples to develop vaccines and other therapeutics.[9]

This system is less formal but nevertheless crucial for other infectious diseases. Sampling and transfer of human immunodeficiency virus (HIV) has been essential to the development of antiretroviral therapies that have drastically reduced its public health burden.[10] The transfer of samples out of Guinea, Liberia, and Sierra Leone during the 2014–16 outbreak led to rapid diagnostics for Ebola, expanded knowledge

protective against a later infection, and the administration of antiviral medications, which are chemicals that interfere with viral replication.")

[5] Kumanan Wilson, Barbara von Tigerstrom, and Christopher McDougall, *Protecting Global Health Security through the International Health Regulations: Requirements and Challenges*, 179(1) CMAJ 44 (2008), available at www.ncbi.nlm.nih.gov/pmc/articles/PMC2464486/. David P. Fidler and Lawrence O. Gostin, *The New International Health Regulations: An Historic Development for International Law and Public Health*, 34 JLME 85, 86–87 (2006).

[6] Kane, *supra* note 4 at 1153–55. ("In an effort to document the patent landscape of the field, the WHO has undertaken a project to map where patents have been sought on any of the relevant H5N1 viral materials. This research demonstrates that a small cluster of patent applications have been filed on various sequences and proteins of H5N1 and several patents have been issued, but the report further notes that patent landscaping must continue as the field matures. The sequence of the H5N1 and novel H1N1 influenza viruses have been determined. The WHO provided notice that genetic sequences from one novel H1N1 virus isolate were available on the GISAID database within several days of the first reports of the outbreak ... Three separate groups of international researchers filed U.S. patent applications on the DNA sequences of the virus.")

[7] *Id.*

[8] Samples are often collected from hospitals, clinics, and other laboratories. *Id.*; *see also* MARIE WILKE, THE WORLD HEALTH ORGANIZATION'S PANDEMIC INFLUENZA PREPAREDNESS FRAMEWORK AS A PUBLIC HEALTH RESOURCE POOL, COMMON POOLS OF GENETIC RESOURCES: EQUITY AND INNOVATION IN INTERNATIONAL BIODIVERSITY LAW (*hereinafter* COMMON POOLS OF GENETIC RESOURCES), 315–43 (2013).

[9] Reichman, *supra* note 2 at 44.

[10] Paul Sharp and Beatrice Hahn, *The Evolution of HIV-1 and the Origin of AIDS*, 365(1552) PHILOS TRANS R SOC LOND B BIOL SCI. (2010).

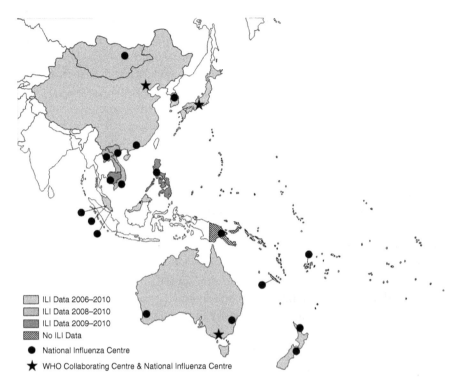

FIGURE 0.1 Epidemiological and Virological Characteristics of Influenza in the Western Pacific Region of the World Health Organization, 2006–2010 PLoS One. 2012;7(5): e37568. doi: 10.1371/journal.pone.0037568. Epub 2012 May 29.

about mechanisms of action for pharmaceutical treatments and several promising vaccine candidates.[11]

Yet proprietary claims over biological resources have fundamentally altered the sharing paradigm in global infectious disease research. In 2006, Indonesia withheld H5N1 avian flu samples from the WHO system, compromising efforts to monitor and produce vaccines in response to an avian flu outbreak that had not only spread worldwide but threatened to become easily transmissible from birds to humans and then between humans.[12] Indonesia asserted that its decision was a response to an

---

[11] Ana Henao-Restrepo et al., *Efficacy and Effectiveness of an rVSV-vectored Vaccine Expressing Ebola Surface Glycoprotein: Interim Results from the Guinea. Ring Vaccination Cluster-Randomised Trial.* 386 Lancet 857–866 (2015).

[12] David Fidler, *Influenza Virus Samples, International Law, and Global Health Diplomacy,* 14(1) Emerg Infect Dis. 88–94 (2008). ("This controversy began toward the end of 2006, when Indonesia decided not to share influenza A virus (H5N1) samples with WHO for risk assessment (e.g., surveillance) or risk management (e.g., vaccine development) purposes. Indonesia's decision reportedly stemmed from its reaction to an Australian company's development of an avian influenza vaccine derived from a virus strain that Indonesia provided to WHO. WHO's acknowledgment that patents had been sought on modified versions of influenza (H5N1) samples shared through the Global

Australian company's development of a vaccine derived from a virus sample Indonesia provided to the WHO.[13] The cycle demonstrated the inequities inherent in the global vaccine distribution system: "Developing countries provided information and virus samples to the WHO-operated system; pharmaceutical companies in industrialized countries then obtained free access to such samples, exploited them, and patented the resulting products, which the developing countries could not afford."[14] "Without access to Indonesia's influenza strains, global surveillance was jeopardized, as was the refinement of diagnostic reagents and the development of intervention strategies, which depend on the information surveillance provides."[15]

The norms of sharing for global infectious disease research had deep historical and economic roots. Because life as a general matter (including seeds, plants for agriculture, and other biological resources) was historically viewed as the "common heritage" of humanity, there were few barriers to researchers, firms or even foreign governments transferring biological resources out of one country and to another, often from a country with less technological capacity for research to one with more. Customs and import laws regulated biological samples as they moved across borders, but for the most part, those laws rarely interrupted infectious disease research.[16] Within the scientific community, this large-scale transfer of resources occurred through three primary channels: conveyance, field work, and annexed research sites.[17]

The scientific process relies upon verification of analyses and conclusions, exchange of data and other resources, and attribution to researchers for contributions that advance knowledge. Consequently, researchers formed (and form) sharing and reciprocity customary practices that encourage scientists to share samples and related data with colleagues in countries with more advanced laboratory and technical capabilities or the former may request inputs from the latter. Under this model, researchers request biological samples including human pathogens from colleagues, sometimes with the understanding that some other resource or knowledge will be shared with the researcher who responds to the request. For example, Ali Mohamed Zaki, an Egyptian physician working in Saudi Arabia, contacted scientists at Erasmus Medical Center in the Netherlands for technical help after he suspected a novel virus (MERS-CoV) caused the severe respiratory symptoms and death of a patient.[18] According to Zaki:

Influenza Surveillance Network (GISN) without the consent of the countries that supplied the samples reinforced Indonesia's discontent.")

[13] *Id.*
[14] *Id.* at 88.
[15] *Id.*
[16] Olive Sturtevant, *The ABCs of Importing and Exporting Products, Samples and Biologics across International Borders* available at https://c.ymcdn.com/sites/www.celltherapysociety.org/resource/resmgr/2014_AnnualMtgPresentations/QO4_O.Sturtevant.pdf.
[17] Patricia Garcia, *International Partnerships: View from the South*, available at www.mcgill.ca/global health/files/globalhealth/09PattyGarcia.ppt.
[18] Islam Hussein, *The Story of the First MERS Patient*, NATURE MIDDLE EAST, June 2, 2014, available at www.natureasia.com/en/nmiddleeast/article/10.1038/nmiddleeast.2014.134. ("Zaki had diagnosed 'patient zero' of the deadly virus at a Saudi Arabia virology diagnostic laboratory established in 1993. Besides

[Erasmus] confirmed my initial findings and asked me to send them a small portion of patient zero's sample because they wanted to do some more testing and they were running out of RNA. I didn't have any mechanism to ship a live virus sample while maintaining the cold chain during transit. So, I filtered the sputum sample and mixed the filtrate with Vero cells, packaged the tightly capped tube in appropriate biohazard containers and shipped it with a private carrier at room temperature as a diagnostic sample. It worked. They received it in the Netherlands and managed to recover the live virus, the first genetic analysis of this novel virus published in *New England Journal of Medicine*.[19]

The scope of acquisition of biological samples represented by Dr. Zaki's experience is vast.[20] There were millions of such transfers over the course of the twentieth century.[21]

"Field work," as used here, refers to the acquisition of biological samples in a country by a foreign researcher who later returns to his or her country to conduct research on the collected samples.[22] For example, in the early 2000s, French researchers conducted interviews in Brazil and French Guiana to find out about local antimalarial remedies, including those derived from the indigenous *Quassia amara* shrub, and also returned to France with samples of *Quassia amara*.[23] "Field work" acquisition is the kind of transfer specifically regulated by the Convention on Biological Diversity and the Nagoya Protocol.[24]

coronavirus, Zaki also diagnosed Dengue fever for the first time in Saudi Arabia in 1994. And in 1997, he isolated a new tick-born flavivirus, known as Alkhurma, which causes severe hemorrhagic fever.")

[19] *Id.*

[20] Maryam Shabikhani et al., *The Procurement, Storage, and Quality Assurance of Frozen Blood and Tissue Biospecimens in Pathology, Biorepository, and Biobank settings*, 47 CLIN. BIOCH. 258–66 (2014). ("The world population has seen exponential growth and is projected to increase from the current 7.2 billion to 9.6 billion by the year 2050 [1]. With this sizeable expansion in the human population, there will be a correspondingly large increase in biomedical biospecimens. In the United States alone, the number of biospecimens is estimated to have tripled over a decade to reach approximately 600 million in 2010 [2]. Furthermore, there has been a rapid evolution of increasingly affordable 'next-generation' technologies that permit global or targeted evaluation of the genome, epigenome, proteome, and metabolome of tissues and cells and that are critical to personalized medicine- the tailoring of targeted therapies for each patient.")

[21] Jimmie Vaught, Marianne Henderson, and Carolyn Compton, *Biospecimens and Biorepositories: from Afterthought to Science*, 21 CANCER EPIDEMIOL BIOMARKERS PREV. 253–55 (2012). ("Given the millions of samples collected for clinical and research purposes, for most of the history of biobanking there has been a serious lack of attention to controlling the quality and consistency of collection, processing and storage of biospecimens.")

[22] Florian Rabitz, *Biopicacy after the Nagoya Protocol: Problem Structure, Regime Design and Implementation Challenges*, 9(2) BRAZILIAN POLITICAL SCIENCE REVIEW 30, 37 (2015).

[23] N. Cachet et al., *Antimalarial Activity of Simalikalactone E, a New Quassinoid from* Quassia amara L. (*Simaroubaceae*), 53 ANTIMICROB AGENTS CHEMOTHER. 4393–98 (2009), available at www.ncbi.nlm .nih.gov/pubmed/19667291. ("We report the isolation and identification of a new quassinoid named simalikalactone E (SkE), extracted from a widely used Amazonian antimalarial remedy made out of *Quassia amara* L. (Simaroubaceae) leaves. This new molecule inhibited the growth of *Plasmodium falciparum* cultured in vitro by 50%, in the concentration range from 24 to 68 nM, independently of the strain sensitivity to chloroquine.")

[24] Daniel Robinson, *Locating Biopiracy: Geographically and Culturally Situated Knowledges.* 42 ENVIRONMENT AND PLANNING, 38–56 (2010).

Annexed research sites are essentially the extension of a research institution located in another country. Samples of genetic resources may be collected locally, and part of the research on those genetic resources is conducted within the host country. This may be done by foreign or local researchers.

Over the many decades in which biological resources flowed from originator countries to laboratories across the world, systems developed to both commercially exploit those resources and to build specific systems that addressed matters of particular concern to the international community. GISRS, mentioned above, facilitated the collection and transfer of influenza samples from all over the world. The Spanish influenza pandemic of 1918–19 killed approximately 3 percent of the world's population and the influenza virus thereafter became an important area of international cooperation.[25]

The GISRS system monitors the evolution of influenza viruses and provides recommendations as to which candidate vaccine viruses should be included in seasonal and pandemic vaccines.[26] The system is structured around six WHO collaborating centers located in Australia, China, Japan, the UK, and the US, four WHO essential resource laboratories, and 141 institutions recognized by the WHO as national influenza centers (NICs) located in 111 countries. NICs collect clinical specimens for the detection of influenza viruses through national surveillance networks. Until 2006, this system regularly collected influenza samples from around the world, distributed them to collaborating centers, and shared them with non-profit and for-profit actors to develop vaccines and antivirals.[27]

THE TRANSITION FROM OPEN SCIENTIFIC EXCHANGE TO PROPRIETARY CONTRACTS

Over the course of the 1960s and 1970s, many low- and middle-income countries reexamined the directional flow of global biological research as part of a broader evaluation of the distribution of technological capacity worldwide, and the importance of technology for development and for meeting basic human needs. In 1964,

---

[25] Sam Halabi and John Monahan, *Regulatory Capacity in Low- and Middle Income Countries: Lessons from the H1N1 Pandemic. in* FOOD AND DRUG REGULATION IN AN ERA OF GLOBALIZED MARKETS (S. F. Halabi ed., 2015). ("The historical and global dimensions of influenza-related mortality are astounding and explain why since at least 1918 there have been vocal groups of public health activists who have warned of the catastrophic potential of future influenza pandemics and encouraged investments in community readiness.")

[26] WHO, Self-Assessment of the WHO Global Influenza Surveillance and Response System (GISRS), Report to the PIP Advisory Group (2014) available at www.who.int/influenza/pip/virus_sharing/gisrs_self_assessment.pdf.

[27] David Fidler, *Negotiating Equitable Access to Influenza Vaccines: Global Health Diplomacy and the Controversies Surrounding Avian Influenza H5N1 and Pandemic Influenza H1N1,* 7(5) PLoS MED. (2010). ("Similarly, states in which vaccines and drugs are manufactured have sovereignty over the manufacturing process and the products themselves, until they are exported. States that import vaccines and drugs then have sovereignty over such resources and, absent a binding obligation, may allocate them however they wish.")

the United Nations Conference on Trade and Development (UNCTAD) formed in order to pursue commerce and trade-related development policies.[28] UNCTAD's mandate encouraged it to "maximize the trade, investment and development opportunities of developing countries and assist them in their efforts to integrate into the world economy . . ."[29] Building technological capacity was a crucial part of this agenda.[30]

Because the development of a technological base was perceived as intricately tied to control over industrial processes applied to raw materials, it was sovereignty over natural resources that informed much of the technology distribution debate. On April 19, 1972, Mexican President Luis Echeverria urged the adoption of a Charter of Economic Rights and Duties of States aimed at exerting greater authority over natural resources.[31] At the time, those resources were thought to be mostly commodities like petroleum, rubber and agricultural goods.[32] But the general call for control over natural resources expanded in the early 1990s to include biological and genetic resources, including human pathogens. Biodiverse rich but economically poor countries argued that there was a "unidirectional flow of samples" out of developing countries for both commercial and noncommercial research and development.[33] These countries emphasized the need for biological research to enhance "the development of local capacity, infrastructure and expertise" of the originating countries.[34]

[28] John Toye, UNCTAD AT 50: A SHORT HISTORY 3 (2014).
[29] D. N. Dwiveldi, INTERNATIONAL ECONOMICS: THEORY AND PRACTICE 464 (2013).
[30] UNCTAD, SECOND SESSION OF THE UNITED NATIONS CONFERENCE ON TRADE AND DEVELOPMENT, SECOND SESSION (UNCTAD II). 31 JANUARY–29 MARCH 1968. NEW DELHI (INDIA) 272 available at http://unctad.org/en/Docs/td97vol1_en.pdf.; PETER DRAHOS, GLOBAL GOVERNANCE OF KNOWLEDGE: PATENT OFFICES AND THEIR Clients xiv (2010).
[31] Summary of Address, UNCTAD Proceedings, Third Session, U.N. Doc. TD/180, Vol. 1A, Part I at 184, 186 (1972). ("Unless direct foreign investment shared managerial responsibility, transferred technological innovations, and. provided access to benefits obtained from foreign markets, it merely prolonged colonial domination. Multinational companies could also make a, significant contribution to modernizing the economies of the developing countries, whose national capacity for creating, assimilating and adapting technology must be increased.")
[32] Charles N. Brower and John B. Tepe Jr. *The Charter of Economic Rights and Duties of States. A Reflection or Rejection of International Law?*, 9 INT'L. LAWYER 295 (1975). ("All states have the right to associate in organizations of primary commodity producers in order to develop their national economies to achieve stable financing for their development, and in pursuance of their aims assisting in the promotion of sustained growth of the world economy, in particular accelerating the development of developing countries.")
[33] Daniel Yergin and Joseph Stanislaw, THE COMMANDING HEIGHTS: THE BATTLE BETWEEN GOVERNMENT AND THE MARKETPLACE THAT IS REMAKING THE MODERN WORLD 88–90 (1998).
[34] Ciara Staunton and Keymanthrj Moodley, *Data Mining and Biological Sample Exportation from South Africa: A New Wave of Bioexploitation under the Guise of Clinical Care?*, 106(2) SOUTH AFRICAN MEDICAL JOURNAL 136 (2016). ("The data from these biological samples and the samples themselves are a valuable resource in medical research, helping to identify the roles that genes play in disease development and accelerating new drug development. For decades there has been a unidirectional flow of samples out of Africa to various destinations in developed countries, with no benefit to local populations or local researchers. Such 'parachute research' has impacted negatively on the

Sam Halabi and Rebecca Katz

In 1972, the UN also held the first of many global conferences, on the Human Environment at Stockholm, Sweden.[35] In the decade after the 1972 conference, scientists and nongovernmental organizations had elevated the issue of biodiversity as a global policy priority.[36] In 1987, the governing council of the United Nations Environmental Programme resolved to create a working group to explore the possibility of developing a legally binding treaty to protect biological resources.[37] In 1991, formal multilateral negotiations began on a Convention for Biological Diversity.

Eventually these preparatory meetings culminated in the 1992 UN Conference on Environmental and Development (or "Earth Summit") held in June 1992 in Rio De Janeiro, the result of which included the Rio Declaration, the Convention on Biological Diversity (CBD), the UN Framework Convention on Climate Change, and the UN Convention to Combat Desertification. The CBD traced a direct line to the 1962 United Nations General Assembly's Declaration on Permanent Sovereignty over Natural Resources, which asserted that it was the inalienable right of each state to handle natural resources as they saw fit and that exploitation of these resources – commercially, technologically, etc. – should be shared "between investors and the recipient state."[38]

Some governments made it more difficult for foreign scientists and bio-prospectors to obtain resources from their territories.[39] Other governments began to limit or question their participation in one of the critical hubs of the Green Revolution, CGIAR (Consultative Group for International Agricultural Research).[40]

The CBD resulted, codifying in a legal instrument that developing countries should not only control access to genetic resources, but also benefit from any commercial value generated from their utilization.[41] The CBD adopted as one of its objectives the promotion of conservation, and sustainable use, of biological

development of local capacity, infrastructure and expertise. As genomic research is advancing in SA, every effort should be made to encourage its development and ensure that SA biological samples and data are used locally. International collaborations can further develop and improve local capacity, but this must be non-exploitative and involve a sharing of facilities, expertise and expense.")

[35] Declaration of the United Nations Conference on the Human Environment (Stockholm Declaration, 1972).

[36] D. H. Janzen, *The Future of Tropical Ecology*, 17 ANNUAL REVIEW OF ECOLOGY AND SYSTEMATICS 305 (1986). ("But the real future of tropical ecology lies in whether, within our generation, the academic, social and commercial sectors can collaboratively preserve even small portions of tropical wildlands to be studied and used for understanding, for material gain, and for the intellectual development of the society in which the wildland is embedded.")

[37] UNEP Resolution 14/26, adopted in 1987.

[38] Permanent Sovereignty over Natural Resources, G.A. Res. 1803, U.N. GAOR, 17th Sess. Supp. No. 17. U.N. Soc. A/5127, 15 (1962); Stockholm Declaration, G.A. Res. 2998, U.N. Doc. A/CONF/48/14 (Dec. 15, 1972).

[39] Reichman et al., *supra* note 2, at 89–90.

[40] Some countries began to demand the return of resources that they fear would be the subject of attempts at patenting or obtaining other intellectual property rights. *Id.* at 90.

[41] Convention on Biological Diversity, *open for signature* June 5, 1992, 1760 U.N.T.S. 79. There are 198 states party to the CBD. The United States is not a party.

diversity while seeking "fair and equitable" sharing of benefits derived.[42] The CBD's goal of "access and benefit sharing" includes both plant genetic resources as well as the relevant technology associated with their development.[43] It also codified the protection of indigenous peoples and the traditional knowledge they had developed especially for medical and agricultural applications, including a principle of compensation when firms or others commercialized that knowledge.[44] The CBD created a legal zone in which biodiverse rich countries could set terms for exploitation and the protection of their citizens to share in the benefits of any commercialization of their resources.[45] More than sixty nations have created Access and Benefit Sharing (ABS) regimes via their domestic laws, with particular activity from biodiverse rich states like Brazil, China, Costa Rica, Kenya, the Philippines, and South Africa.[46]

Article 2 of the CBD defines "genetic resources" as "genetic materials of actual or potential value" which includes "any material of plant, animal, microbial, or other origin containing functional units of heredity."[47] Subsequent agreements expanded this definition. Even then, the broadness of "actual or potential value" allows consideration of "nonmonetary benefits" into the equation of benefit sharing. Article 15 incorporates prior informed consent (PIC) and mutually agreed terms (MAT) as conditions for both access and use of resources.[48] Article 16 incorporates the demand for technology transfer as a form of benefit that could be available to

---

[42]   CBD art. 1.

[43]   Jonathan Carr, *Agreements that Divide: TRIPS vs. CBD and Proposals for Mandatory Disclosure of Source and Origin of Genetic Resources in Patent Applications*, 18 J. OF TRANSNAT'L LAW AND POLICY 131, 133 (2008). ("In Article 16(3), countries of origin, especially developing countries, are given access to technology that incorporates the use of that country's biological resources. This includes patentable biotechnology. A key aim of the CBD is to promote the sustainable use of natural resources, while incorporating power to impact the application of intellectual property rights on the biotechnological industry.")

[44]   CBD art. 8.

[45]   Michiel Korthals and Bram De Jonge, *Two Different Ethical Notions of Benefit Sharing of Genetic Resources and Their Implications for Global Development*, 28 NEW GENETICS AND SOCIETY 87, 89 (Mar. 2009).

[46]   Nicolas Pauchard, *Access and Benefit Sharing under the Convention on Biological Diversity and Its Protocol: What Can Some Numbers Tell Us about the Effectiveness of the Regulatory Regime?*, 6 RESOURCES 1–15 (2017). (" Concerns about the possible free use of GR despite the adoption of the Convention incited the States Parties to implement a set of binding rules dealing with the ABS elements of the CBD. In 2002, in Cancun (Mexico), several megadiverse countries set up the Group of Like-Minded Megadiverse Countries (GLMMC) (Bolivia, Brazil, China, Colombia, Costa Rica, Democratic Republic of the Congo, Ecuador, Ethiopia, Guatemala, India, Indonesia, Iran, Kenya, Madagascar, Malaysia, Mexico, Peru, Philippines, South Africa, and Venezuela). The origins of this group of countries go back to 1998, when Conservation International, a US non-profit environmental NGO established a list of the countries harboring the majority of Earth's species, the 17 megadiverse countries (Australia, Brazil, China, Colombia, Democratic Republic of the Congo, Ecuador, India, Indonesia, Madagascar, Malaysia, Mexico, Papua New Guinea, Peru, Philippines South Africa, United States, and Venezuela). This group is the political expression of the interests of this minority of Southern States accounting for the majority of the existing GR.")

[47]   CBD art. 2.

[48]   CBD art. 15(2).

provider countries.[49] It specifically ties terms of access to intellectual property rights providing that "patents and other intellectual property rights may have an influence on the implementation of [the Biodiversity Convention], [so Parties] shall cooperate in this regard subject to national legislation and international law in order to ensure that such rights are supportive of and do not run counter to its objectives."[50]

While the CBD permits the possibility of regional and multilateral approaches to the issues the treaty covers, it implies by its terms prior informed consent and an agreement be negotiated with every provider/user transaction.[51] The bilateral approach, if implemented effectively, potentially provides an enormous amount of control over intellectual property rights asserted over genetic resources in developing countries.[52] Article 15's requirement for informed consent for access presumes the commercial potential of all research efforts.[53]

Article 15 of the CBD required "fair and equitable sharing of benefits arising out of the utilization of genetic resources," which in turn shaped many countries' "bioprospecting" laws.[54] Before 2010, CBD Article 15 had been largely guided by the nonbinding Bonn Guidelines on Access to Genetic Resources and Fair and Equitable Sharing of the Benefits Arising Out of Their Utilization. The Bonn Guidelines recommended the following provisions for contracts between sovereign states and commercial entities:

(a) Regulating the use of resources in order to take into account ethical concerns of the particular Parties and stakeholders, in particular indigenous and local communities concerned;
(b) Making provision to ensure the continued customary use of genetic resources and related knowledge;
(c) Provision for the use of intellectual property rights include joint research, obligation to implement rights on inventions obtained and to provide licences by common consent;
(d) The possibility of joint ownership of intellectual property rights according to the degree of contribution.[55]

The Convention on Biological Diversity (and the negotiations leading to it) thus paved the way for the transfer of biological resources to take place through mediums

---

49   CBD art. 16(1).
50   CBD art. 16(5).
51   Reichman et al., *supra* note 2, at 96.
52   *Id.* at 106.
53   *Id.* at 109.
54   Thomas Kursar, *What Are the Implications of the Nagoya Protocol for Research on Biodiversity?*, 61(4) BioScience 256–57 (2011). ("The CBD has promoted conservation and defended against biopiracy, but the expectation has not been met that the CBD would substantially propel biodiversity research partnerships. The stagnation over an 18-year period has been frustrating. The core problems are that for fear of biopiracy, developing countries have inhibited biodiversity research, and developed nations, for fear of financial and legal hurdles, have failed to promote studies on the uses of biodiversity.")
55   Bonn Guidelines Paragraph 43.

of proprietary claims – especially government permits and material transfer agreements – often regulated by governments, rather than through informal sharing through scientific networks.

In late 2006, Indonesia withheld H5N1 avian flu samples from the WHO GISRS system described above, a significant measure since the H5N1 avian flu outbreak that had spiked from early 2005 was not only spreading along avian flyways but threatened to become transmissible between humans; those infected experienced a 50 percent fatality rate.[56] Indonesia asserted that its decision was a response to an Australian company's patent on a vaccine derived from a virus sample Indonesia provided to the WHO.[57] More importantly for purposes of human pathogen sharing, Indonesia argued that the H5N1 virus samples that came from its territory constituted the same kinds of natural resources as theretofore petroleum or rubber would have been considered as well as a form of biodiversity protected under Articles 15 and 16 of the Convention on Biological Diversity. Indonesia agreed to resume sharing under an interim agreement that granted it access to antivirals and vaccines, and the promise to develop a broader international agreement on influenza pathogen access and benefit sharing. Indonesia's actions introduced to the scientific sharing process the theretofore unknown concept of "viral sovereignty."[58]

Soon after, CBD countries negotiated the Nagoya Protocol on Access to Genetic Resources and the Fair and Equitable Sharing of Benefits Arising from their Utilization (Nagoya Protocol). The treaty required "prior informed consent" of governments over their sovereign genetic resources and "mutually agreed terms" for the return of benefits should those resources, including human pathogens, be

[56]   J. S. Peiris, M. D de Jong, and Y. Guan, *Avian Influenza Virus (H5N1): a Threat to Human Health*, 20 (2) CLINICAL MICRO REV. 243–67 (2007) doi:10.1128/CMR.00037-06. ("The highly pathogenic avian influenza virus subtype H5N1 is already panzootic in poultry, with attendant economic consequences. It continues to cross species barriers to infect humans and other mammals, often with fatal outcomes. Therefore, H5N1 virus has rightly received attention as a potential pandemic threat. However, it is noted that the pandemics of 1957 and 1968 did not arise from highly pathogenic influenza viruses, and the next pandemic may well arise from a low-pathogenicity virus. The rationale for particular concern about an H5N1 pandemic is not its inevitability but its potential severity.")

[57]   Fidler, *supra* note 12. ("This controversy began toward the end of 2006, when Indonesia decided not to share influenza A virus (H5N1) samples with WHO for risk assessment (e.g., surveillance) or risk management (e.g., vaccine development) purposes. Indonesia's decision reportedly stemmed from its reaction to an Australian company's development of an avian influenza vaccine derived from a virus strain that Indonesia provided to WHO. WHO's acknowledgment that patents had been sought on modified versions of influenza (H5N1) samples shared through the Global Influenza Surveillance Network (GISN) without the consent of the countries that supplied the samples reinforced Indonesia's discontent.")

[58]   Dennis Normile, *Indonesia to Resume Sharing under New Terms*, 316(5821) SCIENCE 37 (Apr. 6, 2007). ("Indonesia has agreed to resume sharing samples of the H5N1 avian influenza virus with the World Health Organization in return for a promised rewrite of WHO's rules governing the use of donated viral samples. The new 'Terms of Reference' for handling viral samples, which will be hammered out over the next several months, may include a clause giving countries that provide flu samples more control over how and whether WHO can pass the virus on to third parties, such as companies making vaccines. Indonesia had halted sharing its samples over concerns that it would not have access to any H5N1 vaccine ultimately produced.")

shared.[59] The Nagoya Protocol regulates commercial, nonprofit, university-driven, and all other forms of microbiological research that lead to drugs, medical therapies, vaccines, and other products derived from genetic resources in member states and, given the limited reach of current international instruments, fundamentally changes the nature and process of international scientific research.

The Nagoya Protocol aimed to encompass the broader universe of drugs, medical therapies, agrochemical products, vaccines, and other products derived from genetic resources not regulated by other international instruments.[60] The Nagoya Protocol, formed to give specific content to Article 15 of the Convention on Biological Diversity, regulates access to genetic resources in party states and establishes mechanisms for "fair and equitable sharing of benefits arising out of the utilization of genetic resources."[61] It portends potentially drastic changes to agricultural, nutritional, and biomedical research undertaken on genetic resources located in developing countries.[62]

Countries adopting legislation or regulation pursuant to the treaty ensure that any genetic resources within the territory of that country condition access to those materials with prior informed consent not only of the country of origin but also "in accordance with domestic law," the consent of indigenous and local communities.[63] Moreover, once access to genetic resources results in a commercially viable product, "benefits arising from the utilization of genetic resources as well as subsequent applications and commercialization shall be shared in a fair and equitable

[59]   Wan Izatul Asma Wan Talaat, *Protection of the Associated Traditional Knowledge on Genetic Resources: Beyond the Nagoya Protocol*, 91 PROCEDIA – SOCIAL AND BEHAVIORAL SCIENCES 673–78 (2013). ("It is obvious that the full benefits (for both parties) of Article 15 can only be realised within a framework of LAP measures that address the main components of ABS, namely by establishing and identifying the authorities responsible for granting Prior Informed Consent, establishing an appropriate benefit sharing arrangements and procedures; and creating an inventory of existing traditional knowledge and a register of owners of such knowledge from among the indigenous population.")
[60]   Nagoya Protocol on Access to Genetic Resources and the Fair and Equitable Sharing of Benefits Arising from their Utilization to the Convention on Biological Diversity, Oct. 29, 2010, UNEP/CBD/COP/DEC/X/1 of 29. COP 10 Decision X/1: X/1.Access to genetic resources and the fair and equitable sharing of benefits arising from their utilization, Convention on Biological Diversity, www.cbd.int/decision/cop/?id=12267.
[61]   Thomas Kursar, *What Are the Implications of the Nagoya Protocol for Research on Biodiversity?*, 61(4) BIOSCIENCE 256–57 (2011).
[62]   Evanson Chege Kamau, Bevis Fedder, and Gerd Winter, *The Nagoya Protocol on Access to Genetic Resources and Benefit Sharing: What Is New and What Are the Implications for Provider and User Countries and the Scientific Community?*, 6(3) L. ENV'T & DEV. J. 246 (2010). ("In order to ensure utilisation of genetic resources in accordance with PIC and MAT requirements once the genetic resource has left the provider state, user states must have adopted measures on monitoring. These measures include primarily 'checkpoints' designated by the user state, which monitor legitimate uses of genetic resources and traditional knowledge. Those checkpoints can be the front institutions that are responsible for the individual research project, such as universities, companies, and scientific journals, as well as administrative supervisory bodies that supervise the supervisors. This means that besides the rules of the provider state the researcher will also have to inquire about the relevant rules of the user state where his or her research is conducted.")
[63]   Nagoya Protocol art. 7.

way with the Party providing such resources that is the country of origin of such resources or a Party that has acquired the genetic resources in accordance with the Convention."[64] The precise nature of benefit sharing, both monetary and nonmonetary, is left to the states themselves to negotiate with those who generate commercialized products.

The purpose of the Nagoya Protocol was explicit. The CBD, as it was originally formed, lacked an agreed upon legal framework for cross-border enforcement of its international regime, diminishing the ability for providers subjected to misappropriation of their resources to seek adequate redress. Additionally, user country governments were in no way obligated to address complaints or assist with providing redress. After six years of negotiations, the Nagoya Protocol brought "greater legal certainty and transparency" regarding the exchange of genetic resources while "reaffirm[ing] and clarif[ying] the [CBD] broad economic scope."[65] It further addressed issues concerning scientific research, also neglected by the CBD and created new enforcement provisions for user and provider nations to implement within their respective national legal systems.[66]

Article 2 of the Nagoya Protocol provides definitions that expand the economic scope of the CBD and address some of its ambiguities, while Article 5 makes benefit sharing legally binding. The "functional units of hereditary" language of the CBD is expanded to include a broader scope in its definition for "utilization of genetic resources," bringing biochemical compounds encoded by genes into the scope of its regime.[67] The Protocol also made the CBD applicable to naturally occurring biochemical as well as "traditional knowledge associated with genetic resources."[68] Further, Article 2 made utilization coextensive with research and development. Article 8 also requires Contracting Parties to create and implement ABS legislation and regulation that seek to "create conditions to promote and encourage scientific research" via "simplified measures" on research oriented access while also addressing the tendency for non-commercial research to become commercial.[69] The Protocol allows individual scientists to exchange nonmonetary benefits for their noncommercial research and afford providers freedom to negotiate nonmonetary benefits in their agreements.

Article 4 established in broad strokes the relationship between the Nagoya Protocol and other international agreements "relevant" to it.[70] Article 4 does not affect rights and obligations under those agreements "except where the exercise of those rights and obligations would cause a serious damage or threat to biological

---

[64] Nagoya Protocol art. 5.
[65] *Id.*
[66] *Id.*
[67] Gerd Winter, Knowledge Commons, Intellectual Property, and the ABS Regime, Common Pools of Genetic Resources (2013).
[68] Nagoya Protocol, Preamble (2010).
[69] Nagoya Protocol, art. 8.
[70] Nagoya Protocol, art. 4.

diversity"[71] and parties may engage in "other relevant international agreements" so long as they "do not run counter to the objectives of the [CBD and the Protocol]."[72] Article 4 also allows for specialized instruments – like the Pandemic Influenza Preparedness Framework described below – that regulate access and benefit sharing in particular areas of genetic resources.

Articles 5 through 18 of the Nagoya Protocol provide for the specific mechanisms by which prior informed consent for access to genetic resources may be obtained, the protection of traditional knowledge and indigenous communities, and the mutually agreed terms for benefit sharing. Contracting Parties are required to "take legislative, administrative, or policy measures" to enforce benefit sharing.[73] Provider countries are specifically required to give prospective users "clear and transparent written decision[s]" regarding use of resources that come from a "competent national authority," along with the issuance of a permit or some equivalent to approved users.[74] In fact, all Contracting Parties must designate national focal points by which applicants can find necessary information on PIC and MATs, complete with one or more "designated national authorities."[75] Article 15 specifically required Parties to engage in measures designed to address noncompliance and to cooperate with alleged cases of violation of legislative and regulatory requirements regarding access and benefit sharing.[76] Articles 15 and 16 together create liability for member states when violations occur within their territories and require Parties to monitor genetic resource use within their jurisdictions, providing regular updates on overall compliance.[77]

The Nagoya Protocol endeavors to promote both "defensive" protection of traditional knowledge – preventing those outside a community from obtaining intellectual property rights to that communities traditional knowledge and "positive protection" – granting proprietary rights to communities in order to "promote their traditional knowledge, control its uses and benefit from its commercial exploitation."[78] The treaty's flexibility allows it to accommodate sharing regimes that exist currently like the Global Influenza Surveillance and Response System.[79]

Bolivia, Brazil, Colombia, Costa Rica, Ecuador, Peru, South Africa, and Venezuela, for example, have adopted strong laws regulating access to genetic

[71] *Id.*
[72] *Id.*
[73] *Id.*
[74] Reichman et al., at 157 (2016). The permits act as "internationally recognized certificate[s] of compliance" to show that genetic resources used have been accessed via PIC and MATs. *Id.* at 159.
[75] Nagoya Protocol, art. 14.
[76] Nagoya Protocol, art. 15.
[77] *Id.*
[78] WIPO, *Traditional Knowledge and Intellectual Property*, available at www.wipo.int/pressroom/en/briefs/tk_ip.html.
[79] 2.3 Bioprospecting, Trips, CBD and Traditional Medicines: Concepts and Questions. Report of an ASEAN Workshop on the TRIPS Agreement and Traditional Medicine, Jakarta (Feb. 2001) *available at* http://apps.who.int/medicinedocs/en/d/Jh2996e/6.3.html.

material from their territories driven by both CBD and the Nagoya Protocol.[80] The Philippines was the first country to enact laws responding to the CBD passing legislation that required compensation and collaboration with local scientists along with the informed consent of local tribes from the areas where resources were being sampled.[81] South Africa's Regulations on Bio-Prospecting, Access and Benefit-Sharing, for example, require firms to obtain a permit from the government if they intend to use South African genetic resources for research or patenting. These permits can only be obtained with a benefit-sharing agreement with relevant stakeholders. South Africa integrates this system with its patent application system as well, so that patent applications must identify indigenous biological resources or forms of traditional knowledge leading to the patentable subject matter.[82]

Other countries have also made important efforts to compile databases of non-codified, often orally based, traditional knowledge.[83] In Venezuela, the BioZulua project documented medicinal plants and food crops of the country's twenty-four Amazonian ethnic groups.[84] This database, with genetic profiles of each plant as well as GPS coordination of specific plant locations, is a distinguishable example of non-codified traditional knowledge preservation.[85]

Similar efforts have been undertaken in South Africa via the Ulwazi program, an online traditional knowledge database focused on the indigenous knowledge of local communities in Durban, South Africa.[86] The database collects traditional knowledge such as "clothing, [] proverbs, folk tales, spiritual herbs, and traditional agricultural methods" in a wiki-style website that allows contributions and

---

[80]   RACHEL WYNBERG, DORIS SCHROEDER AND ROGER CHENNELLS, INDIGENOUS PEOPLES, CONSENT AND BENEFIT SHARING: LESSONS FROM THE SAN HOODIA CASE (2009).

[81]   K. N. NINAN, CONSERVING AND VALUING ECOSYSTEM SERVICES AND BIODIVERSITY: ECONOMIC, INSTITUTIONAL AND SOCIAL CHALLENGES 300–01 (2009).

[82]   Neil R. Crouch, Errol Douwes, Maureen M. Wolfson, Gideon F. Smith and Trevor J. Edwards, *South Africa's Bioprospecting, Access and Benefit-Sharing Legislation: Current Realities, Future Complications, and a Proposed Alternative*, 104 SOUTH AFRICAN JOURNAL OF SCIENCE 355 available at www.biopirateria.org/download/documentos/otros-documentos/sistema-abs-convenio-diversidad-bio logica/Crouch%20et%20al.pdf. ("South Africa's Department of Trade and Industry (DTI) has subsequently published the Patents Amendment Act of 2005, which requires an applicant for a patent to furnish information relating to any role played by an indigenous biological resource, or traditional knowledge, that may form part of the submitted invention and, if so, provide proof that applicant(s) have received permission to make use of the indigenous resource or traditional knowledge or traditional use.")

[83]   Stephen B. *Brush, Farmers' Rights and Protection of Traditional Agricultural Knowledge*, 35 WORLD DEVELOPMENT 1499, 1510 (2007)

[84]   R. Lakshmi Poorna et al. *Preservation and Protection of Traditional Knowledge – Diverse Documentation Initiatives across the Globe*, 107(8) CURRENT SCIENCE 1240–46 (2014). ("The information is collected by field researchers and stored in a searchable database administered by the Foundation for the Development of Mathematics and Physical and Natural Sciences. The database provides genetic profiles of every plant entry and global positioning system coordinates of plant locations and the entries are complemented with geographical references, bibliographies and digital images.")

[85]   *Id.*

[86]   *Id.* at 1244.

modifications from a variety of users.[87] The program is a part of the community's public library network and any content within is owned by the communities themselves, with the libraries acting as "moderator[s] and custodians of [the] knowledge."[88]

As of 2015, only thirteen countries had submitted legislative, administrative or policy measures in furtherance of the Nagoya Protocol but many of the sixty or so countries that have adopted ABS measures pursuant to the CBD are updating those laws. The result is that international research involving pathogens will become more affected by legal review and the terms of material transfer agreements. Indeed, in the context of Zika and MERS-CoV, Brazil and Saudi Arabia respectively have taken preliminary positions as to their ownership of potential therapeutics developed through viruses taken from their territories. As Brendan Coolsaet, Tom Dedeurwaerdere, and John Pitseys have noted, "the [Nagoya Protocol's] redistribution of resources among the stakeholders, allows the state to level the playing field, thereby strengthening weaker actors and, thus, fostering fairer agreements."[89]

While more complex and lengthier, "prior informed consent" and "mutually agreed terms" may be reached through specialized international instruments, envisioned in Article 4 of the Nagoya Protocol.[90] The resolution to Indonesia's complaints about the Global Influenza Surveillance and Response System was the 2011 Pandemic Influenza Preparedness Framework (PIP Framework).[91] The PIP Framework was explicitly committed to "increase the access of developing countries to vaccines and other pandemic related supplies."[92] Under the PIP Framework, firms retain their ability to access samples shared through GISRS, but now firms using the system must contribute towards half the cost of its maintenance.[93]

Additionally, firms must promise to share either intellectual property, products developed through use of the system or other medical countermeasures critical to pandemic response. The PIP Framework provides:

> For manufacturers of vaccines and/or antivirals, the recipient shall commit to at least two of the following options:

---

[87] *Id.*

[88] *Id.*

[89] Brendan Coolsaet, Tom Dedeurwaerdere and John Pitseys, *The Challenges for Implementing the Nagoya Protocol in a Multi-Level Governance Context: Lessons from the Belgian Case*, 2(4) Resources 555–80 (2013).

[90] Nagoya Protocol, art. 4.

[91] *Pandemic Influenza Preparedness: In Search of a Global Ethos*, www.ghwatch.org/sites/www.ghwatch .org/files/B8.pdf, 149–50.

[92] *Pandemic Preparedness Framework*, available at WHO www.who.int/influenza/pip/en/.

[93] Lawrence O. Gostin et al., *Virus Sharing, Genetic Sequencing, and Global Health Security*, 345 SCIENCE 1295, 1296 (Sep. 12, 2014). ("The framework brought together the WHO secretariat, member states, and the pharmaceutical industry in an unprecedented way. Traditional international law creates state obligations, but rarely, if ever, binds the private sector. The PIP Framework – which is not in the form of a treaty – uniquely creates legally enforceable contractual obligations on participating private and academic partners that manufacture vaccines, antivirals, or diagnostics.")

influenza.[102] The government of Saudi Arabia asserted (and continues to assert) legal claims over MERS-CoV based upon the Convention on Biological Diversity.[103] According to the Saudi Ministry of Health, Erasmus had obtained the virus illegally and the conditions it imposed for access by other researchers (they must "contractually agree not to develop products or share the sample without the permission of Erasmus and the Fouchier laboratory") have delayed development of treatments and vaccines.[104] Negotiations between the US and Saudi governments for virus samples involved elaborate demands for research in Saudi territory, participation by Saudi scientists, and other technological requirements.[105]

The effect of these movements has been profound. Nagoya established a complex framework for researchers including botanical gardens, universities, libraries, and for-profit firms to conduct research across the world. Under Nagoya, a researcher would, ideally, contact the country's national focal point (NFP) for access and benefit sharing, an administrative body suggested by the treaty. The NFP, in turn, would identify the correct "competent national authority" to discuss prior informed consent and mutually agreed terms for benefit sharing. While this seems straightforward, the competent national authority may be a ministry of health, environment, indigenous issues, interior, or other department. In some countries, up to five ministries may have jurisdiction over the pathogen at issue.

Slower and more complicated access to biological samples, including human pathogens, is occurring simultaneously with a growing scientific consensus that the next infectious disease threat is likely to emerge in biodiverse countries. Collaborations between scientists in biodiverse but resource-scarce countries and those in wealthier countries are growing in an effort to sample, identify, biobank, and research potentially human pathogenic viruses. These collaborations are essential to the detection, prevention, and response to infectious disease threats.

There are multiple mechanisms by which access and benefit sharing may be formalized in the context of biological research. Some countries have adopted legislation, especially in light of the CBD, that requires foreign researchers to register with specific national offices, establish partnerships with local scientists, and seek various approvals from national bureaucracies.[106] The Nagoya Protocol itself envisions a system of Internationally Recognized Certificates of Compliance that attest to a researcher's proper consultation and permissions from a national

---

[102] Fidler, *supra* note 12, at 88–94.

[103] Laurie Garrett, *Why a Saudi Virus Is Spreading Alarm*, COUNCIL ON FOREIGN RELATIONS EXPERT BRIEF, May 29, 2013, available at www.cfr.org/expert-brief/why-saudi-virus-is-spreading-alarm.

[104] *Id.* See also E. Hammond, *Material Transfer Agreement underlying the controversy over patent rights and the Middle Eastern Respiratory Syndrome Virus.* Third World Netw. 2013. www.twn.my/title2/biotk/2013/biotk130502.htm.

[105] David Fidler, *Who Owns MERS? The Intellectual Property Controversy Surrounding the Latest Pandemic.* FOREIGN AFF. 2013. www.foreignaffairs.com/articles/saudi-arabia/2013-06-06/who-owns-mers.

[106] David Smith et al., *Explanation of the Nagoya Protocolon Access and Benefit Sharing and Its Implication for Microbiology*, 163 MICROBIOLOGY 289, 294 (2017).

authority (in the language of the treaty, a Competent National Authority). One of the most prominent, and spreading, mechanisms is the material transfer agreement. The material transfer agreement, or MTA, regulates relationships, especially between researchers (academic, commercial, nonprofit) in different countries using the biological or genetic resources themselves as the focal point. The terms of the agreement outline how the samples are to be used and stored, whether the samples may be kept after the term of the initial permission, whether they should be returned to the provider or destroyed, and whether the samples or any part thereof may be transferred to third parties and under which conditions. Benefit sharing terms cover items such as how the research results will be disseminated, how related data will be managed, intellectual property rights including monetary terms for royalties and licenses, and how the provider country ought to be acknowledged in research publications.

Surveys and interview-based studies of researchers have concluded that access to biological samples is increasingly preceded by negotiations over material transfer agreements.[107] MTAs are used in connection with the transfer of materials for multiple purposes including safekeeping, storage (for instance, storage in gene banks), intellectual property rights, prohibitions on sharing with third or other downstream parties, and attribution of credit in peer-reviewed journals.[108] MTAs are contracts protected by law. If one of their provisions is violated, the contract is breached and the aggrieved party may initiate a lawsuit against the other.

While MTAs originated when the distinction between upstream research – evaluation of basic inputs, analysis of organisms, genes, proteins and molecules – and downstream applied research – focusing on the development of products used by consumers and patients – was sharper, they are now ubiquitous.[109] MTAs appear in diverse forms as well, from letters of understanding accompanying shipments of

[107] Victor Rodriguez, *Material Transfer Agreements: Open Science versus Proprietary Claims*, 23 NATURE BIOTECHNOLOGY 489–91 (2005). ("Now increasingly being used by public sector laboratories and academia, they may take a variety of forms, from letters accompanying a shipment of materials to detailed and formally negotiated contracts signed by both parties before a transfer of materials is made in or out of research units. Outbound agreements are often associated with having patent rights to the material in question, whereas inbound agreements may include terms that impose research restrictions that infringe upon academic freedom or the dissemination of research results, and may conflict with specific requirements of funding agreements.")

[108] Tania Bubela, Jenilee Guebert, and Amrita Mishra, *Use and Misuse of Material Transfer Agreements: Lessons in Proportionality from Research, Repositories, Litigation*. PLOS BIOLOGY 2015 Feb. available at http://journals.plos.org/plosbiology/article?id=10.1371/journal.pbio.1002060 ("These agreements provide a mechanism to protect the interests of the owners of discoveries and inventions, while promoting data and material sharing in the research community. The latter is an admirable goal in an age where research is increasingly collaborative, multinational, and multidisciplinary. Yet MTAs have a bad reputation among researchers for being overly complex and, in practice, hindering the exchange of research reagents.")

[109] Wendy Streitz and Alan Bennett, *Material Transfer Agreements: A University Perspective*, 133(3) PLANT PHYSIOLOGY 10 (2003). ("Scientists have traditionally shared research materials freely, and indeed an important criterion for scientific publication has been the unfettered ability of other researchers to experimentally reproduce and thereby test published results. That ability to replicate

materials to detailed and formally negotiated contracts signed by two or more parties before a transfer of materials takes place.

The volume of these agreements is large and increasing. For example, "One large pharmaceutical company indicated that it had six administrators dealing with more than 1,000 MTAs in 2000, and many of these agreements required lengthy negotiation."[110] Material transfers between private and public sector institutions are typically the most complex kinds of negotiations and are much more prone to failure.[111] The ascent of material transfer agreements has also created a feedback effect. When a provider declares it owns the results of research using its material, or even requires its permission to conduct certain kinds of research, it may become difficult or impossible to complete follow up research, because an entirely new MTA is required for the new, secondary material or data created.[112]

The relatively scant evidence suggests that the increasing requirements for material transfer agreements is restricting research efforts.[113] In 2004, 18 percent of academic requests for genetic materials were denied, while industry requests were similarly denied 33 percent of the time.[114] Most problems arise from material transfer agreements and associated delays.[115] For example, researchers hoping to develop "combination microbes" must overcome challenges in "obtaining sufficient information about the properties of needed materials."[116] Genetic resources are not typically sources of much market value, but instead, in market terms, are just "precompetitive inputs" that require combination with "large quantities of [other] genetic materials" to result in biomedical breakthroughs.[117] With MTAs, researchers encounter high transaction costs, substantial delays, and even refusals to negotiate for access or use.[118]

　　results will often rely on access to the underlying biological materials or information, but that access is not assured today. So what has changed? Probably the most significant factor has been the narrowing of the gap between fundamental research and commercial developments, particularly in the biomedical arena, but it is also evident in agricultural biology.")

[110]　Alan Bennet and Wendy Streitz, *Specific Issues with Material Transfer Agreements. in* Intellectual Property Management in Health and Agricultural Innovation; A Handbook of Best Practices (Krattiger, Mahoney and Nielsen et al., eds. 2007) at 699.

[111]　Streitz and Bennett, *supra* note 109, at 12.

[112]　A. Mishra and T.Bubela, *Legal Agreements and the Governance of Research Commons: Lessons from Materials Sharing in Mouse Genomics*, 18(4) OMICS 254, 256 (2014).

[113]　*Id.*

[114]　*Id.; see* John P. Walsh, Wesley M. Cohen, and Charlene Cho, *When Exclusivity Matters: Material versus Intellectual Property in Academic Biomedical Research*, 36 Res. Pol'y 1191 (2007).

[115]　Zhen Lei, Rakhi Juneja, and Brian D. Wright, *Patent versus Patenting: Impediments of Intellectual Property Protection for Biological Research*, 27 Nature Biotechnology 36, 38–39 (2009).

[116]　*Id.*

[117]　Jerome H. Reichman, Paul Uhlir, and Tom Dedeurwaerdere, Governing Digitally Integrated Genetic Resources, Data, and Literature: Global Intellectual Property Strategies for a Redesigned Microbial Research Commons, 106–07 (2016).

[118]　Mishra and Bubela, *supra* note 112. In one case entomologist studying the Western Ghat in India were forced to abort their project by local authorities due to biopiracy fears. *See* K. S. Jayaraman,

This book provides a comprehensive evaluation of the substantial changes under-way in the global system for infectious disease research as influenced by the balance between access and benefit sharing principles embodied in the CBD and the Nagoya Protocol on the one hand and the need for robust sharing on the other. Instead of the open system of sharing bacterial and viral human pathogens that characterized the research system for much of the twentieth century, conceptions of "viral sovereignty," access made contingent on sharing research benefits, and com-plex negotiations are far more common. The increasing barriers to the flow of research material and related data like genetic sequencing information are posing threats to the development of diagnostics, therapeutics, and vaccines. The book assesses the extent of these barriers and proposes approaches that may address the global inequalities behind material transfer negotiation issues.

THE PLAN OF THIS BOOK

The views presented in this book document the perspectives of clinicians, epide-miologists, governments, international lawyers, representatives from major interna-tional organizations, and scholars who have not only shaped the discourse around access and benefit sharing with respect to research on genetic resources, but have worked to forge frameworks under which crucial research may be undertaken while respecting the sovereign rights of countries under new international treaties. The various chapters investigate a wide range of activities by national and international public health leaders; the geopolitical history leading to the adoption of the CBD and Nagoya; the role of the International Health Regulations (2005); alternative forms of material transfer agreements (e.g., simple letters, MTAs specific to emer-gencies) to address specific disease threats; and the construction of multilateral solutions including repositories and international agreements that fit within the Nagoya Protocol.[119]

The book is divided into three parts. Part I outlines the geopolitical landscape of access and benefit sharing, especially as conceptions of "viral sovereignty" have informed long-running requests for technology transfer and the intersection with regulations and treaties aimed at protecting global health security. It also provides a specific case study of a multicountry study with both animal and human research subjects. Part II is devoted to the ethical and social implications of these develop-ments, including patient rights and biosecurity implications, which may inform the legal mechanisms analyzed in Part III. Part III is dedicated to solutions. The chapters in Part III analyze material transfer agreements, repositories, specialized international instruments, and other forms of cooperative frameworks that may

---

Entomologist Stifled by Indian Bureaucracy, 452 NATURE 7 (Mar. 5, 2008), available at www.nature .com/news/2008/080305/full/452007a.html.
[119] Sam Halabi, Rebecca Katz, and Amanda McClelland, *International Institutions and Ebola. Response: Comparing the 2014 West Africa and 2017 DRC Outbreaks*, 88 ST. LOUIS U. L.J. 44 (2019).

reduce the costs of ensuring access and benefit sharing while promoting public health research using genetic resources covered by the CBD and the Nagoya Protocol. The chapters in these sections contribute unique insights on coordination, resource and regulatory problems in global infectious disease governance and implications for debates over the future of assuring the integrity of the global infectious disease research system as it unfolds over the next several years.

In Chapter 1, Michelle Rourke, a virologist from the Australian military, with a PhD in law focused on understanding the changes she faced as a researcher, traces the general historical and contemporary division between technologically advanced countries of the Global North and biodiverse countries of the Global South. The value of genetic resources over most of the twentieth century was earned by the former while the latter endeavored to assert that natural resources, including genetic resources like human pathogens, were the "common heritage of [hu]mankind." After the value of genetic resources became clearer over the course of the 1970s and 1980s, poorer countries demanded sovereign rights over natural resources and labeled activities traditionally undertaken by scientists in wealthier countries "biopiracy." Rourke identifies the 1993 Convention on Biological Diversity as the most important turning point in this history. Under the CBD, low- and middle-income countries asserted under the Charter of the United Nations and the principles of international law, the sovereign right to exploit their own resources pursuant to their own policies and to demand "the fair and equitable sharing of the benefits arising out of the utilization of genetic resources." Thereafter, low- and middle-income countries demanded that access to genetic resources be allowed only with mutually agreed terms and prior informed consent.

Rourke establishes that the first application of the CBD to human pathogens – H5N1 samples from Indonesia in 2006 – gave rise to the phrase "viral sovereignty" – that countries could demand access to benefits to share pathogens originating in their territories including but not limited to upfront payments, milestone payments, royalties, joint ownership of intellectual property, sharing of research results, collaboration, cooperation and participation, knowledge and technology transfer, capacity building, contributions to local economies, and favorable licensing terms. These demands have shifted the traditional paradigm of human pathogen sharing for infectious disease research from one of science and understanding to commercial exploitation and equity.

Benjamin Krohmal, an ethicist at Washington Hospital Center, served as bioethics faculty at the US National Institutes of Health during the time when Indonesia made its proprietary claims over the highly pathogenic H5N1 influenza virus spreading globally. He designed a survey aimed at understanding the attitudes of scientists working in both high-income and middle-income countries about sample transfer, related research and attribution rights, and distributive questions as to benefits resulting from transferred samples. Drawing upon evidence from a survey administered to over one hundred scientists in five countries, Krohmal and his team examined whether and under what circumstances scientists in low-income countries (as opposed to their governments) believe that benefits from research must be shared in order for them to share biological samples, what steps researchers from wealthy countries should take to involve partners from low- and middle-income countries, and whether or not the system overall is equitable in terms of distributing gains from scientific inquiry. In Chapter 2, Krohmal assesses the survey's findings after ten years, identifying where researchers have adopted lessons the survey communicated, and where there has been change, if any, in the global research landscape.

In Chapter 3, Brian Bird, a veterinarian and public health researcher whose expertise in Ebola spans both emergency response with the US Centers for Disease Control and Prevention and routine research with a thirty-country viral pathogen detection study, describes the field capture of animals, clinical sampling of animals and people, analysis for genetic sequencing data, transfer of samples to reference laboratories outside of low- or middle-income countries, and how confirmed infections are reported to public authorities for both public health and sovereign resource reasons. Bird argues that the process by which researchers now obtain data requires far more bureaucratic barriers, but that correspondingly, researchers are more likely to partner with local scientists and institutions, thus building capacity for disease surveillance and response should an infectious disease threat emerge. Bird's chapter shows how extensive global infectious disease research has become, how dependent it is upon international collaboration, and how critical it is that those research networks operate as smoothly as possible to ensure global health security.

Part II, Implications, opens with Chapter 4 by Haley Sullivan and Benjamin Berkman from the US National Institutes of Health Bioethics Center. Berkman and Sullivan analyze the implications for genetic research in countries with less technological capacity, primarily related to healthcare access, than countries where genomic analysis has conventionally been undertaken and applied. Increasingly, it is not only the biological samples of human pathogens that are vital for development of medicines, diagnostics and vaccines, but genetic sequencing data (GSD). While obtaining GSD used to be slow and costly, it is now fast and declining rapidly in price. The effect of these trends are to make more genetic information available, about more people, in more parts of the world. While this problem was long anticipated and prepared for in richer countries – for example, the Genetic Information Nondiscrimination Act in the US – there is little or no infrastructure for managing genetic findings in many low- and middle-income countries. Berkman and Sullivan survey the risks to research participants and the ethical and practical obligations of researchers to protect genetic information in low- and middle-income countries.

In Chapter 5, Sam Halabi, Co-Chair (with Gian Luca Burci) of the Global Virome Project's Ethical, Social, and Legal Implications Committee, analyzes the ethical criteria under which pathogen research may be undertaken during public health emergencies in low- and middle-income countries. He examines criteria applicable both to individuals and communities. Halabi emphasizes that these ethical criteria include the "importance of doing research during a public health emergency and afterward, including the collection of samples and data during and after the outbreaks." He discusses mechanisms by which ethical research may be catalyzed. He draws a distinction between ethical criteria for human pathogen research and pervasive legal ambiguities, and zealous lawyers create the false sense that there are ethical ambiguities when the use of broad consent forms for future research, detailed material transfer agreements and harmonized systems for managing samples resolve most ethical problems. For example, most roles and responsibilities for researchers and volunteers are captured in the informed consent process. Broadly, Halabi argues that ethical reasoning requires that social value of research be considered when weighing whether terms for benefits to low- and middle-income countries satisfy "fairness" inquiries and criticisms.[120]

Beyond the ethical implications explored by Berkman, Sullivan and Halabi, there are critical questions related to pathogen transfer and biosecurity. In Chapter 6, Joshua Teperowski Monrad and Rebecca Katz, Director of Georgetown University's Center for Global Health Science and Security, examine the issue of biosecurity as low- and middle-income countries hold samples until mutually agreed terms for sharing are reached. In the aftermath of the 2014–16 West Africa Ebola outbreak, there were thousands of Ebola samples that went unaccounted for as well as virus samples stored in facilities that did not have an appropriate level of biosecurity and biosafety. Monrad and Katz review the existing global governance mechanisms for addressing this biosafety and biosecurity concern, and the ongoing debate amongst donor countries as to the best path forward. They describe efforts to support the Government of Sierra Leone to find and secure Ebola samples as foreign labs shut down. They identify the challenges of tracking all Ebola samples and their associated data, and efforts to place those samples in suitable inventoried repositories by local health authorities. They conclude with recommendations for governments around the world to ensure that plans, procedures, and regulations are in place prior to the chaos of an emergency in order to ensure that dangerous pathogens are handled in safe and secure manner, that data are preserved for research, and appropriate practices are implemented.

In Chapter 7, Alexandra Phelan, who worked closely with the World Health Organization on implications of the Nagoya Protocol for public health research, studies the disputes over proprietary claims to human pathogens and reframes them as human rights problems. The human right to the highest attainable standard of health, as the World Health Organization constitution articulates it, requires both that scientific sharing for biomedical advances take place but also that the benefits of research must be distributed so as to ensure that humans have access to essential medicines. Each of these principles requires separate analysis and doing so, Phelan argues, limits the number and severity of potential conflicts between appropriate

---

[120]   Sam F. Halabi, *The Origins and Future of Global Health Law: Regulation, Security, and Pluralism*, 108(6) GEO. L.J. 1 (2020).

access and benefit sharing, on the one hand, and access to diagnostics, medicines and vaccines, on the other.

The pace of low- and middle-income countries' demands to share the benefits of biomedical research resulting from the use of human pathogens taken from their territory has exceeded the development of legal mechanisms to balance equity and science. While MTAs formed under Nagoya and other access and benefit sharing laws ensure benefits flow to low- and middle-income countries, for example, they also restrict and impede research and development.[121] Part III is committed to finding the balance between research promotion and equity, to finding solutions to unnecessary barriers to public health research. Some of these solutions now exist on a small scale as they were developed to address experiences in individual countries, especially the United States. However, they may be expanded either within the national jurisdiction of individual countries or established and operated at a global scale, especially for research areas of particular concern to global population health.

In Chapter 8, Sherry Brett-Major, an attorney representing parties in technology transfer transactions, dissects material transfer agreements as contracts that regulated collaborative relationships. She identifies typologies of MTAs, areas of rights allocation where disputes are frequent and key decisions that shed light on current MTA negotiation custom and practice.

In Chapter 9, Maria Julia Marinessen, Ruvani Chandrasekera, John Simpson, Theodore Kuschak, and Lauren Barna apply Brett-Major's principles to emergency contexts experienced by governments in Canada, the United Kingdom and the United States in the context of MERS-CoV and Zika. The government authors describe their respective efforts to reach agreement with transferring countries over pathogens, the development of an emergency use simple letter agreement to facilitate transfer, and the ways in which transfers during emergencies have changed from 2012 to 2019. The authors identify difficulties in identifying countries that possessed relevant biological samples and data, protracted negotiations over location, collaboration and benefit sharing of research, and the development of standard agreements afterwards that aimed at reducing transaction costs for access to crucial research inputs. During the Zika public health emergency, the US government developed a specific "emergency use simple letter agreement" (EUSLA) under which Zika samples could be shared for "any legitimate purpose" which broadened the typical language used for material transfers.[122] This EUSLA was adopted at the international level through the Global Health Security Initiative with the World Health Organization as an advisor to the project.[123] The EUSLA facilitated approximately 160 transfers of Zika resource materials with academic, government, and industry researchers.[124] This chapter drives

[121] ASEAN-EU STI, *Material transfer agreements: a multipurpose tool for international cooperation* (2014) at https://sea-eu.net/object/document/117 at 6.
[122] www.atcc.org/Products/All/~/media/61A2C1304E8B4857963D980FB8995A1E.ashx.
[123] https://meeting.federallabs.org/.../FLC-Award-Panel-180425-HHS-FINAL-180423.ppt.
[124] *Id.*

home the implications of the changing system of pathogen sharing in the contexts of national, regional, and global biosecurity.

In Chapter 10, Michael Mowatt and Mukul Ranjan, technology transfer experts at the US National Institutes for Allergy and Infectious Diseases (NIAID), identify the history of scientific sharing, the evolution of sharing paradigms to proprietary claims often embodied in material transfer agreements and the ensuing effort by scientists and researchers to minimize transaction costs to sharing through standard material transfer agreements and repositories. Their contribution provides an invaluable perspective from one of the major funders of scientific research worldwide.

In Chapter 11, Anne Huvos, manager of the Pandemic Influenza Preparedness Framework Secretariat at the World Health Organization, Steven Solomon, principal legal officer at WHO, and Claudia Nannini, legal officer at WHO, describe the technical process behind the PIP Framework's negotiations, and provide an overview of the challenges to, and opportunities for, the PIP Framework moving forward. They analyze how the Nagoya Protocol on Access to Genetic Resources and the Fair and Equitable Sharing of Benefits Arising from their Utilization (Nagoya Protocol) has influenced the global system of human pathogen sharing as seen from the World Health Organization's viewpoint. The most important treaty implementing the access and benefit sharing provisions of the Convention on Biological Diversity, the Nagoya Protocol establishes claims that countries may make when human pathogens are transferred from their territories of origin. Identifying a "path forward" between claims of "biopiracy" and obstruction of scientific progress, the authors analyze the provisions of the Nagoya Protocol that create win-wins for rich and poor countries and illustrate these possibilities with the Pandemic Influenza Preparedness Framework, a system that requires firms to promise to donate medicines and vaccines to poor countries in exchange for accessing influenza samples from a WHO-run system. The instrument developed to facilitate access to influenza samples from the GISRS is through two types of standard material transfer agreements (SMTA-1 and SMTA-2), the latter of which governs the obligations of research institutions and firms when using samples drawn from the system.[125] Since these MTAs are standardized, they help to reduce transaction costs normally associated with exchange and transfer, and through less involvement of lawyers and governments. They help protect national or sovereign rights by stipulating the specific use of the material, limiting or prohibiting commercial use, and restricting possible illegitimate or unacceptable claims on intellectual property.[126] SMTAs may require recipients to make all non-confidential information from the research available, to make the material available to others in case of conservation/storage, and further distribution of the material must be conducted under a new SMTA.[127] The authors clarify legal pathways available to facilitate sample sharing, including specialized international instruments under Nagoya Protocol Article 4, complexities raised by

---

[125] World Health Organization, Pandemic Influenza Preparedness Framework (2011).
[126] *Id.*
[127] *Id.*

digital sequence information, and the role of the World Health Organization in working with the CBD to promote global public health.

In the Conclusion, Gian Luca Burci, who served as the World Health
Organization's Principal Legal Adviser over much of the early history of access
and benefit sharing debates in the lead-up to the Nagoya Protocol and continues
to oversee major projects dedicated to addressing public health implications,
assesses the legal landscape as it has changed over the last fifteen years. He also
anticipates changes and opportunities.

Given that researchers must be active voices in the material transfer process, Burci
argues that researchers must be more integrated into the negotiation process.
International research collaborations in the field of infectious disease increasingly
require researchers to be more extensively knowledgeable about regulations covering
the sampling of biological resources, terms of material transfer agreements and formal
agreements establishing research partnerships. As most analysts of the problem have
concluded, knowledge of "prior informed consent," "mutually agreed terms," and
"access and benefit sharing" must be integrated with the education and research process
as researchers must now work more actively and in partnership with lawyers to ensure
that access to human pathogen samples continues as expeditiously as possible.[128]

Burci notes that access and benefit sharing regulations have changed the way that
some research scientists from museums, biobanks, universities, and government
research institutes collect and share samples. However, the perception that genetic
resources are in the public domain persists in the biological sciences, and many
researchers are still unaware of the legal requirements surrounding the collection
and use of environmental genetic resources for research purposes.[129] Burci anticipates a future where researchers and policymakers are more closely integrated – for
the better – in order to reach the balance between equity and public health research
promotion.

---

[128] Kate Davis, Martin F. Smit, Martin Kidd, Suzanne Sharrock, and Pamela Allenstein, *An Access and
Benefit-Sharing Awareness Survey for Botanic Gardens: Are They Prepared for the Nagoya Protocol?*, 98
SOUTH AFRICAN JOURNAL OF BOTANY, 148–56 (2015). ("Global socio-economic region and international
involvement were significantly related to several measures of familiarity and preparedness.
The survey demonstrates a need for more effective communication with government authorities
and within institutions. Capacity-building initiatives and practical tools are needed to enable gardens
and their networks to understand access and benefit-sharing, comply with new legislation, build trust
and safeguard their role in conservation.")

[129] Claire Lajaunie and Calvin Wai-Loon Ho, *Pathogens Collections, Biobanks and Related-Data in a
One Health Legal and Ethical Perspective* (2017) 1 PARASITOLOGY 2 (2017). ("Research on emerging
infectious diseases calls for a work on collections of pathogens (including hosts or vectors from which
the pathogens were isolated), related to human and animal health, to wildlife or on the environmental material. In this respect, the adoption of a One Health perspective is determined by the need
for a common approach to consider the collection, storage and use of pathogens coming from human
or non-human sources, and particularly when the same pathogen is taken from different environments ... The legal and ethical cutting-edge research on Biomedical Big Data is particularly
stimulating when it comes to address challenges related to collections or biobanks of pathogens
such as prior informed consent and accessibility, Material Transfer Agreement or benefit sharing.")

PART I

The Geopolitical, Historical, and Scientific Context

The History of Accessing and Sharing Human Pathogens for Public Health Research

Michelle Rourke[*]

1.1 INTRODUCTION

Public health researchers have always had to manage practical barriers to accessing pathogens. Anyone collecting or transferring pathogen samples must consider how they will access an outbreak area, issues of patient privacy when collecting diagnostic samples, appropriate sample packaging, cold chain transport and safe storage, sample degradation, and international import and export controls. These requirements all generate costs. But over the past four decades, the process of accessing pathogen samples for public health research has become legally fraught for reasons beyond these practical considerations. Government authorities and nongovernment institutions have started claiming various forms of ownership over pathogen samples, monetizing these vital inputs to the scientific process and increasing the costs of public health research.

Pathogens were once treated as public domain or common pool resources, where researchers were free to access and use whatever pathogen samples they required for their research.[1] Isolates of pathogens were transferred informally between scientific collaborators around the world.[2] If there were ownership claims of any sort vested in these isolates, it was by virtue of the fact that someone had spent the time collecting the sample and isolating the pathogen, and continues to invest the resources required to store and share those isolates.[3] Any ownership-like claims over a pathogen isolate were effectively exhausted when that isolate was transferred to the next party.

---

[*] The author wishes to thank Professor Charles Lawson for feedback and helpful discussions.

[1] Claire Lajaunie & Calvin Wai-Loon Ho, *Pathogens Collections, Biobanks and Related-Data in a One Health Legal and Ethical Perspective*, 145 PARASITOLOGY 688, 689 (2018).

[2] "Historically, the global sharing of pathogens was primarily done informally. In many instances, pathogens were shared without formal permission from national authorities, written agreement, or ongoing research collaborations between provider and recipient countries. Recipients often failed to acknowledge the contributions of provider countries or to share other benefits derived from the use of pathogens." World Health Organization, *Implementation of the Nagoya Protocol and Pathogen Sharing: Public Health Implications* (2016), www.who.int/influenza/pip/2016-review/NagoyaStudy AdvanceCopy_full.pdf?ua=1.

[3] Lajaunie & Wai-Loon Ho, *supra* note 1, at 2.

This chapter examines the enclosure of pathogen samples in two legal domains: intellectual property and the sovereign domain of the nation-state. The extension of intellectual property protections and sovereignty form different and sometimes conflicting ownership claims over pathogens that can impede their access and utilization for public health research. The enclosure of pathogens in these legal domains has closely followed the history of other (nonpathogenic) genetic resources, leading to the "hyperownership" of genetic materials.[4] The open sharing of pathogens between scientific collaborators is a dying practice,[5] and pathogens are being encased in the same proprietary claims that apply to other nonpathogenic genetic resources.[6]

This chapter traces the history of these legal developments. It will first describe the enclosure of genetic resources in intellectual property protections. It will then examine how intellectual property claims over biological resources precipitated the "grand bargain" of the United Nations' Convention on Biological Diversity in 1992[7] and how this treaty was foundational to the pivotal events of 2007 that saw countries start to exercise sovereign control over pathogens under international access and benefit-sharing laws. It will demonstrate, by way of example, that the extension of conflicting intellectual property and sovereignty over pathogens has led to confusion as to whom is allowed to conduct research and development on certain pathogens. The chapter concludes that the enclosure of pathogens in multiple legal domains of ownership have turned pathogens into articles of trade. Other chapters in this volume will examine how both intellectual property protections and access and benefit-sharing regulations practically impact the process of accessing pathogen samples for public health research, so it is important to first understand how we got here.

1.2 INTELLECTUAL PROPERTY

The enclosure of genetic resources in the intellectual property space was aligned with the overall strengthening of intellectual property protections around the world

---

[4] This chapter borrows heavily from Safrin's thesis that the "legal enclosure of genetic material" has come about through the extension of the patent system by developed countries and, in response, the assertion of sovereign rights over genetic materials by developing countries. This is true for pathogens, a specific subset of the genetic materials that Safrin was referring to, albeit a subset whose enclosure in these legal domains came about a couple of decades behind the developments she describes. *See* Sabrina Safrin, *Hyperownership in a Time of Biotechnological Promise: The International Conflict to Control the Building Blocks of Life*, 98 AM. J. INT'L L. 641 (2004).

[5] JEROME H. REICHMAN, PAUL F. UHLIR, & TOM DEDEURWAERDERE, GOVERNING DIGITALLY INTEGRATED RESOURCES, DATA, AND LITERATURE 255–56 (2016).

[6] For most public health researchers (who do not have a view to commercializing their research) their experiences with both intellectual property and sovereignty are likely to have been through the institutional material transfer agreement (MTA). *See* Philip Mirowski, *Livin' with the MTA*, 46 MINERVA 317 (2008).

[7] Kerry Ten Kate & Sarah A. Laird, *Biodiversity and Business: Coming to Terms with the 'Grand Bargain'*, 76 INT'L AFF. 241 (2000).

in the 1980s.[8] This was part of a larger trend towards commercializing scientific outputs and the scientific process itself.[9] Throughout the 1980s the percentage of industry funding for scientific research was increasing in Western countries, relative to government funding,[10] and the business models of universities were starting to change from operating as educational institutions to commercial entities. Intellectual property, including patents, trademarks and trade secrets, came to be considered a vital part of many universities' and research institutions' asset portfolios.

Patents had been awarded for nucleotides (and nucleotide derivatives) since the mid-twentieth century,[11] but two events of 1980 are often cited as being essential (but not themselves sufficient) to the envelopment of genetic resources in intellectual property.[12] First is the United States Supreme Court Case *Diamond v. Chakrabarty* which ruled that genetically modified living organisms were patent eligible subject matter.[13] Second, the Bayh-Dole Act encouraged university researchers to patent their innovations even if they came about through publicly funded research. These, and other events,[14] helped "to spur a soft but rapid arms race in patenting molecular biology"[15] or what Koepsell has called an "unprecedented landgrab"[16] where applicants sought patents on isolated gene sequences even when they had no obvious commercial potential.

Pathogens were not immune to these developments. In 2003, government researchers from the United States, Canada and Hong Kong applied for patents on different selections of gene sequences from the Severe Acute Respiratory Syndrome (SARS) coronavirus genome.[17] Granted patents afford the holder monopoly rights to exclude

---

[8] PHILIP MIROWSKI P, SCIENCE-MART: PRIVATIZING AMERICAN SCIENCE 14–15 (2011).

[9] *See Id.*

[10] *Id.* at 21.

[11] Jacob S. Sherkow & Henry T. Greely, *The History of Patenting Genetic Material*, 49 ANN. REV. GENETICS 161, 164–65 (2015). ("Soon after Francis Crick and James D. Watson famously discovered the molecular structure of DNA in 1953, several researchers began to patent nucleotide derivatives, some of them naturally occurring. In 1957, for example, Har Gobind Khorana, who in 1968 would receive the Nobel Prize in Physiology or Medicine for his work on deciphering the genetic code, received a patent for synthesized nucleoside polyphosphates. Similarly, in 1957, Charles Heidelberger, then a researcher at the University of Wisconsin, received US Patent No. 2,802,005, for a derivative of uracil, one of the four nucleotide bases used in RNA.")

[12] Keeping in mind that both these events occurred in the United States, yet the enclosure of genetic resources in intellectual property protections occurred across the technologically advanced countries of the Global North.

[13] Diamond v. Chakrabarty, 447 *U.S.* 303 (1980).

[14] *See* Sherkow & Greely, *supra* note 11. ("The last major event in this annus mirabilis occurred on December 12, 1980: the signing of the Bayh-Dole Act by lame-duck President Jimmy Carter. Prior to the Bayh-Dole Act, inventions created with any federal funding were owned, at least in part, by the federal government. Because many such inventions were created at large research institutions, such as universities, this discouraged institutions of higher education from commercializing their faculty's inventions and dissuaded research into the applied sciences. By allowing institutions themselves to be assignees to, and hence owners of, their faculties' inventions, the Bayh-Dole Act encouraged universities to engage in patentable research, perhaps nowhere more actively than in the life sciences.")

[15] *Id.* at 166.

[16] DAVID KOEPSELL, WHO OWNS YOU? SCIENCE, INNOVATION, AND THE GENE PATENT WARS 79 (2015).

[17] *Id.* at 338.

others from using the patented subject matter for a defined period, however, when it comes to isolated gene sequences, it is not entirely clear what uses can be excluded.[18] Despite these uncertainties, patents for isolated pathogen gene sequences begat further patents: the SARS researchers from Hong Kong reportedly submitted their patent applications simply because the other researchers had done so.[19]

In 1994, the World Trade Organization's (WTO) Agreement on the Trade Related Aspects of Intellectual Property (TRIPS Agreement) took patent law from being a predominately domestic issue to one of international trade law.[20] Safrin has noted that: "By the early 1990s, not only were biological goods subjected to a range of intellectual property rights, but developing countries were facing pressure, particularly from the United States, to extend intellectual property protection to such goods in their own countries."[21] While the TRIPS Agreement "is only indirectly concerned with biological resources,"[22] it obliged WTO Member States to grant patents on living organisms, where this had previously been optional.[23] With the adoption of international minimum intellectual property standards under TRIPS, the uncertainties in domestic law surrounding the patenting of isolated gene sequences became global uncertainties. This was said to have had a stifling effect on public health research, as "some patent holders [sought] to use patents primarily to preempt others' research efforts and to profit from such pre-emption."[24] Oldham and Forero have noted that "[t]he increasing 'enclosure' of biology using patents is seen as a threat to basic scientific research and the free sharing of knowledge through the public domain."[25]

[18] *See* Kembrew McLeod, Freedom of Expression: Overzealous Copyright Bozos and Other Enemies of Creativity 40 (2005).
[19] Peter K. Yu, *Virotech Patents, Viropiracy, and Viral Sovereignty*, 45 Ariz. St. L.J. 1563, 1597 (2014). ("Regardless of how the CDC, the BCCA, and Versitech would ultimately handle their patents if they were granted, their eagerness to patent the virus to promote the public interest has raised intriguing questions about the need for "defensive patenting." In this case, the agencies were not patenting to profit from a monopoly over technology involving the claimed isolated sequences. Instead, by patenting the technology and subsequently introducing free licenses, these agencies sought to prevent others from abusing such a monopoly.")
[20] Charles Lawson & Barbara Ann Hocking, Accessing and Benefit Sharing Avian Influenza Viruses through the World Health Organization, A CBD and TRIPS Compromise Thanks to Indonesia's Sovereignty Claim? in Incentives for Global Public Health: Patent Law and Access to Essential Medicines (Thomas Pogge, Matthew Rimmer, & Kim Rubenstein eds., 2010).
[21] Safrin, *supra* note 4, at 646.
[22] Philippe Cullet, *Property Rights Regimes over Biological Resources*, 19 Envt. and Planning C: Gov't and Pol'y 651, 656 (2001).
[23] Sampath notes that in accordance with Article 27(3)(b) of TRIPS, countries can deny patents on plants and animals but not on microorganisms. Padmashree G. Sampath, Regulating Bioprospecting: Institutions for Drug Research, Access and Benefit-Sharing 42 (2005).
[24] Yu, *supra* note 19, at 1595.
[25] Paul Oldham, Stephen Hall, & Oscar Forero, *Biological Diversity in the Patent System*, 8 PLoS ONE e78737 at 2 (2013). *See also* Charles Lawson, *Patenting DNA Sequences After the Myriad Decision: New Frontiers or Just More of the Same?*, 33 Biotech. L. Rep. 3 (2014).

Since the recent *Myriad* rulings,[26] it is unlikely that isolated gene sequences that are not materially different to genetic variants found in nature will be considered patent eligible in major jurisdictions.[27] The status of existing patents on pathogen gene sequences is therefore uncertain. However, the overzealous patenting of gene sequences by technologically advanced nations resulted in an ownership backlash from developing countries, which manifested as the vigorous assertion of sovereignty over genetic resources in the early 1990s.[28]

1.3 RESOURCE SOVEREIGNTY AND ACCESS AND BENEFIT-SHARING

Since the middle of the twentieth century, biological resources were said to be the common heritage of humankind. Cullet has noted that: "Common heritage does not imply an absence of property rights, but rather the possibility for various actors to use and enjoy the fruits of a given resource without being stopped by the assertion of monopoly rights."[29] The common heritage concept was a "convenient construct" for developed countries[30] that routinely took genetic resources from the global commons and asserted limited term monopoly rights over them (and their derivatives) in the form of patent protections, eroding "[t]he traditional paradigm that genetic resources were part of the global commons."[31] Furthermore, forcing developing countries to comply with the very Western notion of intellectual property (by making membership in the WTO conditional upon acceding to TRIPS) was seen by many developing countries as an extension of the colonization process.[32] Thus, the extension of sovereignty over genetic resources can be seen as a developing country-led backlash against the enclosure of genetic materials in intellectual property by developed nations, particularly the United States.[33]

Interestingly enough, the watershed agreement that codified sovereignty over genetic resources in a binding international treaty, the Convention on Biological Diversity (CBD) was supported by the United States during the negotiation phase.[34] This is because recognizing "the sovereign rights of States over their natural resources" and that States have "the authority to determine access to genetic

---

[26] *See, e.g.*, Ass'n for Molecular Pathology v. Myriad Genetics Inc., 569 U.S. 576 (2013) and D'Arcy v. Myriad Genetics Inc., 258 CLR 334 (2015) (Austl.).

[27] Although, the European Patent Convention does expressly permit gene sequence patenting. ANDREW STEWART ET AL., INTELLECTUAL PROPERTY IN AUSTRALIA 414–16 (6th ed., 2018). *See also* Sherkow & Greely, *supra* note 11, at 175.

[28] Safrin, *supra* note 4, at 647.

[29] Cullet, *supra* note 22, at 662.

[30] REICHMAN ET AL., *supra* note 5, at 4.

[31] Safrin, *supra* note 4, at 645.

[32] *See* JOHANNA GIBSON, COMMUNITY RESOURCES: INTELLECTUAL PROPERTY, INTERNATIONAL TRADE AND PROTECTION OF TRADITIONAL KNOWLEDGE ch. 4 (2005).

[33] Safrin, *supra* note 4, at 674.

[34] *See* RANEE K. L. PANJABI, THE EARTH SUMMIT AT RIO: POLITICS, ECONOMICS AND THE ENVIRONMENT 116 (1997).

resources,"[35] was a necessary precondition to employing a market-based solution to environmental conservation: access and benefit-sharing. That is, the exchange of facilitating access to genetic resources for the benefits associated with their use; what some have called the "grand bargain."[36] Mirowski has stated: "The best way to initiate the privatization program in any area that had previously been subject to communal or other forms of allocation is simply to get the state to institute a new class of property rights."[37] Such a position originally suited the United States, who in the early 1990s was eager to pursue market-based solutions for many social problems,[38] however the United States never ended up becoming party to the CBD owing to the intellectual property concessions included in the final text of the agreement.[39]

Cullet has stated that "the assertion of sovereign rights by the state is conceptually similar to private property rights."[40] Sovereign rights, like intellectual property protections, can thus be considered a form of monopoly.[41] But unlike intellectual property, which is a term-limited monopoly, sovereignty may be interpreted as a more enduring form of monopoly rights: a conceptual "tether" that links genetic resources to their place of origin,[42] perhaps in perpetuity.[43] In implementing the access and benefit-sharing provisions of the CBD countries have "introduce[d] concepts of ownership and property rights into the collection, exchange and use of genetic resources, and their parts and components" within their domestic laws and regulations.[44] The CBD requires that access to genetic resources "be subject to prior informed consent" of the provider[45] and exchanged "on mutually agreed terms" between the provider and user of the genetic resources.[46] While the CBD encourages States "to create conditions to facilitate access to genetic resources,"[47] the access and benefit-sharing transaction mechanism requires that the initial access is somewhat restricted (with States determining the level of restriction through domestic laws).

[35] Convention on Biological Diversity art. 15(1), 1992.

[36] *See, e.g.,* Ten Kate & Laird, *supra* note 7.

[37] MIROWSKI, *supra* note 8, at 30.

[38] *See* PANJABI, *supra* note 34, at ch. 3.

[39] Article 16(5) of the CBD "recogniz[es] that patents and other intellectual property rights may have an influence on the implementation of this Convention" and asks parties to "ensure that such rights are supportive of and do not run counter to [the CBD's] objectives." For an explanation of the US position, *see* Joseph Straus, *Patents on Biomaterial – A New Colonialism or a Means for Technology Transfer and Benefit-Sharing?* in BIOETHICS IN A SMALL WORLD 54 (Felix Thiele et al. eds., 2005).

[40] Cullet, *supra* note 22, at 655.

[41] *Id.*

[42] Amy Hinterberger & Natalie Porter, *Genomic and Viral Sovereignty: Tethering the Materials of Global Biomedicine*, 27 PUB. CULTURE 361 (2015).

[43] *See* Michelle F. Rourke, *Never Mind the Science, Here's the Convention on Biological Diversity: Viral Sovereignty in the Smallpox Destruction Debate*, 25 J.L. & MED. 429 (2018).

[44] CHARLES LAWSON ET AL., *Information as the Latest Site of Conflict in the Ongoing Contests about Access to and Sharing the Benefits from Exploiting Genetic Resources*, 10 QUEEN MARY JOURNAL OF INTELLECTUAL PROPERTY 7 (2020).

[45] Convention on Biological Diversity art. 15(5), 1992.

[46] *Id.* at art. 15(4).

[47] *Id.* at art. 15(2).

The CBD regulates access to "any material of plant, animal, microbial or other origin containing functional units of heredity," "of actual or potential value."[48] This broad definition certainly captures pathogens,[49] although, given their seemingly doubtful status as objects worthy of environmental conservation efforts, pathogens did not receive much attention with respect to the international regime on access and benefit-sharing until 2007. This is when Indonesia withheld samples of avian influenza virus from the World Health Organization's (WHO) Global Influenza Surveillance Network, claiming that they had sovereignty over their viruses under the CBD.

Indonesia's claim of "viral sovereignty"[50] over the H5N1 avian influenza viruses isolated from within their territory came as a shock to many in the international community.[51] In its historical context, however, this event and the developments stemming from it were predictable. Indonesia's position comported with a line of argument that had become entrenched in the international community: that genetic resources were no longer the common heritage of humankind and were now considered to lie within the sovereign domain of the nation-state.[52] Pathogens were simply the last genetic materials to move out of the public domain and into a legal regime of nationally regulated access.[53]

Pathogens certainly meet the definitional criteria of "genetic resources" laid out in the CBD.[54] Many countries felt (and the United States still holds) that pathogens

[48] *Id.* at art. 2.

[49] *See* Frederick M. Abbott, *An International Legal Framework for the Sharing of Pathogens: Issues and Challenges*, ICTSD Issue Paper No. 30 (2010) and Michelle Rourke, *Viruses for Sale: All Viruses Are Subject to Access and Benefit-Sharing Obligations under the Conventional on Biological Diversity*, 39 EUR. INTELL. PROP. REV. 79 (2017). Abbott notes that "[t]he conclusion that pathogen materials probably are covered by the CBD is not intended to suggest that the CBD is better equipped than the WHO to address the sharing of pathogen materials in the public health context, but rather addresses the existing or 'default' legal situation." *See* Abbott, p. vii.

[50] The term "viral sovereignty" was coined by Richard Holbrooke and Laurie Garrett. *See* Richard Holbrooke & Laurie Garrett, *"Sovereignty" That Risks Global Health*, THE WASHINGTON POST (August 10, 2008), www.washingtonpost.com/wp-dyn/content/article/2008/08/08/AR2008080802919.html.

[51] *See* Laurie Garrett & David P. Fidler, *Sharing H5N1 Viruses to Stop a Global Influenza Pandemic*, 4 PLoS MED.e330 (2007); David P. Fidler, *Influenza Virus Samples, International Law, and Global Health Diplomacy*, 14 EMERGING INFECTIOUS DISEASES 88 (2008); Kelley Lee & David Fidler, *Avian and Pandemic Influenza: Progress and Problems with Global Health Governance*, 2 GLOBAL PUB. HEALTH 215 (2007); Arthur L. Caplan & David R. Curry, *Leveraging Genetic Resources or Moral Blackmail? Indonesia and Avian Flu Virus Sample Sharing*, 7 AM. J. BIOETHICS 1 (2007); and Holbrooke & Garrett, *supra* note 50.

[52] *See, e.g.*, G.A. Res. 1803 (XVII) (Dec. 14, 1962); G.A. Res. 2158 (XXI) (Nov. 22, 1966); G.A. Res. 3016 (XXVII) (Dec. 18, 1972); G.A. Res. 3171 (XVIII) (Dec. 17, 1973); G.A. Res. 3281 (XXIX) (December 12, 1974); G.A. Res. 3201 (S-VI) (May 1, 1974), and, of course, the Convention on Biological Diversity 1992.

[53] Although this might also be characterized as States having always had sovereignty over their genetic resources and the CBD simply codifying that claim in a binding international treaty.

[54] Viruses and bacteria do not form a bulk product for consumption, they evolve and contain genes, functional units of heredity and have scientific value. That means that they meet the definition of genetic resources under the CBD/NP ABS regime. *See* Morten W. Tvedt, *Beyond Nagoya: Towards a Legally Functional System of Access and Benefit Sharing* in GLOBAL GOVERNANCE OF GENETIC RESOURCES: ACCESS AND BENEFIT SHARING AFTER THE NAGOYA PROTOCOL 168–70 (S. Oberthür & G.

should not be included in the scope of the CBD as they are not suitable candidates for environmental conservation efforts, rather, pathogens are a scourge the international community seeks to eradicate.[55] Leaving aside the point that storing pathogen samples is an act of conserving a scientifically valuable (and sometimes commercially valuable) genetic resource, the conservation argument ignores the fact that the CBD was not *just* about conservation. The objectives of the CBD are "[1] the conservation of biological diversity, [2] the sustainable use of its components and [3] the fair and equitable sharing of the benefits arising out of the utilization of genetic resources."[56] It is this third objective that brings about the access and benefit-sharing transactional mechanism for "genetic material of actual or potential value."[57] Pathogens are valuable for foundational and applied biotechnological research and are of undeniable commercial value to the pharmaceutical sector.[58] The exchange of pathogens is, therefore, "an essential aspect of the ABS [access and benefit-sharing] system";[59] a system that is also recognized in the UN's Sustainable Development Goals, two of which "contain targets calling for the promotion of access to and fair and equitable sharing of benefits arising from the utilization of genetic resources and associated traditional knowledge."[60]

To settle the impasse with Indonesia, the WHO negotiated the Pandemic Influenza Preparedness Framework (PIP Framework), passed as a nonbinding resolution in May 2011.[61] This specialized ABS framework "recognize[s] the sovereign right of States over their biological resources" but applies only "to the sharing of H5N1 and other influenza viruses with human pandemic potential."[62] That is, the WHO acceded to the notion that countries have sovereign authority over their pathogens as per the CBD, but chose to provide guidelines for the sharing of only a minute subset of those pathogens: influenza viruses with human pandemic potential. This effectively left all other pathogens within the remit of the CBD.

Before the PIP Framework was finalized, Abbott warned that if the WHO created a specialized access and benefit-sharing instrument for pandemic influenza viruses

K. Rosendal eds., 2014). Furthermore, pathogens are nonhuman genetic resources even if derived from a human sample; the human is simply the environment for those pathogens. Even still, countries have already exercised sovereign authority over access to their nationals' human genetic material. *See* Safrin, supra note 4, at 662.

55 Fidler, *supra* note 51, at 90.
56 Convention on Biological Diversity art. 1, 1992.
57 *Id.* at art. 2.
58 Reichman, Uhlir and Dedeurwaerdere have noted that "microbial genetic resources ... are increasingly perceived as potentially valuable commodities in their own right." REICHMAN ET AL., *supra* note 5, at 43.
59 Tvedt, *supra* note 54, at 170.
60 Food and Agriculture Organization of the United Nations, *Access and Benefit-Sharing: SDG Commitment and Challenge for the Food and Agriculture Sector* (2018), www.fao.org/sustainable-development-goals/news/detail-news/en/c/1045012/.
61 WORLD HEALTH ASSEMBLY, PANDEMIC INFLUENZA PREPAREDNESS: SHARING OF INFLUENZA VIRUSES AND ACCESS TO VACCINES AND OTHER BENEFITS (2011).
62 *Id.* at 3.1.

and failed to address access to "pathogen materials more generally under the auspices of the ABS protocol and/or the CBD" they risked creating "a two-tiered system" of pathogen access.[63] Unfortunately, this is precisely what happened, and the international public health community is still grappling with the consequences of this "missed opportunity,"[64] as is demonstrated in the events following the emergence of the Middle East respiratory syndrome (MERS) coronavirus in 2012, discussed in the following section.

Negotiations for the PIP Framework overlapped with negotiations for the Nagoya Protocol on Access to Genetic Resources and the Fair and Equitable Sharing of Benefits Arising from their Utilization to the Convention on Biological Diversity.[65] This optional but binding supplemental agreement was created to clarify the access and benefit-sharing provisions outlined in the CBD.[66] It was signed in October 2010 and entered into force on 12 October 2014.[67] During negotiations for the Nagoya Protocol, the European Union introduced a provision that would have effectively invalidated sovereign claims over pathogens.[68] "The proposals by the developed countries were hence seen as an attempt to preempt the outcome of the WHO [PIP Framework] negotiations. And to lock developing countries into a position that would perpetuate an inequitable situation."[69] The proposal was roundly rejected by developing countries and the provision on pathogens that appears in the final version of the Nagoya Protocol is included in Article 8 on Special Considerations. It states, in part, that parties to the Nagoya Protocol shall: "[p]ay due regard to cases of present or imminent emergencies that threaten or damage human, animal or plant health, as determined nationally or internationally. Parties may take into consideration the need for expeditious access to genetic resources and expeditious fair and equitable sharing of benefits arising out of the use of such genetic resources."[70] That is, the Nagoya Protocol only asks countries to consider accelerating the access and benefit-sharing transaction during public health emergencies. It does not require countries to sideline the process altogether.

[63] Abbott, *supra* note 49, at viii.
[64] Adam Kamradt-Scott & Kelley Lee, *The 2011 Pandemic Influenza Preparedness Framework: Global Health Secured or a Missed Opportunity?*, 59 POL. STUD. 831 (2011).
[65] Conference of the Parties to the Convention on Biological Diversity, *Report of the Tenth Meeting of the Conference of the Parties to the Convention on Biological Diversity* ¶ 103 and Annex (Decision X/1, Annex – Nagoya Protocol) (2010).
[66] The Nagoya Protocol expanded upon some of the ABS obligations found in the CBD, including for the use of traditional knowledge associated with genetic resources (*see* art. 8(j)), simplified measures for accessing genetic resources for non-commercial research purposes (art. 8(a)), provisions for ABS compliance and monitoring (arts. 15–18) and, importantly, provisions for a global multilateral benefit-sharing mechanism (art. 10 and 11).
[67] *Parties to the Nagoya Protocol*, CONVENTION ON BIOLOGICAL DIVERSITY (2019), www.cbd.int/abs/nagoya-protocol/signatories/default/shtml. At the time of writing, the Nagoya Protocol has 116 parties.
[68] Gurdial S. Nijar, *The Nagoya Protocol on Access and Benefit Sharing of Genetic Resources: Analysis and Implementation Options for Developing Countries*, SOUTH CENTRE RESEARCH PAPER NO. 36, 115–16 (2011), www.southcentre.int/wp-content/uploads/2013/08/Ev_130201_GNjar1.pdf.
[69] *Id.* at 16.
[70] Nagoya Protocol 2010, *supra* note 65, art. 8(b).

The original intent of the access and benefit-sharing mechanism in the CBD and expanded upon in the Nagoya Protocol was laudable, and the inclusion of pathogens within this legal scheme is now undeniable.[71] Unfortunately, however, access and benefit-sharing has proven to be a flawed mechanism that has not yet been successful at achieving its aims.[72] Between 2007 and 2011, the WHO really did miss the opportunity to lead the international community in building a consensus about how access to pathogens *should* be regulated and whether the extension of owner-ship rights (both intellectual property and sovereign rights) is appropriate for the regulation of pathogen access. The WHO appears to be optimistic about the opportunities that the Nagoya Protocol to the CBD presents for pathogen sharing,[73] but realistically, until there is another 2007-like event forcing parties to the negotiat-ing table the current "two-tiered system" for pathogen access (where the PIP Framework covers a subset of influenza viruses and all other pathogens remain under the remit of the CBD and Nagoya Protocol) is likely to remain.[74] The regulation of pathogens under the CBD encourages countries to engage in bilateral negotiations for pathogen access in order to leverage benefits, and at no time do countries have more leverage than when the pathogen in question is killing people.

1.4 CONFLICTING OWNERSHIP CLAIMS OVER MERS

In June 2012, an Egyptian physician working in Jeddah, Saudi Arabia, had difficul-ties identifying the causative agent of his patient's severe respiratory infection. The physician sent a clinical specimen to the Erasmus Medical Center (EMC) in the Netherlands.[75] On 20 September 2012, a ProMED-mail report authored by the physician alerted the world to the isolation of a novel coronavirus, later named the Middle East respiratory syndrome coronavirus (MERS-CoV).[76] Three days later, the team from EMC (along with the physician) filed a 182-page patent application

---

[71] In both definitional and practical terms, as countries are indeed choosing to exercise their sovereign authority by regulating access to pathogens within their domestic ABS regulations. *See* Rourke, *supra* note 49.

[72] *See, e.g.*, Charles Lawson, *Conserving Genetic Resources, Access and Benefit Sharing, Intellectual Property and Climate Change* in INTELLECTUAL PROPERTY AND CLEAN ENERGY – THE PARIS AGREEMENT AND CLIMATE JUSTICE (Matthew Rimmer ed., 2018); DANIEL F. ROBINSON, BIODIVERSITY, ACCESS AND BENEFIT-SHARING 175, 179 (2015).

[73] World Health Organization, *supra* note 2, at 23.

[74] *See* Abbott, *supra* note 49, at viii.

[75] Further details about the 2012 MERS-CoV outbreak in Saudi Arabia, and the conflicting ownership claims that resulted in delays to accessing specimens, can be found in A. E. Bollinger, *E-MERS-GENCY: An Application and Evaluation of the Pandemic Influenza Preparedness Framework to the Outbreak of MERS-CoV*, 29 TEMPLE INTERNATIONAL & COMPARATIVE LAW JOURNAL 1 (2015), and David P. Fidler, *Who Owns MERS? The Intellectual Property Controversy Surrounding the Latest Pandemic*, FOREIGN AFFAIRS (June 6, 2013), www.foreignaffairs.com/articles/saudi-arabia/2013–06-06/who-owns-mers.

[76] Ali M. Zaki, *Novel Coronavirus – Saudi Arabia: Human Isolate*, PROMED-MAIL (Sept. 15, 2012), www.promedmail.org/direct.php?id=1302733.

over "the nucleic acid and/or amino acid sequences of the MERS-CoV genome" and associated "diagnostic means and methods, prophylactic means and methods and therapeutic means and methods."[77] The Saudi government was "unhappy that, although the virus was first isolated in their country, [the physician's] action [had] resulted in handing sovereign and intellectual-property rights on the first diagnostic tests or treatments over to an institute in the Netherlands."[78]

A press release from EMC in May 2013 stated that "[i]t is clearly a misunderstanding that [EMC] owns the virus. Only specific applications related to it, like vaccines and medicines can be patented."[79] This, however, highlights the considerable confusion surrounding gene patents. The EMC's patent application specifically claims the "nucleic acid and/or amino acid sequences of the MERS-CoV genome."[80] Lawson and Hocking have stated that: "existing patents claiming a virus, or part of a virus composition per se, or a step in the development of a vaccine using a virus, or part of a virus composition per se, may prevent the use of that composition or require consent of the patent holder to exercise the patented product, process or product of the process."[81] Furthermore, McLeod has astutely noted that "[d]espite the fact that companies say they don't technically own a gene, they have *de facto* control over the way that gene's sequence can be used – which is only a slight rhetorical distance from actual ownership."[82]

The disputed claims over MERS-CoV revealed the conflict inherent in the two legal regimes: intellectual property and access and benefit-sharing.[83] Fidler summarized the situation:

> If Saudi Arabia has sovereign rights over the sample, moreover, [EMC] is ignoring these rights and engaging in a form of "biopiracy" by exploiting a Saudi genetic resource without Saudi consent. This argument implicates the Dutch government because the Netherlands and Saudi Arabia are CBD parties, and the Dutch government has not intervened to protect Saudi Arabia's rights recognized by this treaty.[84]

[77] At the time of writing, the patent had not been granted. Bartholomeous L. Haagmans et al., Human Betacoronavirus Lineage c and Identification of N-Terminal Dipeptidyl Peptidase as Its Virus Receptor. Patent Application, Int'l Patent No. WO2014045254A2 (filed Sept. 23, 2012), https://patenti mages.storage.googleapis.com/4a/48/3e/c84fe4ebeac669/WO2014045254A2.pdf.

[78] Declan Butler, *Tensions Linger over Discovery of Coronavirus*, NATURE NEWS (Jan. 14, 2013), www .nature.com/news/tensions-linger-over-discovery-of-coronavirus-1.12108.

[79] Press Release, Erasmus Medical Center, Erasmus MC: no restrictions for public health research into MERS coronavirus (May 24, 2013), www.erasmusmc.nl/perskamer/archief/2013/4164294/?lang=en.

[80] The abstract to the patent application reads: "The invention provides an isolated essentially mammalian positive-sense single stranded RNA virus classifiable as belonging to the Order: Nidovirales; Family: Coronaviridae; Subfamily: Coronavirinae; Genus: Betacoronavirus; and non-Lineage A, non-Lineage B or non-Lineage D, human betacoronavirus."

[81] Lawson & Hocking, *supra* note 20, at 298.

[82] McLeod, *supra* note 18, at 40.

[83] This has been the topic of some interesting scholarship. See, e.g., Lawson & Hocking, *supra* note 20; G. KRISTIN ROSENDAL, THE CONVENTION ON BIOLOGICAL DIVERSITY AND DEVELOPING COUNTRIES (2000); Straus, *supra* note 39, at 69; Sampath, *supra* note 23, at 45.

[84] Fidler, *supra* note 75.

Throughout the standoff, WHO Director General Margaret Chan made comments that appeared to rebuke both EMC and Saudi Arabia.[85] At the 2013 World Health Assembly she encouraged countries to share their MERS-CoV samples through WHO Collaborating Centres, and not bilaterally.[86] After recognizing sovereignty over viruses just two years before in the PIP Framework, it was impossible for the WHO to now take the stance that Saudi Arabia did not have a claim to the virus that was the subject of EMC's patent application. Thus, States have every incentive to exercise sovereignty and enter into whatever agreements (bilateral or multilateral) they feel are going to be in their own best interest. In later years the WHO acknowledged the confusion caused in such incidents:

> during recent public health emergencies of international concern … the international response was impacted by a lack of clarity over such questions as: which government entity could grant access to pathogens, which entity became the custodian of the pathogens after transfer, whether intellectual property rights could be sought over the pathogens and whether benefit-sharing obligations were linked to access.[87]

These issues remain unresolved. The WHO continues to recognize States' sovereign authority over not only their pathogens, but also over epidemiological data related to pathogens.[88] This means that States currently have no incentive to share their sovereign pathogens in a multilateral manner unless benefits are provided in return. This is especially so if they feel they are effectively relinquishing their sovereign rights the moment the pathogen samples leave their territorial borders.[89] In this instance, the Saudi government may well have had theoretical sovereignty over the MERS-CoV sample that became the subject of EMC's patent application, but they had lost all functional control of that sample the moment the physician sent it outside of Saudi Arabia. The WHO's vagueness on these ownership issues has encouraged states to maintain functional control over pathogen samples until they can leverage some sort of benefit from the situation (noting that such benefits could ultimately be put towards the public health response to the infectious agent in question).

[85] Jeremy Youde, *MERS and Global Health Governance*, 70 INT'L J. 119, 135 (2015).
[86] Laurie Garrett, *Why a Saudi Virus Is Spreading Alarm*, COUNCIL OF FOREIGN RELATIONS (MAY 29, 2013), www.cfr.org/expert-brief/why-saudi-virus-spreading-alarm.
[87] Noting, of course, that the MERS outbreak was never officially declared a Public Health Emergency of International Concern (PHEIC) by the WHO. World Health Organization, *supra* note 2, at 23.
[88] *See, e.g.*, World Health Organization, *Developing Global Norms for Sharing Data and Results during Public Health Emergencies* WORLD HEALTH ORG. (2015), www.who.int/medicines/ebola-treatment/data-sharing_phe/en/. *See also*, Director-General of the World Health Organization, *Report of the Review Committee on the Role of the International Health Regulations (2005) in the Ebola Outbreak and Response*, WORLD HEALTH ORG. (2016) (stating "[i]t is important to emphasize that data and specimens belong to the country that generated it").
[89] *See* Michelle F. Rourke, *Access by Design, Benefits If Convenient: A Closer Look at the Pandemic Influenza Preparedness Framework's Standard Material Transfer Agreements*, 97 MILBANK Q. 91 (2019).

1.5 "HYPEROWNERSHIP": THE NEW REALITY FOR ACCESSING PATHOGENS

Pathogens were the last of the world's genetic resources to be subject to sovereign claims in the access and benefit-sharing space. Public health scientists and "microbiologists have often escaped from the restrictive coils of the proprietary ethos by engaging in an informal system of exchanging genetic materials solely on the basis of mutual trust and reciprocity,"[90] but the increasingly complex legal terrain is making informal pathogen exchange practices near impossible. Overlapping ownership claims over pathogens has made the process of accessing these vital genetic resources legally fraught, even for scientists engaged in public health research with no immediate commercial intent. This has already caused confusion, increased costs and, most concerningly, caused delays in the public health response to infectious disease outbreaks.

The enclosure of pathogens in both the intellectual property and access and benefit-sharing spaces cannot alone describe the difficulties of accessing pathogens for public health research today. These developments are part of a much larger economic and political picture that has seen the increasing commercialization of the scientific endeavor more generally.[91] International developments since the mid-twentieth century (and accelerated from 1980) eroded the notion that pathogens are the common heritage of humankind. The belief that science is a public good is beginning to seem "hopelessly passé,"[92] and "the idea of an open scientific commons where knowledge is freely shared almost seems quaint rather than something that was central to Western science for centuries,"[93] particularly when the multiple international access and benefit-sharing forums are now negotiating the capture of information (not just physical genetic resources) in the sovereign domain of States.[94]

Since the recent *Myriad* decisions, the validity of gene patents in many jurisdictions have become doubtful.[95] Thus, patents describing the genetic components of pathogens are unlikely to be enforced (or perhaps enforceable). But the extension of patents to genetic resources (including pathogens and pathogen-derived products) was a major driving force behind the extension of sovereign rights over genetic resources. Pathogens can be considered to have been effectively captured within the sovereign domain of the nation state after 2007, and by acceding to this notion with the adoption of the PIP Framework in 2011, the WHO have guaranteed that further negotiations about accessing pathogens for public health research is predicated on

---

[90]   REICHMAN ET AL., *supra* note 5, at 255–56.

[91]   See MIROWSKI, *supra* note 8.

[92]   *Id.* at 31.

[93]   McLeod, *supra* note 18, at 37.

[94]   *See, e.g.*, Charles Lawson et al., *The Future of Information under the CBD, Nagoya Protocol, Plant Treaty, and PIP Framework*, 22 J. WORLD INTELL. PROP. 103 (2019).

[95]   *See, e.g.*, Section II, Sherkow & Greely, *supra* note 11, and Lawson, *supra* note 25.

the idea that nation states effectively own their pathogens, and can trade them as they see fit.

The WHO is currently discussing the introduction of multilateral access and benefit-sharing mechanisms, like that contained in the PIP Framework, for the sharing of other human pathogens. However, this may not be a palatable option to Member States if they feel that they can secure benefits more effectively by engaging in bilateral ABS negotiations under the auspices of the CBD and Nagoya Protocol.[96] Therefore, in many ways, the public health community is now stuck with these conceptions of viral sovereignty and pathogen ownership, and will likely have to navigate them anew each time there is a novel infectious disease outbreak.

---

[96] Michelle Rourke, Sam Halabi, Gian Luca Burci and Rebecca Katz, *The Nagoya Protocol and the Legal Structure of Global Biogenomic Research*, 45 YALE J. INT'L. L. 133 (2020).

2

Attitudes towards Transfers of Human Research Samples across Borders

A Multicountry Perspective

Benjamin Krohmal

Pandemic risk has been identified as one of the most severe and underappreciated threats facing humanity.[1] Global travel, increased population density, factory farming, and human expansion into previously uninhabited areas could facilitate the rise and spread of dangerous new disease variants, while advances in biotechnology raise the prospect of intentional or accidental release of engineered pathogens. A key component of epidemic risk mitigation is the establishment of global networks for monitoring outbreaks and collecting samples – often in developing countries – and transferring them to laboratories – often in developed countries – that are best equipped to study them and quickly respond.

The rules and norms governing the transfer of these samples have been subject to protracted disagreement over the equitable distribution of the benefits of research on samples identified and collected in one country and studied in another. The positions of the governments involved in this debate are a matter of public record and generally

---

[1] Commission on a Global Health Risk Framework for the Future; National Academy of Medicine, Secretariat. THE NEGLECTED DIMENSION OF GLOBAL SECURITY: A FRAMEWORK TO COUNTER INFECTIOUS DISEASE CRISES (2016) available at www.ncbi.nlm.nih.gov/books/NBK368390. ("Pandemics and epidemics have killed countless millions throughout human history. Highly virulent infectious diseases, such as the plague, cholera, and influenza, have repeatedly swept through human societies, causing death, economic chaos, and, as a consequence, political and social disorder. In the past 100 years, the 1918 influenza pandemic killed approximately 50 million; HIV/AIDS took the lives of more than 35 million. Although more recently-emerging epidemics, such as severe acute respiratory syndrome (SARS) in 2003, H1N1 in 2009 – and, most recently, the Ebola epidemic in West Africa – have had lower death tolls, they have nevertheless had a huge impact in terms of both social and economic disruption.") Peter Sands, Carmen Mundaca-Shah, and Victor J. Dzau, *The Neglected Dimension of Global Security – A Framework for Countering Infectious Disease Crises*, 374 NEW ENGL. J. MED. 1281–87 (2016). ("Advances in medicine have transformed our defenses against the threat of infectious disease. Better hygiene, antibiotics, diagnostics, and vaccines have given us far more effective tools for preventing and responding to outbreaks. Yet the severe acute respiratory syndrome (SARS), the Middle East respiratory syndrome (MERS), and the recent West African Ebola outbreak show that we cannot be complacent. Infectious-disease outbreaks that turn into epidemics and potential pandemics can cause massive loss of life and huge economic disruption.")

break down according to development status. What is less well-known are the views of the individuals who comprise the multinational system of transferors and transferees of biological samples, the people who collect the samples and study them and determine how they are used by local institutions. What little is understood about the views of these individual stakeholders comes largely from a single survey study published in 2010, *Attitudes towards transfer of human tissue samples across borders: An international survey of researchers and policy makers in five countries* (the Attitudes Study).[2] The findings of that research, and its continued relevance to the ongoing debate over the transfer of biological samples, is the focus of this chapter.

The Attitudes Study was conducted in China, Egypt, India, Japan, and South Korea between 2005 and 2008, a period which coincided with growing upheaval in the cross-border sharing of biological samples. The year prior, in 2004, an outbreak of a highly pathogenic H5N1 avian influenza virus was reported in Thailand and Vietnam.[3] Over the following years, the outbreak spread to over fifteen countries, including, coincidentally, the five countries participating in the Attitudes Study.[4] Researchers from around the world raced to create a vaccine using samples of the virus collected in developing countries and shared across national borders through the Global Influenza Surveillance Network (GISRS) operated by the World Health Organization (WHO).[5]

Ultimately, the outbreak was contained and subsided and the international effort resulted in the development of new H5N1 vaccines, which were licensed to private pharmaceutical companies in the US, Europe, and Australia.[6] But what might have seemed like a successful result raised concerns in developing countries. In 2007, the Indonesian Ministry of Health announced that it would halt transfers of domestic

---

[2] Xinqing Zhang, Kenji Matsui, Benjamin Krohmal, Alaa Abou Zeid, Vasantha Muthaswamy, Young Mo Koo, Yoshikuni Kita, and Reidar Lie, *Attitudes towards Transfers of Human Tissue Samples across Borders: An International Survey of Researchers and Policy Makers in Five Countries*, BMC MEDICAL ETHICS 2 (2010), available at https://doi.org/10.1186/1472-6939-11-16.

[3] Thanawat Tiensin, Prasit Chaitaweesub, Thaweesak Songserm et al. *Highly Pathogenic Avian Influenza H5N1, Thailand, 2004.* 11(11) EMERG INFECT DIS. 1664–72 (2005), available at doi:10.3201/eid1111.050608. ("Highly pathogenic avian influenza (HPAI) is a devastating disease in poultry; it is associated with a high death rate and disrupts poultry production and trade. HPAI viruses may be transmitted from birds to humans and they are a potential source of future human influenza pandemics. HPAI outbreaks were relatively rare until 1990 but occurred in many countries in the last decade.")

[4] WHO, *H5N1 Avian Influenza: Timeline of Major Events*, 25 January 2012, www.who.int/influenza/human_animal_interface/H5N1_avian_influenza_update.pdf.

[5] WHO, *Global Influenza Surveillance and Response System (GISRS)*, available at www.who.int/influenza/gisrs_laboratory/en/.

[6] U.S. FDA, H5N1 Influenza Virus Vaccine, manufactured by Sanofi Pasteur Inc. Questions and Answers, available at www.fda.gov/vaccines-blood-biologics/vaccines/h5n1-influenza-virus-vaccine-manufactured-sanofi-pasteur-inc-questions-and-answers. ("On April 17, 2007, FDA licensed the first vaccine in the United States for the prevention of H5N1 influenza, commonly referred to as avian influenza or 'bird flu.' This inactivated influenza virus vaccine is for use in people 18 through 64 years of age who are at increased risk of exposure to the H5N1 influenza virus subtype contained in the vaccine. This vaccine is derived from the A/Vietnam/1203/2004 influenza virus. The vaccine is manufactured by Sanofi Pasteur Inc. of Swiftwater, PA and has been purchased by the federal government for inclusion within the Nation's National Stockpile.")

H5N1 samples to foreign laboratories without legally binding assurances that Indonesia would share in the benefits of the transfer, including intellectual property (IP) rights and access to vaccines developed from research on samples collected in Indonesia.[78]

In response, the WHO initiated an "intergovernmental meeting to develop mechanisms aimed at ensuring the continued sharing of influenza viruses, and the fair and equitable sharing of benefits arising from such sharing."[9] The ensuing negotiations over a Pandemic Influenza Preparedness Framework (PIP Framework) would continue for over four years. A central point of contention between developed and developing countries was over the appropriate contents of standard material transfer agreements (SMTAs). SMTAs were intended to streamline the transfer of biological samples through the GISRS by standardizing a set of invariable terms for transfer agreements, avoiding the need to negotiate terms for each individual transfer. Developing countries involved in the negotiations argued that SMTAs should include legally binding benefit-sharing provisions and limitations on IP developed through research on transferred samples, while developed countries, especially Europe and the US, favored non-binding guidelines on benefit-sharing and no IP limitations, citing the need for financial incentives to motivate vaccine research and development.

The Attitudes Study, published in 2010 as the PIP Framework negotiations were ongoing, reported the views of individuals involved in the transfer of biological samples in countries that had been impacted by H5N1, including individuals in countries then classified by United Nations Development Programme (UNDP) as both developed (Japan and South Korea) and developing (China, Egypt, India).[10] The findings, discussed in detail below, generally suggested more widespread alignment with the developing country position and less consensus for the developed country position than might have been expected.

To be clear, the Attitudes Study was designed before and not planned to address the PIP Framework negotiations. The countries involved were selected because of prior collaborations between the researchers there, and the study addressed attitudes towards the transfer of a category of samples, human tissue samples, that overlaps imperfectly with the virus samples at issue in the PIP Framework.[11] Nonetheless, the

---

7   WHO, *Sharing of Avian Influenza Viruses and Pandemic Vaccine Production*, 16 Feb 2007, www .who.int/mediacentre/news/statements/2007/s02/en/.
8   WHO, *Indonesia to Resume Sharing H5N1 Avian Influenza Virus Samples Following a WHO Meeting in Jakarta*, 27 March 2007, www.who.int/mediacentre/news/releases/2007/pr09/en/.
9   WHO, The Pandemic Influenza Preparedness Framework (2011) available at www.who.int/influ enza/pip/history/en/.
10 UNDP, Human Development Report 2010, the Real Wealth of Nations: Pathways to Development 226–27 (2010) available at http://hdr.undp.org/sites/default/files/reports/270/ hdr_2010_en_complete_reprint.pdf.
11 The distinction may implicate relevantly different treatment under the 1993 Convention on Biological Diversity. Human tissue samples likely constitute "human genetic resources," which are exempt from the equitable access requirements of the Convention, while isolated virus samples would likely be

issues addressed in the Attitudes Study and the categories of individual stakeholders who were surveyed made the study's findings relevant in the context of the PIP Framework negotiations and to ongoing controversies relating to the transfer of biological samples.

2.1 THE STUDY

The Attitudes Study recruited over 1,400 participants (between 100 and 200 each in China, Egypt, India, and South Korea, and over 850 in Japan) who fell into one or more of the following categories of stakeholders: Researchers who study human biological samples; collectors who collect human biological samples; research ethics review board members; and policymakers who have been involved in setting institutional policies regarding stored tissue samples.[12] Survey questions focused on (1) preconditions for international transfers, (2) influence over future research, (3) authorship of publications, and (4) intellectual property rights and access to medicine.[13]

2.2 RESULTS

2.2.1 *Preconditions for International Transfer*

The survey asked stakeholders whether they agreed with certain preconditions for transferring samples out of the country in which they were collected. Majorities ranging from 59 percent to 78 percent, in China, Egypt, and India, the three developing countries, agreed that samples should only be transferred when research facilities were unavailable in the country of origin, while only a minority in Japan (22 percent) and South Korea (43 percent) agreed. Somewhat larger majorities in the developing countries (79 percent to 83 percent) and a majority in South Korea (57 percent) agreed that if samples were transferred to a different country, a portion must be left behind for research in the country of origin, unless special government permission was granted; a significant minority in Japan (43 percent) also agreed.[14] At the greatest extreme, a significant majority in Egypt (81 percent), about 40 percent in China and India, and 20 percent and 30 percent respectively in Japan and Korea agreed that samples should always be kept in the country in which they were collected. While support for preconditions for transferring samples abroad was stronger in developing than in developed countries, it is notable that a substantial

covered, and the status of flu viruses contained in human tissue is unresolved. See Michelle Rourke, *The History of Accessing and Sharing Human Pathogens for Public Health Research*, in Sam Halabi and Rebecca Katz (eds.), VIRAL SOVEREIGNTY, TECHNOLOGY TRANSFER, AND THE CHANGING SYSTEM FOR SHARING PATHOGENS FOR PUBLIC HEALTH RESEARCH (2020).
[12] Zhang, Matsui, Krohmal, Zeid, Muthaswamy, Koo, Kita, and Lie, *supra* note 2.
[13] *Id.*
[14] *Id.* at 3 and 4.

minority in Japan and majorities in each of the other countries supported a requirement that when samples are transferred internally, a portion should remain in the source country.

2.2.2 *Influence over Future Research*

A series of questions addressed whether material transfer agreements (MTAs) should require that scientists in countries where samples are collected retain some control over future research on the samples when they are transferred abroad. Specifically, respondents were asked whether MTAs should require that scientists in the originating country: (1) be consulted before any new use, (2) have some decision-making power over future use, (3) be included in the protocol development team for future research, (4) be included in a joint committee for decision-making about future use, or (5) have veto power over any future use.

Significant majorities in each country agreed with (1), that MTAs should, at the very least, require consultation with originating country scientists before new use of samples, with between 90 percent and 93 percent agreement in the three developing countries, 68 percent agreement in Japan, and 78 percent in South Korea. For (2), (3), and (4), levels of agreement remained high, with slight declines for each increase in the degree of control granted to originating country scientists. Even with respect (5), the most extreme requirement that originating country scientists should have a veto over future uses, there was strong agreement (64 percent to 84 percent) in each country except for Japan, where nearly half were in agreement (48 percent).[15] While these results showed somewhat greater agreement in developing countries than in developed countries, overall, a majority in each country agreed that MTAs should mandate a role for originating country scientists in directing future research on samples, including involvement in protocol development and joint membership on a committee for decision-making about future research.

2.2.3 *Authorship of Publications*

The stakeholders were also asked whether and to what extent MTAs should require that scientists who transfer samples abroad must be credited for authorship on publications resulting from research on the samples. A majority of respondents in each country agreed that MTAs should require that originating country scientists be given the opportunity to provide sufficient intellectual input to be credited for authorship on publications arising from research on transferred samples, although agreement was more widespread in the developing countries (73 percent to 91 percent) than in Japan (52 percent) and South Korea (60 percent). There was less consensus on whether MTAs should simply require that originating country

[15]   *Id.* at 4.

scientists be credited for authorship on either all publications or the first publication resulting from research on transferred samples, without regard to additional contributions beyond collecting and supplying the samples. In each of the developing countries, a majority agreed that MTAs should require authorship credit for originating country scientists on either all resulting publications (79 percent in Egypt and 58 percent in India) or at least on the first publication (60 percent in China), whereas only minorities agreed in Japan (21 percent for all and 28 percent for first) and South Korea (49 percent for all and 41 percent for first).[16] As one might expect, respondents across all countries who had used MTAs as sample transferors were more likely than those who had used MTAs as transferees to agree that MTAs should require authorship credit for originating country scientists on all resulting publications (49 percent versus 33 percent).

2.2.4 *IP, Royalties, and Access to Medicines*

Finally, survey respondents were asked whether MTAs should require sharing IP, royalties, or material products, such as pharmaceuticals, that arise from research on transferred samples. With respect to whether MTAs should require sharing royalties and IP with originating country scientists, half of respondents in Japan (50 percent) and large majorities in each of the other countries (70 percent to 87 percent) agreed. Majorities outside of Japan also agreed that MTAs should require sharing IP and royalties with the population of the country from which the samples were collected, ranging from 52 percent in South Korea to 79 percent in India; only 35 percent of respondents in Japan agreed. With respect to whether MTAs should require that the population of the originating country be given access to pharmaceuticals or other products that result from research on transferred samples, nearly half of respondents in Japan (47 percent) agreed, as did significant majorities in the other countries, ranging from 70 percent in South Korea to 89 percent in Egypt.[17] Interestingly, while there was substantial agreement in both developing and developed countries that MTAs should require certain protections for source country scientists and populations, only in Korea did a majority (63 percent) agree that source country scientists are under pressure to accept unfavorable conditions for the transfer of their sample collections to foreign collaborating scientists with access to more resources; in Japan (22 percent) and the three developing countries (8 percent to 42 percent), only minorities of respondents agreed.

2.2.5 *Discussion of the Attitudes Study*

To the extent the findings of the Attitudes Study were generalizable, they reflected an expected divergence of views between respondents in developed and developing

---

[16]   *Id.* at 5.
[17]   *Id.* at 3.

countries that roughly mirrored the positions taken by governments in the PIP Framework negotiations regarding the inclusion of binding benefit-sharing arrangements in SMTAs and restrictions on IP arising from research on transferred samples: A higher proportion of respondents in developing countries than respondents in developed countries agreed that there should be preconditions for transferring samples abroad, and that MTAs should require that source country scientists have input into future research, authorship opportunities, and a share of IP rights and access to pharmaceuticals for source country scientists and/or populations.

Notably, however, while support for these protections was generally lower among developed country respondents, it was nonetheless substantial, with significant minorities, if not majorities of respondents in Japan and South Korea, expressing agreement with positions typically associated with developing countries. While developed countries argued in the PIP Framework negotiations against any binding benefit-sharing provisions in SMTAs or limitations on IP rights, a majority of respondents in both of the developed countries in the study agreed that MTAs should include at least some substantive benefit-sharing provisions, and a majority of respondents in South Korea and half of respondents in Japan agreed with certain requirements for sharing IP and pharmaceutical products developed from research on transferred samples.

While the study generally showed broader than expected support for developing country positions, not all results fit this narrative. The finding that only in Korea did a majority of respondents agree that source country scientists are under pressure to accept unfavorable terms for transferring samples raises questions about the need for mandatory protections for source country scientists. Other results were hard to explain, such as the finding that 80 percent of Egyptian respondents opposed transferring samples abroad under any circumstances, twice the level of agreement with this position in the next most supportive country (India). Was this a fluke? Are there unique circumstances driving such sentiments in Egypt or elsewhere that might make future transfers of biological samples particularly vulnerable to disruption?

2.3 EPILOGUE

Following publication of the Attitudes Study in 2010, the debate over the international transfer of biological samples has shifted, but the issues addressed in the study remain topical. In the following years, controversies have continued to add friction to the system for sharing biological samples across borders, and this is so especially for non-influenza pathogens. As Sam Halabi and Rebecca Katz note in the introduction, the matters covered by the Attitudes Study have been relevant ever since. In 2012, a researcher in Saudi Arabia isolated a virus from a deceased patient and sent it to a medical center in the Netherlands for further study. Dutch researchers identified the virus as a previously unknown human coronavirus, filed for patents, and required an MTA acknowledging the Dutch institution's rights with respect to the development of diagnosis tests, vaccines, and antiviral treatments as a precondition for sharing samples. Even researchers in Saudi Arabia were not exempt from these requirements. While research in the Netherlands resulted in quick identification of a new pathogen and development of diagnostics for use as the virus spread in at least three countries in the Middle East, the Saudi Ministry of Health expressed outrage that a European institution had asserted control over access to a Saudi-derived pathogen.[18]

Similar concerns regarding source country rights to secondary use of samples arose following the 2014 to 2016 West African Ebola epidemic. During the outbreak, thousands of samples were collected and exported abroad for research.[19] Many of the recipient countries have refused to provide information to the WHO and source countries regarding the Ebola samples they possess.[20] A laboratory in Germany began selling samples collected in Guinea for over 7,000 Euros per milliliter, while Liberian scientists have been unsuccessful in their efforts to obtain and study portions of Ebola samples that were collected in Liberia and exported to the US.[21]

The PIP Framework, meanwhile, only addresses the system for sharing samples of influenza virus. This is one reason that a high-level UN panel recommended revisiting the PIP Framework to make it applicable to novel pathogens in addition to influenza. This may be a desirable alternative, given how national governments appear to be addressing the issue of pathogens and their interest in ensuring that research and technological capacity-building occur in their territories and benefit their scientists.

Reprising its leading role in asserting source country rights in 2007, Indonesia is weighing potential legislation to restrict what it calls "helicopter research" (referred to as "field work" in the Introduction), the practice of foreign scientists collecting samples in Indonesia for analysis abroad with little to no involvement or recognition

---

[18]   Declan Butler, *Tensions Linger over Discovery of Coronavirus*, NATURE (2013), www.nature.com/news/ tensions-linger-over-discovery-of-coronavirus-1.12108. ("Meanwhile, Zaki had mailed a sample of the virus to Fouchier, who sequenced it and found that it was a previously unknown human coronavirus, closely related to one from bats. On 20 September, Zaki announced the discovery on ProMED-mail, an online disease-reporting system. The virus has since been provisionally named human betacoronavirus 2c EMC (hCoV-EMC), after the Rotterdam centre, and researchers wishing to acquire samples of its virus are now required to first sign an EMC material-transfer agreement (MTA).")

[19]   Emmanuel Freudenthal, *Ebola's Lost Blood: Row over Samples Flown Out of Africa as "Big Pharma"* *Set to Cash In*, THE TELEGRAPH (2019), www.telegraph.co.uk/global-health/science-and-disease/ebo las-lost-blood-row-samples-flown-africa-big-pharma-set-cash/.

[20]   *Id.*

[21]   *Id.* ("Now several African scientists and Ebola survivors accuse the laboratories of biological asset stripping. Despite the samples having been taken from thousands of Africans, scientists from these patients' home countries – Sierra Leone, Guinea and Liberia – are unable to access them for their own research. 'When you take samples you should keep them,' says Dr Fatorma Bolay, the director of the Liberian laboratory where Ebola samples were stored before they were shipped to the United States in 2016.")

of Indonesian scientists.[22] A bill submitted to the Indonesian House of Representatives in 2017 and still under consideration would require foreign scientists to submit their raw data to Indonesian authorities, involve Indonesian colleagues as equal partners in research projects, and name all Indonesian researchers involved in a project on every peer-reviewed paper that arises from the work. The bill would also enhance penalties, to include jail time, for failure to obtain a government research permit and adhere to a transfer agreement for removal of samples from Indonesia. Indonesian and foreign scientists have expressed concern that the effort to protect Indonesia's scientific interests could backfire, with the risk of harsh penalties potentially deterring foreign collaboration with Indonesian scientists.[23]

It is likely that future developments will continue to pose challenges to international frameworks for sharing biological samples between countries. To respond to these challenges and work towards a more equitable and more effective system for sharing biological samples across borders, negotiators should seek to understand and take into account the views of the professionals who are most closely involved in collecting and studying these samples.[24]

As an ethical matter, when debating rules concerning the distribution of professional opportunities, the views of the individuals whose careers stand to benefit or suffer as a result of those rules deserve consideration. As a practical matter, these professionals are the experts on the science and logistics of the collection and study of biological samples. Where there is broad agreement among them with respect certain rules, such as preconditions for transferring samples abroad or rules regarding the right to influence future avenues of research, there is at least prima facie reason to believe that such rules would be consistent with the promotion of good

---

[22] *See generally,* Dyna Rochmyaningsih, *Indonesian Plan to Clamp Down on Foreign Scientists Draws Protest,* NATURE (2018), www.nature.com/articles/d41586-018-05001-7. ("The proposals are among several outlined in a draft law submitted to the House of Representatives in August 2017. If the house approves the law, international scientists will have to submit their raw data to the research ministry; involve Indonesian colleagues as equal partners in research projects; and name all Indonesian researchers involved in a project on every peer-reviewed paper that arises from the work. In February, Sadjuga, the research ministry's director of intellectual property, told a conference on international research collaborations that in the past, some international groups had 'disregarded' the contribution of Indonesian scientists and left their names off peer-reviewed papers. Of the 832 international science publications that resulted from foreign research projects in Indonesia between 2010 and 2016, 6% had not named an Indonesian co-author, he says.")

[23] *Id.*

[24] Sam Halabi, *Viral* Sovereignty, *Intellectual Property, and the Changing Global System for Sharing Human Pathogens for Infectious Disease Research,* 28(1) ANNALS OF HEALTH L. 101 (2019). ("Given that researchers must be active voices in the material transfer process, this aspect of modern research must change. International research collaborations in the field of infectious disease increasingly require researchers to be more extensively knowledgeable about regulations covering the sampling of biological resources, terms of material transfer agreements, and formal agreements establishing research partnerships. As most analysts of the problem have concluded, knowledge of 'prior informed consent' 'mutually agreed terms' and 'access and benefit sharing' must be integrated with the education and research process as researchers must now work more actively and in partnership with lawyers to ensure that access to human pathogen samples continues as expeditiously as possible.")

science. There is also reason to think that these professionals would have unique insight into the conditions that foster or erode trust and collaborative partnerships between sample collectors and researchers in different countries. While negotiations over the rules governing the transfer of samples occurs at the intergovernmental level, research collaboration still depends upon relationships between individuals, and these relationships could be strengthened by identifying and incorporating broadly supported standards to increase reciprocity and trust. Finally, these professionals are also among the best situated to understand the professional opportunities needed to develop and maintain the human capital required for defense against pandemic risk. Just as incentives matter in the discussion of IP rights to promote drug and vaccine development, incentives matter for attracting and training optimal numbers of talented scientists and clinicians to devote careers to pandemic preparedness, particularly in developing countries where pandemics are most likely to arise, and where those who collect samples for research may put their own health at risk in the process. Publication opportunities, for example, are a source of professional recognition and promotion which, in turn, is used to prioritize funding applications.[25] Failure to account for these professionals' views on their professional development needs risks a set of rules that under-incentivizes the development and retention of human capital.

This is not to say that the opinions of sample collectors, researchers, and policymakers should always determine the policies governing the international transfer of biological samples. Like other stakeholders, there may well be cases where their preferences diverge from the public interest. For example, it is difficult to defend the broad support found in the Attitudes Study for source country scientists to have veto rights over any future research on transferred samples. Such a requirement could give rise to well-founded concerns about the potential suppression of valuable research that happens to be unflattering to particular countries or scientists. That said, it would be a mistake not to seriously consider the views of the professionals who are most closely involved in research on biological samples. Given their unique expertise, it is appropriate to expect compelling reasons when the rules for sample sharing differ markedly from the views of sample collectors, researchers, and policymakers.

The importance of taking into account the views of researchers in refining the system for sharing samples is underscored by a 2015 WHO briefing paper that was commissioned to analyze potential barriers to data and results sharing in public health emergencies following the 2014 Ebola outbreak in West Africa. The paper's analysis is based on interviews with thirteen researchers and policymakers. Among the identified barriers to effective research collaboration were a reluctance to share data to avoid losing opportunities for professional advancement through academic

---

[25]   World Health Organization. Statement arising from a WHO Consultation held on 1–2 September 2015. www.who.int/medicines/ebola-treatment/blueprint_phe_data-share-results/en/.

publication, a lack of reciprocity that left some researchers feeling exploited, and the need for "capacity building, through more balanced and meaningful collaboration and training ... [to] creat[e] independent academic researchers with a wider range of backgrounds and good knowledge of local datasets, culture, opportunities, politics, and health issues."[26] A better understanding of the views of researchers and other professionals most closely involved with biological samples has the potential to identify broadly supported avenues for avoiding these barriers and realizing opportunities to improve global infectious disease response.

2.4 NEXT STEPS

In a field recognized as neglected relative to its global significance, it is unsurprising that much important work remains to be done in pandemic preparedness. This chapter highlights one avenue where pandemic preparedness, and specifically the policy infrastructure for transferring biological samples between countries, would benefit from further research. There is a paucity of data – really, just one study going on a decade old – that seeks to understand the attitudes of the professionals most closely involved in the collection, transfer, and study of biological samples. That study included only five countries, and even in those countries, it is likely that attitudes have changed in the last ten years with shifts in geopolitics, new infectious disease threats, and new frameworks for sharing samples across borders. In addition to updating and expanding the Attitudes Study to additional countries, follow-on research could provide perhaps the greatest benefit by delving into the reasons for attitudes about how biological samples should be shared, with a goal of leveraging the expertise and experience of professionals closely involved with biological samples to better identify threats and opportunities to improve scientific value, foster trust between researchers and sample collectors in different countries, and ensure an appropriate balance of incentive to optimize devotion of human capital to pandemic preparedness.

---

[26] World Health Organization. WHO consultation on Data and Results Sharing During Public Health Emergencies. Background Briefing. September 2015. www.who.int/medicines/ebola-treatment/back ground_briefing_on_data_results_sharing_during_phes.pdf?ua=1, at 10.

3

The Scope of Global Infectious Disease Research

Field Capture, Quarantine, and Sample Transfer to Detect Emerging Pathogen Threats

Brian Bird

The breadth and depth of international research activity aimed at detecting emerging pathogens have expanded as those pathogens have been increasingly understood to threaten global health. Preceding chapters have explained the origins of international research collaborations and detailed some of the challenges those collaborations have faced as equitable considerations permeate research partnership structure. This chapter is intended to illustrate how extensive and elaborate international research partnerships have become, how those larger partnerships have been affected by equitable considerations when undertaken in low-resource countries, how written agreements between researchers and governments shape data collection, analysis, and exchange, and how those written agreements have worked in favor of the development and expansion of research capacity in low-resource countries.

Using the case study of PREDICT – a large-scale research effort involving approximately thirty countries aimed at detecting novel pathogens that could threaten human health – it describes the field capture of animals, clinical sampling of animals and people, analysis for genetic sequencing data, transfer of samples to reference laboratories outside of low- or middle-income countries, and how confirmed infections are reported to public authorities for both public health and sovereign resource reasons. The chapter argues that the process by which researchers now obtain data requires far more formal and informal negotiation of administrative matters, but that, as a result, researchers now partner more effectively and beneficially with local scientists and institutions, building capacity for disease surveillance and response should an infectious disease threat emerge.

The problem of emerging pathogens has arisen because of trends in human population growth, behavior, and needs. "Emerging" pathogens may be defined as those that have newly appeared in a population or have existed but are rapidly increasing in incidence or geographic range.[1] Among recent examples are HIV/ AIDS and Lyme disease. Many of these appear at the human/livestock/wildlife interface. More than half of the known pathogens infectious to humans are shared with animals (zoonotic diseases) and occur via recurring transmission or an initial spillover event.[2] Globally, more than one billion infections and one million deaths annually are attributable to zoonoses and vector-borne diseases.[3]

As the human population grows, more land is committed to food production, and more interactions between humans and animals (including their parasites) occur. For example, the Nipah virus is transmitted through interaction with infected livestock or eating fruit containing the urine or saliva from infected bats.[4] As those interactions arise in the context of climate change and urbanization, both of which contribute to emergence and spread, conditions for outbreaks become more prevalent.[5] Indeed, annual population growth is now highest in areas that buffer areas reserved for wildlife where these transmissions are likely to occur.

---

[1] Stephen S. Morse, *Factors in the Emergence of Infectious Diseases*, 1(1) PERSPECTIVES 7–15 (1995). ("Specific factors precipitating disease emergence can be identified in virtually all cases. These include ecological, environmental, or demographic factors that place people at increased contact with a previously unfamiliar microbe or its natural host or promote dissemination. These factors are increasing in prevalence; this increase, together with the ongoing evolution of viral and microbial variants and selection for drug resistance, suggests that infections will continue to emerge and probably increase and emphasizes the urgent need for effective surveillance and control.")

[2] Paul D. van Helden et al., *One World, One Health; Humans, Animals and the Environment Are Inextricably Linked – a Fact That Needs to Be Remembered and Exploited in Our Modern Approach to Health*, 14 EMBO REP 497–501 (2013). ("To illustrate the complex, interwoven net of dependencies between humans, animals and the environment, let us consider the parasite *Toxoplasma gondii*. The common host of this protozoan is the domestic cat (Felidae), in which the sexual part of the parasite's life cycle takes place. However, *T. gondii* can infect many other warm-blooded species, from humans to birds, and has become endemic in many areas. Estimates put the number of infected humans at about 500 million, with large regional differences. Although toxoplasmosis is not usually a deadly disease, the infection does have some unpleasant side effects for many species, including its ability to modify the behaviour of rats and mice, making them drawn to, rather than fearful of, the scent of cats – probably a survival strategy for a parasite that requires cats to sexually reproduce. In humans, toxoplasmosis during pregnancy can cause miscarriage and severe health effects if it infects the fetus, and it has been associated with a higher risk of schizophrenia in adults ... Environmental factors determine the spread of toxoplasmosis. Felid hosts shed *Toxoplasma* oocysts with their faeces into the environment, including into water systems, from which the parasite infects other species. The main routes of infection for humans are thought to be direct contact with cats and eating undercooked meat from infected sheep. However, infection could also occur through water and contaminated vegetable or fruit produce.")

[3] *Advancing a "One Health" Approach to Promote Health at the Human-Animal-Environment Interface*, AM. PUB. HEALTH ASSN (2017).

[4] *Nipah Virus.*, WORLD HEALTH ORG., 2018, www.who.int/news-room/fact-sheets/detail/nipah-virus.

[5] Johanna F. Lindal and Delia Grace, *The Consequences of Human Actions on Risks for Infectious Diseases: A Review*, 5 INFECT. ECOL. & EPIDEMIOLOGY (2015). ("Many factors are contributing to disease emergence, including climate change, globalization and urbanization, and most of these factors are to some extent caused by humans. Pathogens may be more or less prone to emergence in themselves, and rapidly mutating viruses are more common among the emerging pathogens. The climate-sensitive

The increasing ease with which people travel across the world means those outbreaks are more likely to become pandemics than in decades past.[6] For much of human history, populations were fairly isolated. Cross-continental exploration, war, and the expansion of communication has redefined global travel. The expansive reach, speed and volume of passengers via air, sea, and land transport provide pathogens and vectors a way to move further, faster, and in greater numbers than ever before.[7] A human's ability to reach almost any part of the world within the incubation period with many stops and layovers along the way means that travelers themselves are serving as sentinels for diseases. The increased displacement of bacteria through global travel and trade can turn what would be a local outbreak into an epidemic.

3.1 ONE HEALTH AND PREDICT

For these reasons, researchers, governments, and public health scholars have promoted what is generally referred to as "one health" approaches to animal, human, and plant health.[8] That humans, animals, and the environment are interconnected and that their respective welfare is interdependent has been acknowledged for centuries. Yet it is relatively recently that public health policies have focused on the nexus between humans, animals (domesticated and wild), and the environment.[9] After the severe acute respiratory syndrome (SARS) epidemic and the H5N1 avian influenza outbreaks, one health approaches expanded to include health service delivery, environmental health, and ecosystem services. "An estimated 75% of emerging infectious diseases are zoonotic, mainly of viral origin, and likely to be vectorborne" and thus an integrated approach to health preparedness and response is required simply to address what we know about the origins of human health threats.[10]

vector-borne diseases are likely to be emerging due to climate changes and environmental changes, such as increased irrigation.")

[6] *Why It Matters: The Pandemic Threat*, CDC, www.cdc.gov/globalhealth/healthprotection/fieldup dates/winter-2017/why-it-matters.html.

[7] Mary E. Wilson, *Global Travel and Emerging Infections*, NAT'L ACAD. OF SCI. 90–104 (2010) at 90.

[8] *Advancing a "One Health" Approach to Promote Health at the Human-Animal-Environment Interface*, AMER PUBLIC HEALTH ASSN (2017), available at apha.org/policies-and-advocacy/public-health-policy-statements/policy-database/2018/01/18/advancing-a-one-health-approach. ("A One Health approach (and related approaches such as veterinary public health, EcoHealth, and Planetary Health) recognizes the integral connections among humans, animals, and the environment in relation to people's health and well-being and promotes interdisciplinary collaborations to more holistically understand and more effectively act against public health threats. More than half of known human infectious disease pathogens have an animal source or origin and result in over a billion cases globally each year, often imposing high financial and societal costs.")

[9] van Helden et al., *supra* note 2.

[10] Bruno B. Chomel, Albino Belotto, and François-Xavier Meslin, *Wildlife, Exotic Pets, and Emerging Zoonoses*, 13(1) EMERG. INFECT. DIS. 6–11 (2007). ("An estimated 75% of emerging infectious diseases are zoonotic, mainly of viral origin, and likely to be vectorborne. The emergence and rapid spread of

A survey of 15,998 studies published between 1912 and 2013 showed results that on the whole, research and research funding is primarily interested with the flow of disease from animals and livestock to humans.[11] However, "one health" emphasizes that all factors of life are interconnected: animals, plants, and humans. Animal health is inherently a human concern, and knowing what affects animals and in what way is good information to have and to begin to study more robustly. This information can yield important results, including a better understanding of how viruses themselves mutate, helping a global population better protect animals, plants, and humans from them. This kind of research into wildlife–livestock and interspecies viral transfer research could produce the highest return on the investment of surveillance.[12]

In 2009, the US government launched its Emerging Pandemic Threats program in an effort to prioritize one health approaches to public health emergency preparedness. The Emergency Pandemic Threats program was comprised of several constituent programs including PREDICT, the focus of this chapter, which prioritizes detection and discovery of zoonotic diseases at the wildlife–human interface. Its specific activities include strengthening surveillance and laboratory capacities in order to monitor wildlife and people in contact with wildlife for novel pathogens that may pose a significant public health threat; characterizing human and ecological drivers of disease spillover from animals to people; strengthening and optimizing models for predicting disease emergence and using this information to improve surveillance; and supporting outbreak response when requested.[13]

PREVENT, by contrast, focuses on characterizing risks associated with disease transmission between animals and people and developing risk-mitigation strategies including characterizing specific practices and behaviors (e.g., bushmeat hunting and butchering, raising wildlife for trade and consumption) that expose people to zoonotic diseases; and developing and deploying risk-mitigation strategies, including a tool for extractive-industry workers to decrease their exposure to emerging zoonoses. IDENTIFY strengthens laboratory capacity to safely diagnose and report common animal and human pathogens.[14] IDENTIFY partners the World Health Organization (WHO), the Food and Agricultural Organization (FAO), and the World Organisation for Animal Health (OIE) to improve laboratory assessment tools to allow for better targeting of technical support and training; developing and

West Nile virus in North America and the monkeypox outbreak in pet prairie dogs have been major awakening public health events that underscored the need for closer collaboration between the veterinary profession, wildlife specialists, and public health personnel. These events emphasized the role that veterinarians and other wildlife specialists can play in surveillance, control, and prevention of emerging zoonoses, as their training in disease recognition and population medicine makes them well suited for early detection networks.")

[11] *Id.*
[12] *Id.*
[13] *Emerging Pandemic Threats*, USAID, www.usaid.gov/news-information/fact-sheets/emerging-pandemic-threats-program.
[14] *Id.*

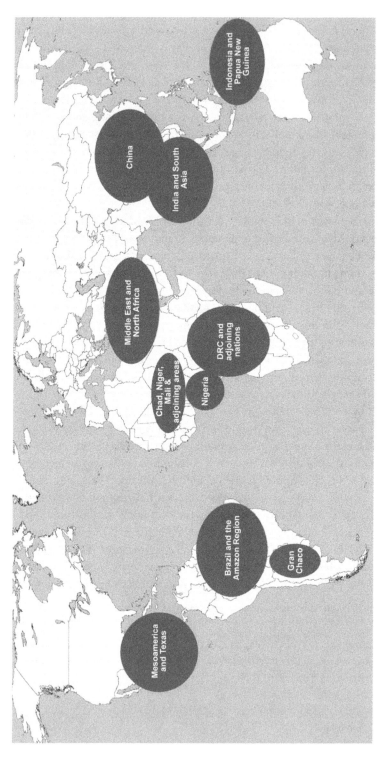

FIGURE 3.1 Global distribution of relative risk of an EID event. Maps are derived for EID events caused by a, zoonotic pathogens from wildlife, b, zoonotic pathogens from non-wildlife, c, drug-resistant pathogens and d, vector-borne pathogens. Global Distribution of Relative Risk of an Emerging Infectious Disease Event as adapted from Jones, Patel, et al., Global Trends in Emerging Infectious Diseases. Nature 451, 990–93: 21 February 2008.

rolling out training modules on diagnosing highly infectious diseases; improving laboratory management practices related to biosafety and biosecurity; "twinning" labs in rich and poor countries; and expanding monitoring of antimicrobial resistance rates among priority bacterial pathogens.[15] RESPOND is dedicated to training "one health" workers – those at the human/animal interface who may both assess spillover events and act as part of a primary healthcare team responding – in Africa and Asia.[16] Because high-risk interfaces occur along tropical and equatorial belts of biodiverse countries, the investments in laboratory, personnel, and technology for pandemic preparedness are concentrated in low-resource countries.

PREDICT's mission is to preempt or combat, at their source, zoonotic diseases that pose a significant threat to public health, or potentially pandemic infections. This involves field studies including the sampling of animals and humans, laboratory analysis of those samples, development of probabilistic models suggesting likelihood of spillover, and, of course, close cooperation with local communities as well as national health and other public authorities about preparedness, training, and dissemination of knowledge.[17] PREDICT's surveillance strategy involved early recognition of "viral shedding" – the expulsion and release of virus progeniture after successful reproduction within a host-cell – in potentially zoonotic viruses in wildlife (including the detection of heretofore unknown viruses) to syndromic surveillance in people to detect disease as well as to assess behavioral risk.

---

[15] *Id.*
[16] *Id.*
[17] C. LeAnn White and Robert J. Duseck, *Wildlife Specimen Collection, Preservation, and Shipment*, 15-C4 USGS 13 (2015). ("Specimens are used to provide supporting information leading to the determination of the cause of disease or death in wildlife and for disease monitoring or surveillance. Commonly used specimens for wildlife disease investigations include intact carcasses, tissues from carcasses, euthanized or moribund animals, parasites, ingested food, feces, or environmental samples. Samples from live animals or the environment (e.g., contaminated feed) in the same vicinity as a mortality event also may be helpful. The type of specimen collected is determined by availability of samples and biological objectives. Multiple fresh, intact carcasses from affected species are the most useful in establishing a cause for a mortality event. Submission of entire carcasses allows observation of gross lesions and abnormalities, as well as disease testing of multiple tissues. Samples from live animals may be more appropriate when sick animals cannot be euthanized (e.g., threatened or endangered species) or for research and monitoring projects examining disease or agents circulating in apparently healthy animals or those not exhibiting clinical signs. Samples from live animals may include collections of blood, hair, feathers, feces, or ectoparasites, or samples obtained by swabbing lesions or orifices. Photographs and videos are useful additions for recording field and clinical signs and conveying conditions at the site. Collection of environmental samples (e.g., feces, water, feed, or soil) may be appropriate when animals cannot be captured for sampling or the disease agent may persist in the environment. If lethal collection is considered necessary, biologists should refer to the policies, procedures, and permit requirements of their institution/facility and the agency responsible for species management (U.S. Fish and Wildlife Service or State natural resource agency) prior to use in the field. If threatened or endangered species are found dead, or there is evidence of illegal take, field personal should contact local wildlife law enforcement authorities immediately and prior to handling the carcass. Prior to collecting samples, it is important to determine the capabilities and submission criteria of the laboratory receiving the samples.")

This strategy means identifying global "hotspots" where spillover risks are highest.[18] In infectious disease epidemiology, "hotspot" is frequently used to refer to areas of elevated disease burden or high transmission efficiency.[19] For the PREDICT project, these hotspots tend to occur in sub-Saharan Africa and Southeast Asia, areas where rapid intensification of agriculture systems, especially with livestock keeping, have increased interactions between animals and humans, and consequently caused significant changes in habits and practices of those communities.[20] An in-depth understanding of global hotspots presented in disease surveillance programs have two general orientations: General surveillance that is interested in the occurrence of any disease, or limited surveillance where the focus is on particular, pre-identified disease.[21]

PREDICT's primary focus is on wildlife and surveillance through biological samples of animals and the people who live nearby in those high-risk areas. High-risk areas include places where domesticated livestock interface with other species (e.g., domesticated camels interacting with poultry or guano collection sites where bats, humans, and other animals interact). PREDICT specifically has undertaken livestock and wildlife sampling in Bangladesh, Cambodia, Cameroon, China, Cote d'Ivoire, Democratic Republic of Congo, Egypt, Ethiopia, Ghana, Guinea, Indonesia, Jordan, Kenya, Lao PDR, Liberia, Malaysia, Mongolia, Myanmar, Nepal, Republic of Congo, Rwanda, Senegal, Sierra Leone, Tanzania, Thailand, Uganda, and Viet Nam.[22] As more fully described below, the coincidence of spillover "hotspots" and low-resource countries where they are largely located provides a significant opportunity to build the capacity for disease detection, preparedness, and response.

PREDICT's focus on wildlife and livestock surveillance is based on the best available evidence as to where threats are likely to emerge. Infectious diseases of livestock are a major threat to global animal health and human welfare. Livestock diseases that impact national and international trade remain endemic in many parts of the world.[23] Seventy-seven percent of known livestock pathogens are capable of

---

[18] Justin Lessler et al., *What Is a Hotspot Anyway?*, 96 Am. J. Trop. Med. Hyg. 1270 (2017), www.ncbi.nlm.nih.gov/pmc/articles/PMC5462559/ ("Hotspots" may be further subdefined as "burden hotspot," "transmission hotspot," and "emergence hotspot," as well as explicit specification of the spatiotemporal scale of interest.).

[19] *Id.*

[20] Lindal and Grace, *supra* note 5.

[21] Tyler Stitt et al., *Opportunities and Obstacles to Collecting Wildlife Disease Data for Public Health Purposes: Results of a Pilot Study on Vancouver Island, British Columbia*, 48 Can Vet J. 83–90 (2007), www.ncbi.nlm.nih.gov/pmc/articles/PMC1716737/.

[22] *PREDICT 2017 Annual Report*, USAID & OFDA, https://pdf.usaid.gov/pdf_docs/PA00TBF1.pdf.

[23] Fiona M. Tomley, *Livestock Infectious Diseases and Zoonoses*, 364 Phil. Trans. R. Soc. B 2637–42 (2009). ("Infectious diseases of livestock are a major threat to global animal health and welfare and their effective control is crucial for agronomic health, for safeguarding and securing national and international food supplies and for alleviating rural poverty in developing countries. Some devastating livestock diseases are endemic in many parts of the world and threats from old and new pathogens continue to emerge, with changes to global climate, agricultural practices and demography presenting conditions that are especially favourable for the spread of arthropod-borne diseases into new geographical areas.")

infecting multiple host species including wildlife affecting around 37 percent of total agricultural gross domestic product.[24] Dynamic and bidirectional, pathogens can transmit freely though wildlife–livestock interface as well as bird-poultry interface through indirect contact in communal areas, shared resources, and via vectors.[25]

In the wildlife sphere, bats, rodents, and primates are of primary importance. The PREDICT project targets detection of novel viruses in bats, rodents, and primates and to characterize high-risk behaviors in people and to identify potential migration channels.[26] Bats, for example, are intricately intertwined into their ecosystems worldwide. Their roles as pollinators, seed dispersers, and pest control agents mean they serve as foundational contributors to the ecosystem.[27] Their nitrogen-rich guano is used as a biological fertilizer.[28] While bats' benefit to humans is significant, they are also a reservoir species for diseases including Ebola, SARS, and Nipah. Understanding why bats host so many zoonotic pathogens that cause lethal diseases in humans and how spillover from bats to humans occurs is important in order to control these, and possibly as-yet-undiscovered, diseases.[29] Unfortunately,

[24]   Anke K. Wiethoelter, *Global Trends in Infectious Diseases at the Wildlife-Livestock Interface*, 112(31) PNAS 9662–67 (2015). ("Globally, livestock constitutes on average 37% of the agricultural gross domestic product and is one of the most important and rapidly expanding commercial agricultural sectors worldwide. Infectious diseases cause direct losses to this sector through increased mortality and reduced livestock productivity, as well as indirect losses associated with cost of control, loss of trade, decreased market values, and food insecurity. Diseases that are shared between species also represent a potential burden to the whole ecosystem, affecting biodiversity, changing behavior or composition of animal populations, and even relegating species to the fringe of extinction.")

[25]   *Current Surveillance Systems for Detecting Zoonoses in Animals*, NAT'L ACAD. PRESS (2008), www.ncbi.nlm.nih.gov/books/NBK207997/; *Global Infectious Disease Surveillance and Detection: Assessing the Challenges – Finding Solutions, Workshop Summary*, NAT'L ACAD PRESS (2007), www.ncbi.nlm.nih.gov/books/NBK52871/; Stitt et al., *supra* note 21.

[26]   *Emerging Pandemic Threats*, USAID, www.usaid.gov/news-information/fact-sheets/emerging-pandemic-threats-program.

[27]   N. Allocati et al., *Bat-man Disease Transmission: Zoonotic Pathogens from Wildlife Reservoirs to Human Populations*, 2 CELL DEATH DISCOVERY (2016). ("Bats, mammals of the Chiroptera order, are present all over the world with the exception of the Arctic, the Antarctic and a few oceanic islands. Bats are the only mammals with the ability to fly and are present in >1100 different species. Bats are essential members of the global ecosystem and humans benefit from their presence in many ways. They are involved in seed dispersal and pollination activity: tropical bats are vital – as an example – in rebuilding cut down forests and in the pollination of wild plants as bananas, avocados and dates. Furthermore, the flying mammals are the major predators of night insects, including crop and human pests. Finally, their guano, which is rich in nitrogen, is used as biological fertilizer.")

[28]   S. H. Newman, H. E. Field et al., *Investigating the Role of Bats in Emerging Zoonoses: Balancing Ecology, Conservation and Public Health Interests*. FAO ANIMAL PRODUCTION AND HEALTH MANUAL. VOL. (2011).

[29]   Viacheslav Y. Fofanov et al., *Guano Exposed: Impact of Aerobic Conditions on Bat Fecal Microbiota*, 8 ECOLOGY & EVOLUTION 5563–74 (2018). ("If guano samples from such deposits are useful for feces-based surveillance, it could significantly ease logistics of sample collection and enable cost-effective, large-scale studies of bat communities. Such studies could offer insights into the state of gut microbiotas, pathogen transmission for pathogens shed in feces, and diet, provided that the stability of the fecal microbiota is not significantly impacted by environmental exposure.")

larger studies of bats and their guano have not been explored due to the time and cost of sample collection, which will be discussed more in depth further below in Section 3.2.

The general flow of field and work operations varies slightly from country to country, but is generally comprised of the field capture of animals and clinical sampling of humans. All field capture and sampling has been approved by ethics review committees. Animal surveillance is guided by standards and codes created by the World Organisation for Animal Health (OIE), whose goals are to encourage countries to see surveillance as a global public good, and establish the necessary infrastructure to do so effectively.[30] "Diseases in wildlife often show up in the form of noticeable concentrations of carcasses, but these may not be noticed if no one is looking for them."[31] Surveillance is coordinated when researchers are looking for a specific source or disease to manifest in a known animal population, but more difficult when researchers do not know what they are looking for, or where.[32] An effort is in place to connect the surveillance data from national groups within countries to bolster the surveillance information held by the global community.

Trapping is a more invasive method of sampling, in which animals are captured and held long enough to produce the samples needed.[33] Trapping can be done to produce guano samples in the case of bats, or blood samples in the case of other wildlife. If it is blood, rather than the raw material getting transferred, chemicals for DNA preservation and anticoagulants are added to the small vials of two to three milliliters and sent to the local lab.

When taking a sample from a human, different procedures are in place to ensure their privacy, informed consent, and welfare. Obtaining samples from people requires that the patient give his or her informed consent, a written document or verbal recording outlining their understanding that a sample is going to be taken from them and analyzed at research institutions to understand the virus in their system.[34]

Once the samples are identified, they are collected by field scientists. Gathering data relies on a variety of samples in different conditions to analyze the underlying factors as well as variable effects, so the samples collected are a mix of sick animals

[30] *Current Surveillance Systems for Detecting Zoonoses in Animals*, NAT'L ACAD. PRESS (2008) at 3.
[31] *Id.* at 4.
[32] *Id.*
[33] Robert S. Sikes and William L. Gannon, *The Animal Care and Use Committee of the American Society of Mammalogists, Guidelines of the American Society of Mammalogists for the use of wild mammals in research*, 92 JOURNAL OF MAMMALOGY, 235–53 (2011).
[34] Ellen Clayton et al., *Informed Consent for Genetic Research on Stored Tissue Samples*, 274(22) J. OF AM. MED. ASS'N, 1786–92 (1995). ("Genetic research using stored tissue samples poses an array of benefits and risks to individuals, researchers, and society ... (1) informed consent is required for all genetic research using linkable samples unless conditions for limitation or waiver are met; (2) informed consent is not required for genetic research using anonymous samples but may be considered if identifiers are to be removed from currently linkable samples; (3) institutional review boards could usefully review all protocols that propose to use samples for genetic research .... ")

that have been euthanized and fresh carcasses found in the course of surveillance.[35] The samples must also be multiple from each species collected, so as to have better empirical representation of what affects the species as a whole.[36] Field personnel are advised to wear disposable gloves, coveralls (or bring a change of clothes), and rubber boots. To maximize results, investment in labor and partnerships can create gains in the number, diversity, and range of samples collected when surveillance program works collaboratively with organizations that already collect wildlife, especially wildlife rehabilitation centers.[37]

Samples are then analyzed for viral families using conventional PCR (polymerase chain reaction) testing. PCR testing allows for the location of specific segments of DNA and sequencing it to clone, reproduce, and analyze it efficiently.[38] Genetic samples are used to analyze DNA for potential viral strains that may be revealed in the feces or blood of animals. This is instrumental in the research of pathogens, and is a technique that has been honed to the point it can be done within the host country in the first step of the process. Later analysis may be done in laboratories abroad, facilitated through material transfer agreements, although one of the benefits in-country is the increasing capability of local researchers to do more analysis

[35] White and Duseck, *supra* note 17, at 4.
[36] *Id.*
[37] Stitt et al., *supra* note 21. ("Few organizations could collect samples for diagnostic evaluation, fewer still maintained records, and none regularly characterized or reported wildlife disease for public health purposes. Wildlife rehabilitation centers encountered the greatest variety of wildlife from the largest geographic area and frequently received submissions from other organizations. Obstacles to participation included the following: permit restrictions; financial disincentives; staff safety; no mandate to collect relevant data; and lack of contact between wildlife and public health agencies. Despite these obstacles, modest investments in personnel allowed novel pathogens of public health concern to be tracked. Targeted surveillance for known pathogens in specific host species, rather than general surveys for unspecified pathogens, was judged to be a more effective and efficient way to provide useful public health data.")
[38] Lilit Garibyan and Nidhi Avashia, *Research Techniques Made Simple: Polymerase Chain Reaction (PCR)*, 133 J INVEST DERMATOL (2013), www.ncbi.nlm.nih.gov/pmc/articles/PMC4102308. ("PCR is a simple, yet elegant, enzymatic assay, which allows for the amplification of a specific DNA fragment from a complex pool of DNA . . . PCR can be performed using source DNA from a variety of tissues and organisms, including peripheral blood, skin, hair, saliva, and microbes. Only trace amounts of DNA are needed for PCR to generate enough copies to be analyzed using conventional laboratory methods. For this reason, PCR is a sensitive assay. Each PCR assay requires the presence of template DNA, primers, nucleotides, and DNA polymerase. The DNA polymerase is the key enzyme that links individual nucleotides together to form the PCR product. The nucleotides include the four bases – adenine, thymine, cytosine, and guanine (A, T, C, G) – that are found in DNA. These act as the building blocks that are used by the DNA polymerase to create the resultant PCR product. The primers in the reaction specify the exact DNA product to be amplified. The primers are short DNA fragments with a defined sequence complementary to the target DNA that is to be detected and amplified. These serve as an extension point for the DNA polymerase to build on. The above mentioned components are mixed in a test tube or 96-well plate and then placed in a machine that allows repeated cycles of DNA amplification to occur in three basic steps. The machine is essentially a thermal cycler. It has a thermal block with holes, into which the test tubes or plates holding the PCR reaction mixture are inserted. The machine raises and lowers the temperature of the block in discrete, precise and pre-programmed steps.")

locally. This analysis is generally done as quickly as possible, to prevent the decomposition of samples.

Viruses have a life span after the host has died, and this life span is affected by the time outside of a host. Ebola for instance has a life span of a few hours on hard surfaces, but several days in samples like blood.[39] The H5N1 virus can survive up to two weeks when in contact with cold surfaces and temperatures, but in the heat it can only survive for a few hours.[40] The collection and preservation of these samples at their window of opportunity is important for ensuring the collection yields workable testing material.

Once the PCR testing is complete, that data and analysis is communicated to the host country's government and local authorities. It is then decided whether or not samples and research data must be transferred to other countries for further analysis. Often, the research capacities of the various laboratories necessitate the transferring of the material either to another laboratory in-country, and sometimes outside the country. The current model favors the building of laboratory capacity of in-country labs, diminishing the need for transfers.

3.2 SAMPLE TRANSFER AND MATERIAL TRANSFER AGREEMENTS

Procedures for shipping specimens differ with different disease diagnostic laboratories and regulatory requirements. There are five major considerations for proper specimen shipment: (1) prevent cross-contamination from specimen to specimen, (2) prevent decomposition of the specimen, (3) prevent leakage of fluids, (4) preserve individual specimen identity, and (5) properly label the package.[41] Dry ice is recommended for smaller specimens (e.g., tissue samples, small carcasses such as passerines) that need to be kept frozen during transit. When transporting samples back for further testing, one must comply with the host countries' regulations. Each country has its own agreement, but there is a preliminary agreement, the material transfer agreement or MTA, that PREDICT uses, which is usually signed by the Ministry of Health and Ministry of Agriculture. An MTA is a legally enforceable contract used by research institutions and others to set the terms on their materials and associated data that may be obtained and used by others. MTAs are used to send the material between the collectors in the field and the laboratory that runs the original tests. They are then used for subsequent transfers, both intra-country and inter-country.

---

[39]   *Ebola (Ebola Virus Disease)*, CTR. FOR DISEASE CONTROL AND PREVENTION (2019), www.cdc.gov/vhf/ ebola/transmission/index.html. ("On dry surfaces, like doorknobs and countertops, the virus can survive for several hours. However, in body fluids, like blood, the virus can survive up to several days at room temperature.")

[40]   American Chemical Society, *Highly Pathogenic Bird Flu Virus Can Survive Months on Steel or Glass at Cooler Temperatures*, SCI. DAILY (2010), www.sciencedaily.com/releases/2010/10/101013124334.htm.

[41]   White and Duseck, *supra* note 17, at 13.

MTAs have developed a reputation for excessive complexity and, at worst, hindering the exchange of research. While in theory they are a way to quickly move through the process of transferring the data and samples where each party is aware of the terms of the agreement without spending time on negotiating, which is both time consuming and costly, it also has its drawbacks. MTAs can be so formulaic that they can mandate terms that one party would not have required if they had drafted the agreement *ab initio*, and can legally complicate scientific work.[42]

Yet MTAs facilitate the process of sending the samples from the entity taking the samples to the next person or laboratory. MTAs can reduce negotiating time, especially as researchers involved in various stages of studying the viral samples are not trained in negotiation with other entities, nor is it in their basic job understanding that they need do so. MTAs also provide information in the form of instructions for cold chain preservation and information for subsequent researchers.[43]

These agreements are also important to assure not only good practices among researchers, but also to respect the law of the host country, which can in turn be part of complying with international law. For example, the MTAs require reporting certain findings to Ministries of Health and Agriculture. These agreements help those ministries determine their international reporting obligations under the International Health Regulations (IHR) (2005). The International Health Regulations set out a collaborative global framework to enhance the world health security through reporting unusual or unexpected health events, and was created to help standardize and set the expectations for all countries in combating global health threats.

3.3 THE TANZANIA CASE STUDY

The above process may appear relatively uncomplicated, but each step may involve significant investments of time and resources. Some of PREDICT's work in Tanzania may help illustrate. Examining the experience of researchers in Tanzania will also help understand the benefits in terms of research and other capacities global infectious disease research may engender. As recently as February of 2018, Tanzania partnered with the World Health Organization to create a One Health Coordination Desk and a National One Health Strategic Plan.[44] This sort of partnership is vitally important to the world's collective knowledge of sample sharing and viral samples: Tanzania has a wide spectrum of biodiversity, allowing for

---

[42] See generally Tania Bubela et al., *Use and Misuse of Material Transfer Agreements: Lessons in Proportionality from Research Repositories, and Litigation*, PLoS BIOL (2015).

[43] *Id.*

[44] *Tanzania Commits to Embrace the One Health Approach*, WORLD HEALTH ORG. (2018), www .afro.who.int/news/tanzania-commits-embrace-one-health-approach.

a larger breadth of understanding how viruses mutate and affect local wildlife.[45] Access to this sect of wildlife allows for larger global understanding of diseases.

In Tanzania, the research effort begins with the employment of Tanzanians for transport and staff and materials. Even at this initial stage, there may be important practical limitations. On average Dar Es Salaam, a major port city and most likely a good starting place from which a research crew could embark, sees upwards of 10 inches of rain in April and 7.9 in May.[46] This rainy season makes it next to impossible to work in the field, let alone get the vehicle transport through the muddy roads. Over the span of the "rainy season," Tanzania will see an average of 23.5 inches of rain, creating a major difficulty in travel.[47]

Tanzania is rich in forests and rural areas. Its population has a high rate of contact with plants and animals.[48] Bats play an important ecological role in Tanzania, pollinating flowers and dispersing fruit seeds; many tropical plant species depend entirely on bats for the distribution of their seeds. Bats are economically important as they consume insect pests, reducing the need for pesticides. They are also an important source of potentially human pathogenic viruses.

How do the zoonotic viruses make the transfer to human beings? A common method of transference is from domesticated livestock to humans, and this has been studied and documented in the surveillance step to attempt to identify any potential for emerging diseases.[49] It is a common understanding that transference of disease from livestock to humans is frequent either in the interface of caretaking of the animals or the consumption of their by-products, and this is an important step to be aware of and cognizant of how viruses can be transferred in this way. But another step in this chain that is not as well researched is the interface from wildlife to livestock, or from a bat to a pig, for example, a transfer that might happen in a number of ways. There is no set form of interaction, and it can come about in any number of ways, but shared access to a communal space (such as a pasture or water source) can be one simple way a virus can migrate from one animal to another.[50]

In order to acquire samples from animals, numerous methods are used. As discussed above, one of the ways to do so is to find an animal carcass that has very recently died and save whole tissue samples (or even the entire animal if it is small enough) and use that as the raw vessel from which the transfer is made. However there are times that samples of whole animals or waiting to happen upon a dead sample is impractical. A simple and effective method of animal sample collecting is through the use of harvesting guano samples from bats. More than 200 viruses are

---

[45] See generally, *Tanzania: Environment*, USAID (2019), www.usaid.gov/tanzania/environment.
[46] *Climate, Tanzania*, WORLD CLIMATE GUIDE, www.climatestotravel.com/climate/tanzania.
[47] *Id.*
[48] *Id.*
[49] Wiethoelter, *supra* note 24, at 9662.
[50] *Id.*

associated with bats, and bats to human transmission of diseases are frequent enough to be the source of many disease outbreaks throughout the world.[51] Bats make a very good species to watch for any emerging patterns of potential viral infections, and taking samples of and analyzing their guano is a good way to do so.[52] This does, however, lead to certain problems itself.

Collecting the animal samples requires specialized personnel depending on the method being used.[53] In the case of bat guano collection, it requires researchers trained in knowing the ways to get to and collect the material without disturbing the bats, all of which is done in the dead of night when the bats are moving from their roosts.[54] A cost-effective strategy that has been considered is to collect the samples with the minimally invasive procedure of using a tarp by a roost's entrance, allowing the tarp to accumulate the guano without disturbing the bats or overextending the research team's resources.[55] The samples also do not have to take as severe a problem as decomposing in the sun when they can be harvested in a single, clean method eight to twelve hours after being left.[56] This is one of the many methods in which researchers can extend less resources and personnel and focus instead on enhancing the lab's capabilities to assess the DNA of the samples themselves.

PREDICT's work on bats in Tanzania shows the benefits to local infectious disease research capacity and the important returns that investment in this research may provide. As local laboratories became adept at undertaking first-level PCR analysis, technicians working in those laboratories became better able to use diagnostics in other disease classes. Take the example of malaria diagnosis. In 2008, the presence of malaria in children under five was around 18.1 percent according to the mRDT (malaria rapid diagnostic test) results able to be performed at the time, while in 2012 the prevalence in mRDT was 9.7 percent and only 4.2 percent when analyzed microscopically.[57] A study conducted in 2015 analyzed the accuracy of mRDT results in a grouping of 600 children under five years old by comparing mRDT results from the health clinics where they were taken and then analyzing them further in a microscopic, individualized way. The results confirmed overall the mRDT results skewed in favor of recognizing malaria and subsequently providing antibiotics, though in actuality the rate of malaria cases was less than the amount caught by field tests.[58] This study was conducted in the three years before Tanzania

---

[51] See generally, Allocati et al., *supra* note 27.
[52] Fofanov et al., *supra* note 29, at 5563.
[53] *Id.*
[54] *Id.* at 5564.
[55] *Id.* at 5571.
[56] *Id.*
[57] Danial Nkonya, Donath Tarimo, and Rogath Kishimba, *Accuracy of Clinical Diagnosis and Malaria Rapid Diagnostic Test and Its Influence on the Management of Children with Fever under Reduced Malaria Burden in Misungwi District, Mwanza Tanzania,* 25 Pan Afr Med J. (2016).
[58] *Id.*

signed on to be a member of the One Health initiative, and thus the only field testing available of human subjects was the mRDT.

As the One Health initiative progresses, the goal will be to allow even greater success rates in accurately diagnosing and detecting disease in the field. With the aid to the Tanzania ramping up to assist in the research and disease detection capacities, the labs themselves will eventually be set to take on this task fully and independently with a low margin for error.

3.4 PREDICT AND CAPACITY-BUILDING

As noted below, PREDICT projects work in support of the IHR (2005). These rules apply in all countries contributing to and working with PREDICT, and themselves represent a legally binding agreement that provides a framework for the coordination of events should a public health emergency occur.[59] Simply, these rules include developing and strengthening specific national public health capacities, maintaining these capacities to build and strengthen as needed, developing national IHR implementation plans, and identifying priority areas for action.[60]

Further, while each country has individual agreements with PREDICT, there is also a standard preliminary agreement signed by the Ministry of Health and Ministry of Agriculture that binds all countries to the same base terms. These terms incorporate the IHR directly and provide uniformity to allow for a cohesive mission amongst all the contributors.

Ultimately, the strategies and tactics of the One Health method and how PREDICT interacts with the surveillance and collection of the raw data all point back to the same common goal: building capacity in the places from which these samples are taken. The world at large benefits when host countries and research stations are better equipped to perform research and disease detection in their own laboratories.

The World Health Organization recognizes that "when assessing a new infectious diseases disease outbreak, [research capacity] is of utmost importance – but enormously difficult."[61] To strengthen research capacities, the United Nations Development Programme challenges scientists to do diagnostic research themselves, as PREDICT now does in thirty countries.[62] PREDICT undertakes training using technology that is best suited for the goals of the country with built-in incentives to empower/enable trainees to train others.[63] PREDICT has trained

---

[59]   David Heymann, *Public Health, Global Governance, and the Revised International Health Regulations*, WORLD HEALTH ORG. *Infectious Disease Movement in a Borderless World: Workshop Summary* 182–95 (2010) at 184.

[60]   *Strengthening Health Security by Implementing the International Health Regulations* (2005), WORLD HEALTH ORG., www.who.int/ihr/procedures/implementation/en/.

[61]   *Strengthening Capacity for Response and Research*, NAT'L ACAD. PRESS (2017).

[62]   *Capacity Development: A UNDP Primer*, UNDP (2009).

[63]   Stitt et al., *supra* note 21.

over 4,200 people, taken 124,000 individual samples from people and animals, and resulted in more than 400,000 laboratory tests in over 60 labs, and the discovery of over 1,000 known and new viruses. This information is shared amongst the network, allowing for fast-paced disbursement of current information. Building this capacity is crucial.[64]

3.5 CONCLUSION

This chapter has analyzed the ascendance of one health approaches to infectious disease threats, described how the PREDICT project works in aid of one health, and has provided some data to support the proposition that investments in one health research have a compounding benefit to low-resources countries because it enhances their research and laboratory capacity. As new infectious disease threats emerge and old pathogens mutate in ways that require continuous vigilance, similar investments are likely to be viewed as a win-win for the global health and global development communities.

---

[64] Marianne I. Martić-Kehl et al., *Can Animal Data Predict Human Outcome? Problems and Pitfalls of Translational Animal Research*, 39 EUR. J. NUCLEAR MED. & MOLECULAR IMAGING 1492–96 (2012), www.ncbi.nlm.nih.gov/pmc/articles/PMC3411287/.

PART II

Health Security, Research Ethics, and Human Rights Implications

4

The Ethics of Conducting Genomic Research in Low-Resource Settings

Haley K. Sullivan and Benjamin E. Berkman[1]

Transnational infectious disease research, effectively illustrated in Chapter 3, aims to predict and prevent global health pandemics by capitalizing on international collaboration and large databanks. Genome sequencing is an important component of this research, and its results are used to analyze both viral and host DNA. Viral genetic data aid vaccine development by illustrating the evolution of the infectious source; these kinds of data help researchers predict yearly influenza viral strains, which enables them to repeatedly produce effective vaccines.[2] Meanwhile, host genetic data help predict individuals' disease progression for viruses like West Nile, HIV-1, and Hepatitis C.[3]

Given the transnational reality of infectious disease, the problem with this latter approach is that existing genetic research has largely been conducted only on people of European descent.[4] In 2009, 96 percent of genome-wide association study

[1] This chapter is adapted from: Haley K. Sullivan and Benjamin E. Berkman, *Incidental Findings in Low-Resource Settings*, HASTINGS CENTER REPORT 48, no. 3 (2018). The views herein are ours and do not represent the views or policies of the Department of Health and Human Services or the National Institutes of Health. This research was supported in part by the Intramural Research Program of the National Human Genome Research Institute at the NIH.
[2] Martha I. Nelson et al., *Fogarty International Center Collaborative Networks in Infectious Disease Modeling: Lessons Learnt in Research and Capacity Building*, 26 EPIDEMICS 116–27 (2019), https://doi .org/10.1016/j.epidem.2018.10.004. ("These activities have provided evidence-based recommendations for disease control, including during large-scale outbreaks of pandemic influenza, Ebola and Zika virus. Together, these programs have coordinated international collaborative networks to advance the study of emerging disease threats and the field of computational epidemic modeling.")
[3] See, e.g., Abigail W. Bigham et al., *Host Genetic Risk Factors for West Nile Virus Infection and Disease Progression*, 6 PLOS ONE, 9 (2011), doi.org/10.1371/journal.pone.0024745 ("Identifying the genetic factors (i.e. risk alleles) that influence the development of WNV disease could help to elucidate pathways important for increased pathogenicity of WNV disease, facilitate the identification of individuals at high risk for severe WNV-induced disease, and provide potential therapeutic targets"); Casado Concepcion et al., *Host and Viral Genetic Correlates of Clinical Definitions of Hiv-1 Disease Progression*, 5 PLOS ONE 6 (2010), doi.org/10.1371/journal.pone.0011079 ("Several studies describe a correlation between disease progression and the extent of HIV-1 genetic variation"); Megan M. Dring et al., *Innate Immune Genes Synergize to Predict Increased Risk of Chronic Disease in Hepatitis C Virus Infection*, 108 PNAS 14 (2011), doi.org/10.1073/pnas.1016358108.
[4] Alice B. Popejoy and Stephanie M. Fullerton, *Genomics Is Failing on Diversity*, 538 NATURE 161–64 (2016), https://doi.org/10.1038/538161a. ("A 2009 analysis revealed that 96% of participants in genome-

(GWAS) participants in the United States were categorized as white or as people of European ancestry: in 2016, the percentage had decreased only to 81 percent.[5] This lack of diversity has generated data and findings that are not necessarily generalizable to a global population and that miss novel genetic variants specific to people not of European ancestry. Because ethnicities and races have different disease-linked variants,[6] non-diverse data limit the "potential for discovery" by missing "associations between variants and diseases … and responses to drugs" in non-European population groups.[7] Including diverse populations in genomic research enables investigators to estimate the risk of disease with greater scientific accuracy and confidence according to participants' ancestry.[8]

To remedy the problem, there has been a commendable recent push for increased genetic research on more global populations. This has particularly been true in transnational infectious disease research, where viral host genome sequencing has become a major part of a larger global health trend toward genetic research to identify disease-linked variants. Much of this new global genetic research employs Whole Genome Sequencing (WGS), which many see as the future of genetic research in a "post-GWAS era" because it provides researchers with large amounts of data and because variants discovered with WGS often have larger effect sizes than disease-associated loci identified through GWAS.[9]

wide association studies (GWAS) were of European descent. Such studies scan the genomes of thousands of people to find variants associated with disease traits. The finding prompted warnings that a much broader range of populations should be investigated to avoid genomic medicine being of benefit merely to 'a privileged few'. Seven years on, we've updated that analysis. Our findings indicate that the proportion of individuals included in GWAS who are not of European descent has increased to nearly 20%. Much of this rise, however, is a result of more studies being done in Asia on populations of Asian ancestry. The degree to which people of African and Latin American ancestry, Hispanic people and indigenous peoples are represented in GWAS has barely shifted.")

5   Anna C. Need and David B. Goldstein, *Next Generation Disparities in Human Genomics: Concerns and Remedies*, 25 Trends in Genetics 489–94 (2009). ("Studies of human genetics, particularly genome-wide association studies (GWAS), have concentrated heavily on European populations, with individuals of African ancestry rarely represented. Reasons for this include the distribution of biomedical funding and the increased population structure and reduced linkage disequilibrium in African populations.") *Id.*

6   National Research Council (US) Panel on Race, Ethnicity, and Health in Later Life; N. B. Anderson, R. A. Bulatao, B. Cohen B, eds. *Critical Perspectives on Racial and Ethnic Differences in Health in Late Life*. Washington (DC): National Academies Press (US); 2004. 8, Genetic Factors in Ethnic Disparities in Health. Available from: www.ncbi.nlm.nih.gov/books/NBK25517/.

7   Nadia M. Penrod, Richard Cowper-Sal-lari, and Jason H. Moore, Systems Genetics for Drug Target Discovery, 32(10) Trends in Pharmacological Sciences 623–30 (2011), https://doi.org/10.1016/j.tips.2011.07.002.

8   A. R. Bentley, S. Callier, and C. N. Rotimi, *Diversity and Inclusion in Genomic Research: Why the Uneven Progress?*, 8(4) J Community Genet. 255–66 (2017), doi:10.1007/s12687-017-0316-6.

9   Galen Wright et al., *Ethical and Legal Implications of Whole Genome and Whole Exome Sequencing in African Populations*, 14 BioMedCentral Med. Ethics 21 (2013) ("Funding agencies and journals often require submission of genomic data from research participants to databases that allow open or controlled data access for all investigators. Access to such genotype-phenotype and pedigree data, however, needs careful control in order to prevent identification of individuals or families. This is particularly the case in Africa, where many researchers and their patients are inexperienced in the

The quantity of data generated through WGS has also led to the generation and discovery of more incidental[10] or secondary[11] findings (IFs) and subsequently, a vigorous theoretical discussion about the ethical obligations that follow from these IFs.[12] After more than a decade of debate in the genetic research community, the issue is not fully settled, although there is a growing consensus that researchers should, at the very least, offer to return IFs that provide high impact, medically relevant information, when it is not unduly burdensome to the research enterprise to do so.[13] A list of fifty-nine highly valuable, actionable secondary findings was released by the American College of Medical Genetics and Genomics, and serves as the reference list for many research studies that choose to return IFs.

Much as genetic research has been limited to US and European settings, the IF debate has primarily focused on research conducted in high-income countries. In a 2015 paper, Alberto Ortiz-Osorno, Linda Ehler, and Judith Brooks note salient differences between the circumstances of research participants in low- and high-resource settings that alter the analysis of when and why IFs should be offered to research participants.[14] This chapter will expand on the Ortiz-Osorno

ethical issues accompanying whole genome and exome research; and where an historical unidirectional flow of samples and data out of Africa has created a sense of exploitation and distrust."); Andreas Ziegler and Yun V. Sun, *Study Designs and Methods Post Genome-Wide Association Studies*, 131 HUMAN GENETICS 1525, 1525–31 (2012). ("The success of GWAs using a large number of unrelated individuals has only been made possible by the great advancements in microarray technology. However, it has also required new developments in statistical methodology. As pointed out by Cardon and Palmer (2003) and others, the importance of population stratification as a cause of non-replicated association outcomes led to a great shift in association study design in the 1990s, away from the traditional case–control approach towards the more costly and less efficient family-based designs. However, family-based association designs are often neither practical nor plausible, especially for pharmacogenetic studies, including personalized medicine. It is therefore only natural that approaches that allow adjustments for population stratification in case control or cohort studies are highly cited.")

[10] Susan Wolf defines an incidental finding as "a finding concerning an individual research participant that has potential health or reproductive importance and is discovered in the course of conducting research but is beyond the aims of the study." *See* Susan M. Wolf et al., *Managing Incidental Findings in Human Subjects Research: Analysis and Recommendations*, 36 J. L., MED. & ETHICS 219 (2008).

[11] A secondary findings is defined by The Presidential Commission for the Study of Bioethical Issues as "a finding that is actively sought by a practitioner that is not the primary target" of the research. *See* Presidential Commission for the Study of Bioethical Issues, *Anticipate and Communicate: Ethical Management of Incidental and Secondary Findings in the Clinical, Research, and Direct-to-Consumer Contexts* at 3 (2013).

[12] *See id., see also* Wolf et al., *supra* note 10 at 219.

[13] Susan M. Wolf, *The Past, Present, and Future of the Debate over Return of Research Results and Incidental Findings*, 14 GENETICS IN MED. 355–57 (2012); Sarah S. Kalia et al., *Recommendations for Reporting of Secondary Findings in Clinical Exome and Genome Sequencing, 2016 Update (Acmg Sf V2.0): A Policy Statement of the American College of Medical Genetics and Genomics*, 19 GENETICS IN MEDICINE 249, 249–55 (2017); Gail P. Jarvik et al., *Return of Genomic Results to Research Participants: The Floor, the Ceiling, and the Choices in Between*, 94 AM. J. HUM. GENETICS 818, 818–26 (2014).

[14] Alberto Ortiz-Osorno et al., *Considering Actionability at the Participant's Research Setting Level for Anticipatable Incidental Findings from Clinical Research*, 43 J. L. MED. & ETHICS 619, 619–32 (2015).

analysis and present a framework for thinking about how investigators' obligations to return genomic data might change in low-resource settings, particularly
in settings where participants do not have access to the medical care needed to
treat, assess, or monitor IFs that are actionable in settings with plentiful
resources.

4.1 A CASE: TRANSNATIONAL STUDY OF GENETICS AND IMMUNOLOGY

Imagine that a research team based in the United States is conducting a multisite
study on the genetic risk factors that exacerbate an individual's response to a set of
serious infectious diseases, a step that might naturally follow the research described
by Brian Bird in Chapter 3.[15] The team hopes to generate WGS data for affected
patients to help understand the genetic basis of immune responses. The research
will be conducted in several low- and middle-income countries in Africa and Asia,
including Nigeria and Thailand.

In the process of analyzing genomic sequence data, researchers may discover IFs
about the research participants, including non-affected family members. The team
believes that it is important to return any medically actionable findings (even when
unrelated to the infectious diseases under investigation) and has previously done so
in similar studies conducted only in the United States.

The researchers' Institutional Review Board (IRB), however, has concerns about
whether it is appropriate to return IFs in low-resource settings. Participants in low-
and middle-income countries may not have the same level of access to healthcare
as participants in the United States do, meaning that it will be less clear that
"actionable" incidental genetic information will actually lead to concrete medical
interventions. For example, some basic preventative services like mammography,
which would be a possible preventative service should there be an IF related to
BRCA1 and an increased risk of hereditary breast and ovarian cancer, are much less
accessible in developing countries like Nigeria, where there are often only
a handful of facilities providing services for an entire region.[16] Even in a country

---

("However, no author has addressed how the 'actionability' of the IFs should be considered, evaluated,
or characterized at the participant's research setting level. This paper defines the concept of
'Actionability at the Participant's Research Setting Level' (APRSL) for anticipatable IFs from clinical
research, discusses some related ethical concepts to justify the APRSL concept, proposes a strategy to
incorporate APRSL into the planning and management of IFs, and suggests a strategy for integrating
APRSL at each local research setting.")

[15]   This description is adapted from a related pair of NHGRI intramural studies.
[16]   Olanrewaju Lawal et al., *Mammography Screening in Nigeria – a Critical Comparison to Other
Countries*, 21 RADIOGRAPHY 348, 348–51 (2015). ("The screening program in Nigeria is largely unstruc-
tured regarding the mode of invitation, frequency of screening, and the age of the participants. For
instance, only one Nigerian state out of the thirty-six reported organising a structured mammography
screening program. Other non-government organisations and multinational cooperation organisations have also been involved in providing mammographic breast screening in Nigeria but it is

with many medical services, and facilities like Thailand, access to them can be inequitable.[17]

Furthermore, the IRB worries that the cultural norms surrounding certain diseases may be different in low-resource settings, perhaps providing additional reasons for being cautious about returning IFs. For example, Nigerian or Thai research participants might be reluctant to learn about a genetic predisposition for depression given the pervasive stigma and superstition associated with mental illnesses in those countries.[18] Certain cancer diagnoses (e.g., breast and cervical) have also been shown to be highly stigmatizing in some developing countries.[19] Despite these concerns, the prospect of having divergent IF policies for different sites seems potentially unfair, and perhaps sets a problematic precedent as international WGS protocols become increasingly common.

4.2 THE ACTIONABILITY PROBLEM

This case highlights an underexplored tension in the IF debate: the actionability problem. The return of IFs is predicated on the idea that the information could lead

haphazard. As there are several important elements involved in the four developed countries' screening programs, the program being evaluated will be discussed using these factors- mode of invitation, frequency of screening, age of the participants, image projections, imaging staff, quality assurance program, and availability.")

[17] Sukanya Chongthawonsatid, *Inequity of Healthcare Utilization on Mammography Examination and Pap Smear Screening in Thailand: Analysis of a Population-Based Household Survey*, 12 PLoS One e0173656 (2017). ("To examine factors associated with the utilization of mammography examination for breast cancer and Pap smear screening for cervical cancer, data from the national reproductive health survey conducted by the National Statistical Office of Thailand in 2009 was examined. The survey was carried out on 15,074,126 women aged 30–59 years. The results showed that the wealthier respondents had more mammograms than did the lower-income groups.")

[18] Theddeus Iheanacho et al., *Attitudes and Beliefs about Mental Illness among Church-Based Lay Health Workers: Experience from a Prevention of Mother-to-Child HIV Transmission Trial in Nigeria*, 9 Int'l J. Culture & Mental Health 1, 1–13 (2016) ("Common mental disorders are prevalent in Nigeria. Due to stigma and a limited number of trained specialists, only 10% of adults with mental illness in Nigeria receive any care."); Christoph Lauber & Wulf Rossler, *Stigma towards People with Mental Illness in Developing Countries in Asia*, 19 Int'l Rev. Psychiatry 157, 157–78 (2007). ("Comparable to Western countries, there is a widespread tendency to stigmatize and discriminate people with mental illness in Asia. People with mental illness are considered as dangerous and aggressive which in turn increases the social distance. The role of supernatural, religious and magical approaches to mental illness is prevailing. The pathway to care is often shaped by scepticism towards mental health services and the treatments offered. Stigma experienced from family members is pervasive. Moreover, social disapproval and devaluation of families with mentally ill individuals are an important concern.")

[19] Dusanee Suwankhong, and Pranee Liamputtong, *Breast Cancer Treatment: Experiences of Changes and Social Stigma among Thai Women in Southern Thailand*, 39 Cancer Nursing 213, 213–20 (2016); Laura Nyblade et al., *A Qualitative Exploration of Cervical and Breast Cancer Stigma in Karnataka, India*, 17 BioMedCentral Women's Health 58 (2017). ("Cancer stigma emerged as a general theme across both data sets. It appeared throughout the transcripts as descriptions of how women with breast or cervical cancer would be treated and talked about by husbands, family and the community (manifestations of stigma) and the reasons for this behavior. Stigma as a theme also arose through discussions around managing disclosure of a cancer diagnosis.")

to clinical benefits – what has been termed actionability.[20] While actionability is always relevant when considering obligations to return IFs, in discussions about IFs and low-resource setting research, actionability is often conflated with access to care. Just because a medical or behavioral action exists that could prevent, mitigate, or cure the condition does not mean a person always has access to the healthcare resources to take that action. Imagine that a woman who participated in the research study described above is contacted by the researchers and told she has a variant of the BRCA1 gene that is linked to higher risk for hereditary breast and ovarian cancers, but that she does not have access to preventative care such as mammograms or preventative mastectomies. She therefore cannot easily gain the same clinical benefit from learning of this so-called actionable IF as can a woman participating at a US study site who received a similar result but has access to care.

Additionally, because certain populations have historically been excluded from genetic research, there is uncertainty about how to interpret certain genetic variants in these under-studied populations. Another woman participating in the same hypothetical study might learn that she has a variant of unknown significance in the BRCA1 gene. Because the ancestral groups in which this particular variant is common were not included in early genetic research, there may not be sufficient evidence to know how the variant affects this woman's personal risk of cancer. Even if she has access to care, clinicians and geneticists might be unsure how to advise her on the meaning of the results.[21]

Although it is clear that the benefit of returning IFs depends on access to care, it is not clear how to analyze access to care. Access could be analyzed at an individual level, but this process would be both difficult and time-consuming and the resources needed to carry it out might detract from the creation of generalizable knowledge. Ortiz-Osorno and colleagues suggest an alternate approach; researchers should assess "actionability at the participant's research setting level" (ASPRL) and consider the average access of people in the research community when determining what IFs

---

[20] There are several definitions of actionability: a narrow medical sense, which includes only information that could provide medical benefit in the form of treatment or prevention; an intermediate reproductive sense, which includes information that could be used for reproductive decision-making; and a broad personal utility sense, which includes any information that someone could find useful in planning their life. We prefer the narrow sense first because researchers only have limited resources and assuming the additional obligation to return IFs reduces the ability to create generalizable knowledge, the central goal of research. Second, the most restrictive definition is useful for argumentation: if researchers do not have obligations to return medically actionable IFs, then they certainly do not have obligations to return IFs under a more expansive conception of actionability. Lisa Eckstein et al., *A Framework for Analyzing the Ethics of Disclosing Genetic Research Findings*, 42 J. L. MED. & ETHICS 2 (2014).

[21] Nicola M. Suter, *BRCA1 and BRCA2 Mutations in Women from Shanghai China*, 13 CANCER EPIDEMIOLOGY BIOMARKERS & PREVENTION 181, 181–89 (2004); Ava Kwong et al., *Characterization of the Pathogenic Mechanism of a Novel BRCA2 Variant in a Chinese Family*, 7 FAMILIAL CANCER 125, 125–33 (2008); Michael J. Hall et al., *BRCA1 and BRCA2 Mutations in Women of Different Ethnicities Undergoing Testing for Hereditary Breast-Ovarian Cancer*, 115 CANCER 2222, 2222–33 (2009).

to return.[22] Such a policy could lead to IFs being offered to participants at some study sites, but not at others.

While we agree with Ortiz-Osorno et al. that the benefit of returning IFs should be analyzed above the individual level, we disagree with their conclusion. We think that their analysis does not deal adequately with the tension between two competing considerations. First, IFs may be less helpful in certain settings, potentially reducing researchers' obligation to return them. Second, treating groups differently seems unfair, particularly when it would disadvantage groups that are already worse off because of lack of access to health care resources. Ortiz-Osorno et al.'s considerations around justice are inadequate: They conclude that "since IFs by definition are not related to the aims of the research but are better considered ancillary benefits, they should not be taken into account in the analysis of 'justice and fairness'" in the context of the distribution of research risks and benefits.[23] However, justice in human subjects research is not limited to the distribution of risk and benefit. Particularly in global research, justice considerations often include the provision of ancillary benefits to research participants. For example, the Council for International Organizations of Medical Sciences (CIOMS) guidelines for ethics in international human subjects research note that "[i]n some cases, in order to ensure an overall fair distribution of the benefits and burdens of the research, additional benefits such as investments in the local health infrastructure should be provided to the population or community."[24]

We believe that a central tenet of human subjects research is to treat all participants equally unless there is a compelling scientific or ethical reason not to. The scientific reasons not to return findings are likely specific to a given study but the ethical reasons are not.

4.3 THE DUTY TO RETURN INCIDENTAL FINDINGS

Although the overall emerging consensus (and our own intuition) is to return actionable IFs that meet a threshold of medical importance in most cases, stakeholders still do not agree on which ethical concepts should ground such an obligation to return IFs.[25] The bioethics literature cites various principles to support returning IFs: The duty to rescue, the duty to warn, general and specific duties of beneficence, and positive autonomy.[26] These different principles suggest different levels of obligation to

---

[22] *See* Ortiz-Osorno et al., *supra* note 14.
[23] *Id.*
[24] Council for Int'l Org. of Med. Sci., *International Ethical Guidelines for Health-Related Research Involving Humans* (2016).
[25] *See* Wolf, *supra* note 13.
[26] Annelien L. Bredenoord et al., *Disclosure of Individual Genetic Data to Research Participants: The Debate Reconsidered*, 27 TRENDS IN GENETICS 41, 41–47 (2011); Elizabeth R. Pike et al., *Finding Fault? Exploring Legal Duties to Return Incidental Findings in Genomic Research*, 102 GEO. L.J. 795 (2014); Henry S. Richardson, *Incidental Findings and Ancillary-Care Obligations*, 36 J. L. MED. & ETHICS 256, 256–70 (2008).

return incidental findings. Analyzing the ethical underpinnings of the possible obligation to return actionable IFs can therefore provide insight about how to grapple with
the actionability problem.

None of these candidate principles or duties fit perfectly, but we find that the duty
to rescue is the most plausible. The duty to warn is generally conceived of as a legal
duty to third parties – doctors may have a duty to warn patients' biological family
members about genetic findings relevant to the family members' health – and as
such is not a good fit for a duty that researchers have to return IFs to research
participants.[27] The imperfect duty of beneficence is a general duty that requires
people do some good in their lives; it does not adequately support a duty to return IFs
because researchers could discharge the duty through many beneficent actions
unrelated to the return of IFs.[28] Giving research participants information to make
informed choices fosters positive autonomy, but the limits as to what kinds of health
information researchers are required to return is not clearly delineated by the
principle and therefore the principle of autonomy does not strongly support a duty
to return IFs.[29]

The duty to rescue is an obligation to provide help to specific people. In the
influential account developed by Tom Beauchamp and James Childress, one has
a duty to rescue a person when (1) the person is in a life- or health-threatening
situation, (2) the action is necessary to prevent harm, (3) the action will likely
succeed in preventing harm, (4) the action will not cause significant risk or burdens
to the rescuer, and (5) the benefit the rescued person will receive will outweigh the
harm to the rescuer.[30] The duty to rescue derives from a duty of general beneficence
and therefore it is a duty that any person owes any other person.[31] In the literature on
IFs, many conclude that such findings fulfills the duty to rescue.[32] Others qualify
such assertions: Laura Beskow and Wylie Burke argue that there are limitations on
what IFs must be returned such that the duty to rescue requires return only when an
IF "clearly indicates a high probability of a serious condition for which an effective
intervention is readily available."[33]

The paradigmatic example of the duty to rescue is often said to be the case of
an adult who sees a child drowning in a shallow pool. The return of incidental
findings does not quite fit with this paradigm in two ways. First, the threat is less

---

[27] Susan M. Wolf et al., *The Law of Incidental Findings in Human Subjects Research: Establishing
      Researchers' Duties*, 36 J. L. Med. & Ethics 2 (2008); *Pate V. Threlkel*, 661 278 (1995); *Safer V. Estate of
      Pack*, 677 1188 (1996); *Abc V. St George's Healthcare NHS Trust* (2017).
[28] Joseph Millum, *Post-Trial Access to Antiretrovirals: Who Owes What to Whom?*, 25 Bioethics 145,
      145–54 (2011).
[29] Tom L. Beauchamp and James F. Childress, Principles of Biomedical Ethics (7th ed. 2012).
[30] *Id.*
[31] *Id.*
[32] *See* Bredenoord et al., *supra* note 26; Michael Ulrich, *The Duty to Rescue in Genomic Research*, 13 Am.
      J. Bioethics 50, 50–51 (2013); Laura M. Beskow and Wylie Burke, *Offering Individual Genetic
      Research Results: Context Matters*, 2 Sci. Translational Med. 38, 38 n. 20 (2010).
[33] Beskow and Burke, *id.*

immediate; genetic findings are probabilistic and disorders may not manifest for years.[34] Because genes interact with other genes, the environment, and behavior, the development of a particular disease or phenotype is not certain or immediate.[35] Second, returning the information without accompanying treatment is not a complete rescue, particularly in low-resource settings; even if returning an IF is necessary to the rescue, it is not *sufficient* unless it is followed by the receipt of care.

Still, we believe that the duty to rescue is the most plausible principle on which to base support for returning IFs. First, it specifies the conditions that must be met for there to be an obligation to return IFs and it thus limits the types of findings that must be returned. Second, it allows for the consideration and balancing of burdens to the investigator or research enterprise. Finally, it allows for analysis of the net benefit of returning the findings. As a result, its framework is helpful when considering the actionability problem.

4.4 THE DUTY TO RESCUE

The conditions identified by Beauchamp and Childress for a duty to rescue have implications for the return of incidental findings, particularly in low-resource settings. The first condition of the duty to rescue, that a person must be in a life- or health-threatening situation, suggests that the IFs that would be returned should predict serious medical conditions, where evidence of the link between genotype and phenotype is strong, similar to the findings on the ACMG list. Developing a list of findings to return in low-resource settings may be complicated because many of the findings related to conditions on the ACMG list have not been sufficiently validated in non-US populations.[36]

The second condition, that the rescue action is necessary to prevent harm, implies that the people who receive IFs should not have other likely pathways of access to the information. For example, if conducting clinical WGS were the standard of care in the United States, then researchers might have less of an obligation to return IFs derived from research using WGS in the United States. However, such a clinical practice does not currently exist in the United States, much less in low-resource settings, and therefore this condition is almost certainly met.

---

[34] Benjamin D. Solomon, *Incidentalomas in Genomics and Radiology*, 370 NEW ENG. J. MED. 988, 988–90 (2014).

[35] *Id.*

[36] Although worries about the validity of existing scientific information for some populations are worth considering, we do not think this is an argument against the duty to rescue. If the findings are not scientifically or clinically valid, then they should not be returned. There may currently be too much uncertainty about how to interpret findings in non-US and European populations such that some IFs should not be returned to certain groups due to lack of validity. However, as more global genetic research occurs, more evidence will be accumulated and more accurate lists can be generated. The ACMG list of variants is a well-known example of a list of actionable findings, but is not the only one.

The third condition requires that the action will likely succeed in preventing the harm. The operative word here is "likely," and it is somewhat difficult to parse because it suggests a threshold. The question of where that threshold should lie is hard to determine. Ortiz-Osorno et al. suggest it should be very high – the research participant receiving the IF should have immediate access to preventative care or treatment. For reasons that we discuss below, we propose a lower threshold of medical actionability: Treatment or preventative care should exist (somewhere in the world) that, given the research participant's access to it, would likely succeed in preventing the harm.

The fourth condition is that the actions would not cause significant burden to the rescuer. At this point, we want to bracket discussions of burden. While the burden to return IFs might be too high in some cases, burden has been cited as a reason to avoid talking about returning IFs altogether.[37] But as analytic tools improve and curated lists of actionable variants proliferate, the standard of care is shifting and returning IFs will probably get even easier. Still, there might be some research settings with unique circumstances that make returning IFs extraordinarily burdensome. More research is needed to determine the extent to which burden arguments are justified, and how these burdens might be mitigated.

The final duty to rescue condition requires that the benefit received by the person rescued outweigh the harm to the rescuer. While determining whether the other conditions are satisfied is straightforward, this final condition requires more analysis. How can we think about the potential benefits of returning IFs to people in low-resource settings who do not currently have access to care? To determine the net benefit that a person receives from the return of IFs, the magnitudes of potential harms and potential benefits must be weighed. If there is no net benefit, then there may be no obligation to return IFs.

4.5 ASSESSING BENEFITS AND HARMS

When balancing the harms and benefits of returning IFs, we first need to decide what counts as a harm and what as a benefit. Generally, in the literature on IFs, the harms of return are psychosocial: Distress, stigma, or other negative emotions that result from learning about genetic information. These harms are often mentioned without accompanying consideration of the likelihood and magnitude of harm. People tend to assume that receiving information about IFs or positive genetic test results will be extremely harmful, even though literature on affective forecasting and studies of people who have undergone genetic testing suggest that these harms are relatively minor and transient.

---

[37] Pilar N. Ossorio, *Letting the Gene out of the Bottle: A Comment on Returning Individual Research Results to Participants*, 6 AM. J. BIOETHICS 24, 24–25 (2006).

First, the affective forecasting literature suggests that people are poor predictors of how they will feel after a particularly intense emotional experience.[38] For example, a study of lottery winners found them to be just as happy as non-lottery winners, contrary to predictions that winning the lottery would increase happiness.[39] When people are asked how they might feel about an injury that results in disability (such as losing a leg), they predict that they will have a much lower quality of life than people with the disability have been found to have.[40] These examples demonstrate that people tend to overestimate the intensity and duration of their emotions after a particularly strong or unexpected emotional experience.

Genetic testing literature suggests that affective forecasting principles also apply in medical contexts. A study of women tested for BRCA1 and BRCA2 found that after women learned they had pathogenic variants, they experienced increased "general and cancer-specific distress" but that levels of distress returned to baseline a year after testing.[41] A review of genetic testing studies found that for several hereditary cancers and Alzheimer's disease, people experienced negative emotional effects that were short-lived.[42] A review of psychosocial distress in people tested for Huntington's disease found an increase in distress between symptomatic Huntington's carriers relative to non-carriers, but there was no difference in distress levels between asymptomatic carriers and non-carriers, a somewhat surprising finding, given that Huntington's disease is not medically actionable.[43]

Although these studies suggest that the current presumption of harm when returning IFs is probably often overstated, their applicability is limited by several important factors. These studies surveyed early adopters of genetic testing. Such early adopters who sought out genetic testing expected information about a particular gene, and likely received follow-up care from their healthcare providers. Research participants receiving IFs are not actively pursuing such results (although they should be made aware during the informed consent process that WGS might generate IFs) and may not always have access to follow-up care. Further research remains to be done on people who receive IFs and on how their experiences with genetic testing and WGS vary from those of early adopters.

Such future studies should also examine the ways in which psychosocial distress varies across communities, cultures, and social circumstances. Not all cultures may

---

[38] Stacey A. Peters et al., *The Future in Clinical Genetics: Affective Forecasting Biases in Patient and Clinician Decision Making*, 85 CLINICAL GENETICS 312, 312–17 (2014).

[39] Philip Brickman et al., *Lottery Winners and Accident Victims: Is Happiness Relative?*, 36 J. PERSONALITY & SOC. PSYCHOL. 917, 917–27 (1978).

[40] Jodi Halpern and Robert M. Arnold, *Affective Forecasting: An Unrecognized Challenge in Making Serious Health Decisions*, 23 J. GENERAL INTERNAL MED. 1708, 1708–12 (2008).

[41] Tammy Beran et al., *The Trajectory of Psychological Impact in BRCA1/2 Genetic Testing: Does Time Heal?*, 36 ANNALS OF BEHAVIORAL MED. 107, 107–16 (2008).

[42] Jodi T. Heshka et al., *A Systematic Review of Perceived Risks, Psychological and Behavioral Impacts of Genetic Testing*, 10 GENETICS IN MED. 19, 19–32 (2008).

[43] Sarah Crozier et al., *The Psychological Impact of Predictive Genetic Testing for Huntington's Disease: A Systematic Review of the Literature*, 24 J. GENETIC COUNSELING 29, 29–39 (2015).

have the same values surrounding health and genetics; for example, risk identification, a common practice in US medical culture could cause US research participants to expect and value risk information, including IFs, more than people in
cultures that do not prioritize risk information.[44] Similarly, the stigma surrounding
health conditions varies cross-culturally.[45] If the research team in the multisite study
case presented at the beginning of the chapter were to find an IF related to a mental
health condition that was highly stigmatized in a particular community, it should
carefully consider the potentially harmful impact of returning the finding.
Researchers should work with community representatives and local IRBs, parties
better situated to understand the ways that cultural circumstances affect views on
genetic testing and the stigma surrounding various health conditions.

Determining what counts as a benefit of returning IFs is even more difficult.
Ortiz-Osorno et al. consider only the immediate benefit of returning IFs: They
require that, at the time the participant receives the information, they should be able
to take a medical action that will prevent or treat the condition associated with the
IF. We argue for a more expansive conception of benefit[46] and identify four pathways by which research participants might benefit from the return of IFs.

First, individuals might benefit from IFs in the near term. A participant might
not have access to treatment or care at the present, but might be able to seek access
(e.g., through medical tourism)[47] after hearing about the IF. Researchers are not
often in a position to know all of the potential avenues to healthcare that
a participant might have and it would be presumptuous for them to assume that
a participant who lives in a low-resource setting has no means of obtaining access
to healthcare, in the present or in the near future. Within a given community,
different people will have more or less access to healthcare – if researchers overlook that some people in a given community will have greater-than-average access
to healthcare and therefore do not return IFs, then some people may never be able
to take advantage of their access and respond to an IF. For example, a woman in
a low-resource setting who learns she has a BRCA1 mutation might, unbeknownst
to the researchers, have a cousin living in the United States who would be willing
to pay for her travel and medical care, so that she could receive a prophylactic
mastectomy. If researchers overlook the possibility of such differences and

[44] Robert Aronowitz, Risky Medicine: Our Quest to Cure Fear and Uncertainty (2015).
[45] Jantina de Vries et al., *Psychiatric Genomics: Ethical Implications for Public Health in Lower- and Middle-Income Countries*, 17 Am. J. Bioethics 17, 17–19 (2017).
[46] This benefit and harm analysis is different from the risk benefit analysis of a protocol that Institutional Review Boards (IRBs) consider. IFs are inherently ancillary to the research and are often not included in IRB analyses. Where an IRB may not consider societal or community benefit as balancing out physical risks, the duty to rescue does not limit what risks and benefits can be considered and therefore, we believe it is appropriate to include expanded conceptions of benefit in our analysis.
[47] This suggests that a duty to rescue might not exist for IFs for which no treatment exists at all, or for variants of unknown significance. Although scientific progress may one day create a cure, what is relevant here is that the barrier to treatment is lack of access.

therefore do not return incidental findings, then some people who might have responded to an incidental finding will not be able to do so.

Second, individuals might benefit in the long-term. Medically actionable IFs already have a treatment or cure. Genetic risk may not manifest for years, if ever; therefore, the need for treatment may be far removed from the time of diagnosis. It is not implausible that a participant's access to already existing healthcare could improve in the time it takes for a genetic condition to develop. For example, a twenty-five-year-old woman with a positive BRCA finding might not have disease manifestation for multiple decades, during which time a community could quite plausibly develop access to mammography and cancer treatment services. However, if the participant is not informed of their risk through the return of IFs, they might not be able to take advantage of future improved access to healthcare and seek out preventative care or treatment.

Third, a participant who learns about an IF for which they do not have access to treatment or care, might use that information to advocate for a reallocation of health resources. This advocacy would be particularly powerful if a community had a high prevalence of a particular disorder and advocacy could be directed toward governmental and non-governmental health organizations. For example, a group of women in a low-resource setting might learn that many of them have mutations in the BRCA1 gene and are at higher risk for hereditary breast and ovarian cancer, and yet they may not have access to preventative care or treatment. After speaking with this group of women, an NGO could decide to partner with the local health ministry to perform periodic mammograms in the community and to provide surgical services to women who elect to pursue them.

Finally, researchers should consider benefits to the community. Even if there are certain research settings where it would be inappropriate and, all things considered, harmful to return individual IFs, researchers should still collect aggregate data on IFs that could be given to the communities as a whole, as well as passed on to local governments, health departments, or aid groups who could collaborate on strategies to provide access to care. Researchers are well positioned to facilitate these kinds of community benefit, particularly if they have existing relationships with local IRBs or community representatives.

There will always be some uncertainty when weighing potential harms and potential benefits to determine whether the final duty to rescue condition is met. Our goal is to clarify the relative magnitudes of these harms and benefits. Clarifying the harms and benefits is important, moreover, even if the duty to rescue is not the best basis for an obligation to return incidental findings. Nearly all possible bases for the obligation require some assessment of the risks and potential benefits of returning incidental findings.

4.6 POLICY POINTS AND PROBLEMS

Our framework has implications for genetic research policy and also raises certain implementation concerns. These problems, which we will address in this section, include how best to return findings, institutional responsibility, and the right not to know genetic information.

The first policy point concerns how IFs are returned. In the United States, genetic testing results are often accompanied by genetic counseling. Some ethicists might suggest that in order to treat research populations equally, IFs in low-resource settings should be returned with equivalent genetic counseling support. We agree that IFs should always be returned with explanation and guidance, even if doing so will be more expensive; however, it is unclear if this information must be provided by genetic counselors. Although the details and funding of infrastructure to facilitate informed return of IFs are not the domain of this chapter, we will quickly sketch several solutions that suggest this problem is not insurmountable. Providing some form of genetic counseling will cost money, but research funders could anticipate these costs when awarding grants. Individual research institutions or affiliated research networks could also reduce costs by creating a single group or department that provides genetic counseling and support for the return of findings for all affiliated researchers. The National Institutes of Health has already explored implementing such a program in the context of its Intramural Research Program.[48] Creating such a shared resource would reduce costs and burden to individual researcher teams by taking advantage of centralized expertise and economies of scale.

A second policy point is about who bears the duty to rescue. Douglas MacKay and Tina Rulli argue that the duty to rescue falls on institutions, rather than individual researchers. They note that researchers do not own research funds and thus are obligated to use the funds for their authorized purpose – research – rather than rescuing people in resource-poor areas.[49] Still, MacKay and Rulli think research institutions might have a duty to help these people. This line of argument is somewhat difficult to contend with in the context of IFs. When MacKay and Rulli talk about the provision of ancillary care, they use examples such as oral rehydration therapy for sick children.[50] Such examples are truly ancillary to research, but IFs fall somewhere in between ancillary care and research related injuries: IFs are discovered through the course of research and would likely not have been discovered had the research not occurred. Jeremy Garrett argues that in research, if scenarios where rescue obligations might arise can be anticipated, then more energy should be spent on preventing such scenarios in the first place.[51] In the case of genetic research, he suggests that

[48] Andrew J. Darnell et al., *A Clinical Service to Support the Return of Secondary Genomic Findings in Human Research*, 98 AM. J. HUM. GENETICS no. 3 (2016).
[49] Douglas MacKay and Tina Rulli, *The Duty to Rescue and Investigators' Obligations*, 27 KENNEDY INST. ETHICS J. NO. 1 (2017).
[50] *Id.*
[51] Jeremy R. Garrett, *Collectivizing Rescue Obligations in Bioethics*, 15 AM. J. BIOETHICS 17, 17–19 (2015).

population-level genetic screenings would prevent investigators from needing to return findings.[52] However, even though IFs can be anticipated in WGS research, we think that it will still take significant time before population level screening can be broadly implemented, especially in low-resource settings. Research will continue in the interim, and investigators, particularly those close to local communities, may be better placed to return anticipatable IFs than institutions.

A final concern is about the right not to know genetic information. Following publication of the ACMG recommendations about incidental findings, there has been an extensive and vigorous debate about the extent to which individuals should be given a choice whether to learn about clinically important, and actionable, IFs.[53] As one of us has argued, there are a number of reasons to be skeptical about the strength of the right not to know generally, but it can be appropriate to actively solicit individual preferences in cases where there are reasons to think that clinical intervention might not be possible or warranted.[54] Given the uncertain utility associated with returning IFs in low-resource settings, it seems prudent to offer participants a choice to learn or not learn clinically important genetic information about themselves.

4.7 EQUALIZING THE BENEFITS OF RESEARCH

Genetic research in low-resource settings is both valuable and necessary as the push toward personalized medicine continues. Yet, as research in low-resource settings proliferates, researchers will have to confront the actionability problem: Tension between the reduced benefit of returning IFs in low-resource settings and the idea of promoting justice by not withholding medical information from populations that already have limited access to healthcare.

We argue that an expanded concept of the duty to rescue best captures an obligation to return IFs and that the conditions for the expanded duty create a framework that can help researchers and ethicists decide when it is obligatory to return medically actionable IFs. Although concerns about actionability in low-resource settings are important to address, there is a risk of too quickly dismissing the possibility of benefit or overselling the possibility of harm from the return of IFs. This is not to say that the benefit of IFs will be as strong in low-resource settings as in well-resourced settings, but rather that it may still exist in sufficient quantity to justify disclosure.

Further research remains to be done on the burdens to the research enterprise generated by the return of IFs in low-resource settings. However, these burdens will probably decrease as advances in genetic research link variants of unknown significance to health outcomes in previously understudied populations. Research on the existence of psychosocial harms resulting from returning IFs in low-resource settings

---

[52] *Id.*

[53] Robert C. Green et al., *ACMG Recommendations for Reporting of Incidental Findings in Clinical Exome and Genome Sequencing*, 15 GENETICS IN MED. 565, 565–74 (2013).

[54] Benjamin E. Berkman, *Refuting the Right Not to Know*, 19 J. HEALTH CARE L. & POL'y 1 (2017).

would also clarify the actual impact of returning information in unique cultural contexts. The current practice of assuming that severe psychosocial harms result from the return of incidental findings should be revisited.

If research suggests that the benefits of returning IFs are low, or that the risks and burdens are exceptionally high, then justice might require the provision of additional benefits to populations where IFs were not returned. Providing additional benefits would keep the potential ancillary benefits of the research equal across all study populations. Researchers should not be incentivized to perform research on disadvantaged groups who lack access to healthcare just because they are the only group where researchers are not required to return IFs.

5

The Ethics of Human Pathogen Research during Public Health Emergencies in Low- and Middle-Income Countries

Lessons from Latin America and the Caribbean

Sam Halabi

Responding to infectious disease emergencies, in all countries, is dependent in part upon the development and deployment of diagnostics, medicines, and vaccines. In emergencies where these are unavailable or unlicensed, biomedical research *during* the emergency may be a priority. Biomedical research during a public health emergency raises difficult questions of informed consent, patient confidentiality, and allocation of resources (e.g., is it even ethical to conduct research when time and money might be used to alleviate suffering?), among others. In low-resource settings, these ethical difficulties are magnified. Recent infectious disease emergencies have raised many of these ethical questions: Is it ethical to conduct research in West Africa during the Ebola outbreak when people are dying and need treatment? Can research be conducted on pregnant women (who are normally excluded) because the Zika virus renders its most devastating effects *in utero*?[1]

Because climate change, urbanization and conflict are causing the emergence of novel pathogens likely to threaten human health security, there is a crucial need to identify these ethical questions now. This chapter addresses this need, in part, by analyzing the relevant work of the Pan American Health Organization (PAHO) which has addressed ethical criteria for biomedical research in both the routine and emergency contexts. Indeed, given that the World Health Organization declared a public health emergency of international concern with respect to the Zika virus on the basis of an extraordinary cluster of microcephaly and other neurological disorders reported in Brazil, PAHO has recent, relevant experience on the ethics of research during public health emergencies.

---

[1] Sam Halabi, *Zika and the Regulatory Regime for Licensing Vaccines for Use During Pregnancy*, 26(2) ANNALS OF HEALTH L. 20 (2017).

5.1 ETHICAL OBLIGATIONS FOR RESEARCH UNDERTAKEN IN PUBLIC HEALTH EMERGENCIES

Over the past decade, lessons learned from previous infectious disease outbreaks highlighted the importance of rapid access to information for a timely public health response and development of medical countermeasures. In 2015, subject matter experts and global stakeholders convened at a WHO consultation to identify norms that should operate during public health emergencies, especially with respect to research and sharing research results for the purposes of advancing development of diagnostics, therapeutics, and vaccines.[2] In 2016, a similar consultation was arranged to address the Zika outbreak in Brazil, which rapidly spread to the rest of the Americas regions.[3]

The 2014–16 Ebola outbreak in West Africa exposed significant limitations in existing ethical norms during public health emergencies. At the time, the existing West African regulatory frameworks were lagging, lengthy, and rarely clearly defined. As the outbreak unfolded, WHO declared Ebola a public health emergency and outlined that there was both a moral and ethical obligation for biomedical research to be an integral part of the response activities. However, the chaotic nature of the emergency, in combination with the lack of formal, codified agreements, resulted in insufficient accountability, delayed research, and bypassed regulations. According to Delaunay et al., the lack of material transfer agreements (MTAs) or other sharing mechanisms in emergency situations can result in severe biosafety and biosecurity risks as well as violations of the rights of human research subjects and/or patients.[4]

Even before Ebola and Zika, the H1N1 public health emergency implicated a different kind of ethical quandary – sharing the resulting products of research undertaken during an emergency.[5] While the H1N1 vaccine was developed quickly after Mexican officials shared samples, the government experienced significant difficulty obtaining the vaccine for itself.

Canada awarded its vaccine contract to a Canadian company because it feared that foreign governments might restrict exports to Canada because of vaccine shortages within their territories. The Australian government made it clear to the Australian manufacturer CSL that it must fulfill the government's domestic needs before

---

[2] Sophie Delaunay et al., *Knowledge Sharing during Public Health Emergencies: From Global Call to Effective Implementation*, 94 BULL. WORLD HEALTH ORGAN. 236–236A (2016); B. Y. Kenneth, C. Monagin, and J. Fletcher, *Promoting Scientific Transparency to Facilitate the Safe and Open International Exchange of Biological Materials and Electronic Data*, 2(4) TROP. MED. INFECT. DIS. 57(2017).

[3] Pan American Health Organization. *Zika ethics consultation: ethics guidance on key issues raised by the outbreak*. Washington, DC: Pan American Health Organization(2016).

[4] *Id.*

[5] Sam Halabi, *Obstacles to pH1N1 Vaccine Availability: The Complex Contracting Relationship Between Vaccine Manufacturers, WHO, Donor and Beneficiary Governments* in M. A. Stoto and M. Higdon (eds.), THE PUBLIC HEALTH RESPONSE TO H1N1: A SYSTEMS PERSPECTIVE 203–16 (2015).

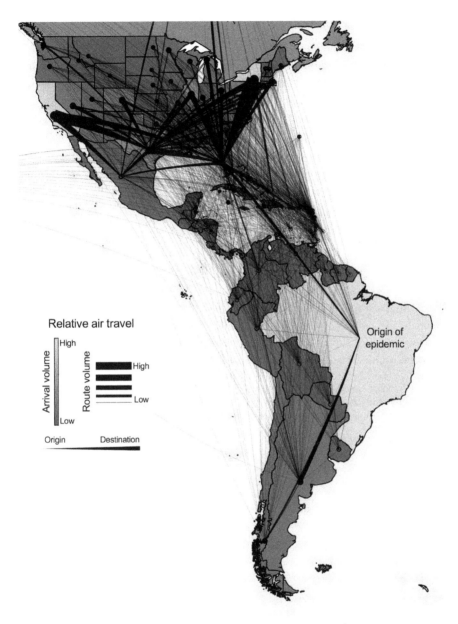

FIGURE 5.1 Geographic spread of Zika virus[6]

exporting vaccine to the United States. The United States pledged on September 17, 2009, to donate 10% of its vaccine purchases to WHO, but on October 28, US Secretary of Health and Human Services Kathleen Sebelius stated that the United

---

[6] https://doi.org/10.1371/journal.pntd.0006194.

States would not donate H1N1 vaccine as promised until all at risk Americans had access, because production problems had created shortages in the United States.[7]

Despite clear acknowledgment that the 2009 outbreak originated in Mexico and leveled its most significant toll there, Mexico had "a terrifically difficult time getting access to the pandemic vaccine."[8]

Over the last twenty years, the Latin America and Caribbean region (LAC) experienced significant growth and development in the field of research ethics education. In 1994, PAHO created its own Regional Program on Bioethics, nearly a decade before the World Health Organization established its Ethics Units.[9] The creation of the PAHO ethics program followed an earlier report outlining important insufficiencies and failures in research ethic oversight in the region. At the time, no ethical review board existed in the region, and research oversight relied largely on health professionals' individual integrity and ethical rigor rather than national standards or regulations. PAHO's Regional Program on Bioethics aimed at addressing these research ethics limitations through sustainable trainings and publications relevant to actors in the region.

According to PAHO guidance, there can be little doubt that not only is there an ethical duty to undertake research during public health emergencies, but that there is a duty to do so as expeditiously as possible.[10] Research results, and even preliminary data, must be shared expeditiously as well.[11] These two obligations – to undertake

7   David P. Fidler, *Negotiating Equitable Access to Influenza Vaccines: Global Health Diplomacy and the Controversies Surrounding Avian Influenza H5N1 and Pandemic Influenza H1NI*, 7(5) PLOS MEDICINE 1 (2010), available at www.plosmedicine.org/article/info%3Adoi%2F10.1371%2Fjournal.pmed.1000247.

8   Richard Knox, *WHO Resolves Impasse Over Sharing of Flu Viruses, Access to Medicines*, NPR Apr. 18, 2011 available at www.npr.org/blogs/health/2011/04/18/135519592/who-resolves-impasse-over-sharing-of-flu-viruses-access-to-vaccines.

9   Pan American Health Organization. Establishment of the Regional Program on Bioethics. 37th Directing Council of PAHO, 45th Session of the Regional Committee of WHO for the Americas; 1993 Sep 28–Oct 1; Washington (DC), US. Washington (DC): PAHO; 1993: (Resolution CD37.R9) available at www.paho.org/english/gov/cd/ftcd_37.htm; Carla Saenz et al., *Twelve Years of Fogarty-Funded Bioethics Training in Latin America and the Caribbean: Achievements and Challenges*, 9(2) J. EMPIR. RES. HUM. RES. ETHICS 80–91 (2014).

10   World Health Assembly. Pandemic influenza preparedness: sharing of influenza viruses and access to vaccines and other benefits, WHA60.28, 23 May 2007; United Nations Environment Program. Convention on Biological Diversity: report of the meeting on the impact of avian influenza on wildlife: note by the executive secretary. UNEP/CBD/COP8/8/ INF/47, 22 Mar 2006; K. Modjarrad, V. S. Moorthy, P. Millett, P.-S. Gsell, C. Roth, and Marie Paule Kieny, *Developing Global Norms for Sharing Data and Results during Public Health Emergencies*, 13(1) PLOS MED (2016): e1001935. Forum on Medical and Public Health Preparedness for Catastrophic Events; Board on Health Sciences Policy; Institute of Medicine. Enabling Rapid and Sustainable Public Health Research During Disasters: Summary of a Joint Workshop by the Institute of Medicine and the U.S. Department of Health and Human Services. Washington (DC): National Academies Press (US); 2015 Apr 6. 2, Science Preparedness: Conducting Research During Public Health Emergencies. Available from: www.ncbi.nlm.nih.gov/books/NBK285426/.

11   C. D. S. Ribeiro et al., *How Ownership Rights over Microorganisms Affect Infectious Disease Control and Innovation: A Root-Cause Analysis of Barriers to Data Sharing as Experienced by Key Stakeholders.*

research expeditiously during emergencies and to share resulting research data – may implicate a further obligation on the part of ethics review committees to expedite or "fast track" applications submitted in emergency circumstances.

Ethics review is a procedural requirement needed to ensure the voluntary and informed consent of human research subjects; even in emergency circumstances, there is a hesitancy to correspondingly adjust existing processes. While there are evident ethical concerns on the use of unapproved experimental products, PAHO experts have continuously asserted that timely access to experimental medical countermeasures should be allowed on humanitarian grounds, when communities are threatened by life-threatening or life-altering diseases with no other existing therapeutic alternatives. Jerome Singh et al. argue that the international community ought to create a governance framework for the use of unapproved medical counter-measures in humanitarian crises. Similarly, during the Zika outbreak in Latin America, PAHO stated that it is an ethical duty to undertake biomedical research and the outcomes to enable timely responses to health emergencies. According to PAHO, because diseases such as the 2016 Zika outbreak carry global implications and impose a potentially global burden, there is a moral duty in undertaking prompt research collaboration and in the delivery of health interventions at the international level.[12]

This is particularly true given the nature of research capacity and where the development of diagnostics, therapeutics, and vaccines is likely to occur.[13] For Type 1 diseases (i.e., those diseases incident in both rich and poor countries, with large numbers of vulnerable populations in each) global biomedical research and development is centered in wealthier countries.[14] Type II diseases (incident in both rich and poor countries, but with a substantial proportion of the cases in poor countries) and Type III diseases (which overwhelmingly affect poorer countries) are generally neglected. Yet even research for Type III diseases is conducted in wealthier countries.[15] These types of diseases "have more than 99 percent" of their disease burden in low-income countries.[16] This concentration renders many low- and middle-income countries (LMICs) dependent on wealthier states to

13(5) PLoS ONE (2018): e0195885. Published 2018 May 2. doi:10.1371/journal.pone.0195885; Modjarrad, Moorthy, Millett, Gsell, Roth, and Kieny, *supra* note 10.

[12] J. A. Singh et al. *Humanitarian Access to Unapproved Interventions in Public Health Emergencies of International Concern*, 12(2) PLoS MED (2015) e1001793; Pan American Health Organization. *Zika ethics consultation: ethics guidance on key issues raised by the outbreak*. Washington, DC: Pan American Health Organization(2016).

[13] Sam F. Halabi and John Monahan, *Regulatory Capacity of National Regulatory Authorities in Low- and Middle-Income Countries* in Sam Halabi ed. FOOD AND DRUG REGULATION IN AN ERA OF GLOBALIZED MARKETS 63–76 (2015).

[14] Gene M. Grossman and Edwin L.-C. Lai, *Parallel Imports and Price Controls*, 39(2) RAND J. ECONOMICS 378–402 (2008).

[15] World Health Organization, DEFINING DISEASE TYPES I, II, AND III available at www.who.int/phi/3-background_cewg_agenda_item5_disease_types_final.pdf.

[16] *Id.*

manufacture and distribute diagnostics, therapeutics, and vaccines in sufficient quantities to address their needs in routine and emergency circumstances.[17]

5.2 ETHICAL OBLIGATIONS AND MATERIAL TRANSFER AGREEMENTS

The duties to undertake research expeditiously and to share it robustly necessitates greater focus on the legal instruments through which the latter obligation, and to some extent the former, are facilitated: MTAs. MTAs raise many ethical questions including those of fairness and equity; distinctions between ethical and legal decisions; and the resulting governance, both ethical and legal, of biological samples and related information used for future research.

Beyond the clear moral significance of MTAs, informed consent forms, and other appropriate clinical and research practice documentation during public health emergencies, there are also important legal liability aspects linked to their use. In 2009, Singh noted that while research-related lawsuits have habitually arisen in developed countries, LMICs have increasingly become new legal battlegrounds.[18] It is evident that MTAs and other clinical research agreements allow for better transparency and fairness during the research process, by stipulating responsibilities and confidentiality clauses, outlining the liability risks of researchers and host institutions, and by obtaining fully informed consent from the participants. During infectious disease crises, MTAs may also serve as legal protections for epidemiologists and on-the-ground responders who are also at risk of legal liability in relation to confidentiality, informed consent, and other privacy concerns. In particular, the question of property rights pertaining to tissue and blood may become subject to potential litigation for researchers without appropriate MTAs in a crisis context. There is a need (if not an ethical obligation) to advance broad consent for future research so that upstream researchers do not try to impede the research process undertaken by downstream researchers through proprietary or other similar claims.

5.3 ETHICAL OBLIGATIONS AND MATERIAL TRANSFER AGREEMENTS IN THE LMIC CONTEXT

There is clear need to fill the gaps created by lack of knowledge and experience in sample sharing and MTAs usage during public health emergencies in low- and low-to middle-income countries. The appropriate use of MTAs would increase trust within the international research community and advance local research

---

[17] Fidler, *supra* note 7.
[18] J. A. Singh, *Research and Legal Liability*, 112(Suppl 1) ACTA TROP S71–S pmid:19665438 (2009); R. Ravinetto, E. Alirol, Y. Mahendradhata, S. Rijal, P. Lutumba, M. Sacko et al. *Clinical Research in Neglected Tropical Diseases: The Challenge of Implementing Good Clinical (Laboratory) Practices*, 10(11) PLoS NEGL TROP DIS (2016) e0004654, https://doi.org/10.1371/journal.pntd.0004654.

capacity-building during public health emergencies. The ethical significance of sample sharing during infectious disease outbreaks was further confirmed in February 2016, after leading research funders, academic journals, and nongovernmental organizations signed a joint declaration of commitment to rapidly share data relevant to the Zika virus outbreak in Latin America and the Caribbean. According to the group, "countries are obliged to give all available information on Zika and be explicit about what is not known."[19]

Yet even in light of that declaration, MTAs are rarely used in Latin America and the Caribbean.[20] According to a study undertaken by the Office of Human Research Protection in 2013, many LAC countries still lack a formal legal structure for the regulation and oversight of human subjects research, including the use of MTAs. Furthermore, according to Eduardo (2015), most LAC countries lack national legislation for the use of stored human samples, which means that norms referring to international transfer of bio-specimens are subjected to international cooperation agreements rather than national regulations. Eduardo argues that these international agreements may be especially challenging in the LAC context. Indeed, these agreements may not be sensitive enough to the cultural context of certain indigenous groups. For examples, Eduardo notes that past biomedical research with blood samples drawn from Mapuches, a group of indigenous inhabitants of south-central Chile and southwestern Argentina, including parts of present-day Patagonia, caused important protests by ethnic leaders in Chile.[21]

Effectively communicating informed consent terms and meanings in these vulnerable communities present significant ethical problems for researchers. Eduardo adds that there is a need to harmonize language used in such international agreements, as some English technical terms are often incorrectly translated into standard Spanish, which can lead to misunderstandings in the LAC context. Lastly, like in other LMICs, bio-sample ownership and benefit-sharing issues need to be clarified and better stipulated in international sharing agreements with LACs, where international research and sample sharing is often viewed with suspicion, which might hinder further collaboration.

---

[19]   PAHO, *Experts Analyze Ethics of Response to Zika in the Americas*, available at www.paho.org/hq/index.php?option=com_content&view=article&id=12082:experts-analyze-ethics-of-the-response-to-zika-virus-in-the-americas&Itemid=41716&lang=en.

[20]   Office for Human Research Protections (OHRP) (2013). *International Compilation of Human Research Standards.* US Department of Health and Human Services, available at www.hhs.gov/ohrp/sites/default/files/2019-International-Compilation-of-Human-Research-Standards.pdf.

[21]   R. Eduardo, *Ethical Issues of Consent for Genetic Research in Latin American Bio-banks*, 6 J. CLINIC. RES. BIOETH. 228 (2015). ("There are concerns with the possibility of invasion of privacy, difficulties in safeguarding confidentiality, ways to avoid discrimination and stigmatization and that bio-specimens may be used in international commercial trade. Numerous international ethical guidance has been produced. Research ethics has established the right of participants to be fully informed of objectives and procedures of research projects and the right to withdraw from a project at any time.")

Ravinetto et al. highlight the additional cultural and contextual challenges linked to undertaking clinical research in developing world communities.[22] Often, these contextual constraints include the complexities in engaging with vulnerable populations, the opacity of informed consent in such communities and lack of on-the-ground qualified staff to undertake the research. However challenging these obstacles may be, it is clear that they should not preclude clinical research in LMICs, nor should they lead to a lowering of ethical standards while conducting such research. Emerson et al. note that ethical considerations are central to all biomedical research in every cultural context, and that failure to attend to them, such as the use of tissues in ways that were not made explicit in the informed consent, can lead to exploitation and eroded trust, especially in LMIC communities. In 2007, Upshur et al. argued that ensuring ethical research with exported tissue samples entails bringing entire communities into the discussion. At minimum, the authors state that legitimate consent should include engagement with communities, as well as "agreed upon and explicit standards for current use, and a process to manage future uses of exported tissue."[23]

The entry of lawyers into this system is not necessarily a panacea for the ethical problems raised by undertaking research in LMICs during public health emergencies nor the negotiation of MTAs that follow. Anecdotally, legal document experts are, in the wake of Zika, playing a greater role in the sample and data transfer process in LAC and the result has not necessarily been either more research nor more robust sharing. Lawyers may actually be hindering the research process in LAC countries because they emphasize legal risks, and are generally ill-equipped to advise in contexts where legal risks must be situated into ethically complex contexts.

For example, law-mkers in many LAC countries have prohibited all research with children, for example, a policy at odds with identifying interventions that may uniquely help children and which are actively supported in jurisdictions like the US and the EU. Patient or human research subject confidentiality is not well protected in the LAC region and, indeed, there is not a widespread discourse around what the ethical concept of confidentiality entails nor how it might be implemented.[24]

[22] Ravinetto, Alirol, Mahendradhata, Rijal, Lutumba, Sacko et al., *supra* note 18.
[23] Ross Upshur, James V. Lavery, and Paulina Tindana, *Taking Tissue Seriously Means Taking Communities Seriously*. BMC MEDICAL ETHICS (2007); C. Weijer and E. Emmanuel, *Protecting Communities in Biomedical Research*, 289 (5482) SCIENCE 1132–44 (2000) 10.1126/science.289.5482.1142.
[24] E. Lamas, M. Ferrer, A. Molina et al. *A comparative analysis of biomedical research ethics regulation systems in Europe and Latin America with regard to the protection of human subjects*, 36 JOURNAL OF MEDICAL ETHICS 750–53 (2010); Office for Human Research Protections (OHRP) (2013). *International compilation of human research standards*. US Department of Health and Human Services. Retrieved from www.hhs.gov/ohrp/sites/default/files/2019-International-Compilation-of-Human-Research-Standards.pdf.

5.4 CONCLUSION

Conducting biomedical and related research in low- and middle-income countries during public health emergencies raises significant ethical problems related to fairness, autonomy, and distribution of resources. In the context of Latin America and the Caribbean regions, these issues have been at least partially addressed by the Pan American Health Organization, especially in light of the Zika public health emergency. The result is the understanding that conducting research, even during an emergency, is an ethical priority, although there is a great deal of work to do to make sure that the legal structures necessary for that priority to be given effect.

6

Biosecurity, Biosafety, and the Management of Dangerous Pathogens for Public Health Research

Joshua Teperowski Monrad and Rebecca Katz

6.1 INTRODUCTION

Biologic agents are essential for public health research, including the development of novel diagnostics, treatments, and vaccines. However, handling pathogenic samples invariably entails biosafety risks (relating to the accidental exposure to dangerous biological agents) and biosecurity risks (relating to the deliberate misuse or release of biological materials). While such risks have existed for as long as dangerous pathogen research has been conducted, recent events have highlighted their significance. In 2001, concerns over biosecurity intensified in the United States when media organizations and senators were targeted by letters laced with *Bacillus anthracis*, or anthrax. More recently, biosafety has been in the spotlight after several incidents occurred at American agencies, including an unintentional exposure to *Bacillus anthracis* spores and a mistaken shipment of a contaminated and highly pathogenic influenza virus.[1]

Globally, concern about biosafety and biosecurity risks grew with the 2014–16 Ebola outbreak in West Africa. The epidemic, which primarily affected the three countries of Guinea, Sierra Leone, and Liberia, involved more than 28,000 reported cases and claimed more than 11,000 lives.[2] After the outbreak was declared a Public Health Emergency of International Concern by the World Health Organization (WHO), the affected countries saw an influx of humanitarian nongovernmental organizations (NGOs), bilateral actors, academic researchers, and commercial research organizations.[3] Hundreds of thousands of samples were extracted from

---

[1] CENTERS FOR DISEASE CONTROL AND PREVENTION, *Report on the Potential Exposure to Anthrax* (2014), www.cdc.gov/labs/pdf/Final_Anthrax_Report.pdf (last visited Feb. 18, 2020); Shay Weiss, Shmuel Yitzhaki and Shmuel C. Shapira, *Lessons to Be Learned from Recent Biosafety Incidents in the United States*, 17 ISR MED ASSOC J 269–73 (2015); Denise Grady, *Deadly Germ Research Is Shut Down at Army Lab Over Safety Concerns*, THE NEW YORK TIMES, August 5, 2019, www.nytimes.com /2019/08/05/health/germs-fort-detrick-biohazard.html (last visited Feb. 18, 2020).

[2] Centers for Disease Control and Prevention, *2014–2016 Ebola Outbreak in West Africa* (2020), www .cdc.gov/vhf/ebola/history/2014-2016-outbreak/index.html (last visited Feb. 18, 2020).

[3] Akin Abayomi et al., *Managing Dangerous Pathogens: Challenges in the Wake of the Recent West African Ebola Outbreak*, 1 GLOBAL SECURITY: HEALTH, SCIENCE AND POLICY 51–57 (2016).

patients – initially for diagnostic purposes, but later utilized for research.[4] During the outbreak, these samples posed a biosafety hazard to the health workers and researchers who handled them, as well as to surrounding populations, since they were often managed – by necessity – without adequate biosafety measures and equipment in place.

In addition to biosafety hazards, the 2014–16 Ebola outbreak also posed biosecurity risks that arose when a large volume of highly pathogenic samples was collected. In November 2014, a cooler containing live Ebola virus (EBOV) blood samples was taken and never recovered when a transport van was robbed in Guinea.[5] While the samples were almost certainly not the objective of the robbery, the event highlights the difficulty of securing dangerous biological materials in resource-limited environments. This issue can be further complicated by the coincidence of an epidemic with an armed conflict, as has been the case in the 2018–19 Ebola outbreak in the Democratic Republic of Congo, where treatment centers have been the targets of armed attacks.[6] Although some considered it unlikely that the virus strain from the 2014–16 outbreak would be targeted for weaponization,[7] both state and non-state actors have historically sought to obtain and utilize EBOV for nefarious purposes.[8] In general, the biosecurity risk associated with dangerous pathogen samples should not be underestimated.

Even as the West African Ebola outbreak was ultimately contained, the biosafety and biosecurity risks associated with EBOV samples persisted. While a large number of samples were destroyed, many were preserved, with some remaining in the affected West African nations while others were transported out of the region – with and without official government agreement.[9] A WHO review from October 2016 identified about 162,000 stored EBOV samples, roughly 10 percent of which were identified as positive samples. According to the WHO review, about 42,000 of these samples were stored in laboratories outside the affected countries.[10] Of the remaining 120,000 identified samples, approximately 28,000 were stored in

4   Emmanuel Freudenthal, *Ebola's lost blood: row over samples flown out of Africa as "big pharma" set to cash in*, THE TELEGRAPH, February 6, 2019 (last visited, Feb. 18, 2020).
5   Associated Press, *Bandits in Guinea steal blood samples believed to be infected with Ebola*, THE GUARDIAN, November 21, 2014, www.theguardian.com/world/2014/nov/21/bandits-guinea-steal-blood-samples-possibly-infected-with-ebola (last visited Feb. 18, 2020).
6   Stephanie Soucheray | News Reporter | CIDRAP News | Jun 05 & 2019, *New violence in Beni, DRC, as Ebola lab targeted*, CIDRAP, www.cidrap.umn.edu/news-perspective/2019/06/new-violence-beni-drc-ebola-lab-targeted (last visited Feb. 18, 2020).
7   Stephen Hummel, *Ebola: Not an Effective Biological Weapon for Terrorists*, 7 CTC SENTINEL 16–18 (2014); Dina Fine Maron, *Weaponized Ebola: Is It Really a Bioterror Threat?*, SCIENTIFIC AMERICAN (2014), www.scientificamerican.com/article/weaponized-ebola-is-it-really-a-bioterror-threat/ (last visited Feb. 18, 2020).
8   JOHN R. HAINES, *Weaponizing Ebola?* (2014), www.fpri.org/article/2014/10/weaponizing-ebola/ (last visited Aug. 23, 2019).
9   Abayomi et al., *supra* note 3.
10 Notably, this is possibly an underestimate, since countries such as the US, UK, and South Africa were reticent about disclosing their holdings of samples. See Freudenthal, *supra* note 4, as well as Erika

Liberia, approximately 58,000 in Guinea, and approximately 33,000 in Sierra
Leone. As Akin Abayomi and coauthors noted in 2016, many of the samples scattered
across the West African nations were poorly accounted for – if at all – and were often
stored in unsafe and insecure environments.[11]

In this chapter, we examine the biosafety and biosecurity issues relating to the
management – including collection, storage, transfer, and handling – of dangerous
pathogen samples. The examination takes as its point of departure the events of the
2014–16 Ebola outbreak in West Africa, yet the discussion herein is highly relevant
for biological materials other than EBOV samples, including nonhuman animal
specimens. The chapter begins with a survey of the relevant mechanisms for
governing pathogen management, discussing both international law and national
regulatory systems. This section is followed by an examination of the distinct
biosafety and biosecurity issues associated with managing pathogens in resource-
limited contexts as well as their implications for policymaking. We then discuss the
challenge of achieving biosafety and biosecurity when conducting public health
research with dangerous biological agents. Finally, the chapter concludes with
recommendations for regulations and policies that can support safe, secure, and
effective management of dangerous pathogens.

6.2 GLOBAL GOVERNANCE MECHANISMS

As the other chapters in this volume demonstrate, international regulatory regimes
like the Convention on Biological Diversity, Nagoya Protocol, and the WHO
Pandemic Influenza Preparedness (PIP) Framework govern the transfer and sharing
of biological materials used for public health research. However, when it comes to
highly pathogenic agents, additional regulations exist to ensure biosafety and biosecurity. In this section, we outline the relevant governance mechanisms relating to
the safety and security of pathogenic samples, and discuss both international laws as
well the role of legal and regulatory systems at the national level.

Various international regulatory systems detail the obligations of countries with
respect to dangerous pathogen management.[12] The International Health
Regulations (IHR), revised and adopted in 2005 and overseen by the WHO, were
intended "to prevent, protect against, control and provide a public health response to
the international spread of disease . . . ."[13] However, while the IHR (2005) established
landmark regulations for governing global public health emergencies, they do not
focus on pathogen management. The regulations do not explicitly address the

Check Hayden, *Proposed Ebola Biobank Would Strengthen African Science*, 524 NATURE 146–47
(2015).
[11] Abayomi et al., *supra* note 3.
[12] *Id.*
[13] WORLD HEALTH ORGANIZATION., *International Health Regulations (2005), 2nd edition* at 1 (2008), www
.who.int/ihr/publications/9789241596664/en/ (last visited Feb. 18, 2020).

biosecurity or biosafety of pathogenic materials, nor do they include guidance on the distribution of genetic sequencing data. Furthermore, and more generally, many countries have struggled to develop core capacities to fully implement the IHR (2005).[14] The precise limits to their capacity have been difficult to document, as the WHO originally relied primarily on country self-assessments.[15] Recognizing these difficulties, and prompted by the work of the Global Health Security Agenda (GHSA), the WHO launched the voluntary Joint External Evaluations Tool (JEE) in 2016, which has now been used by over 100 countries. JEE assessments involve site visits and external evaluations of core capacities for health security in addition to self-reported data from governments. Notably, the JEE – unlike the IHR (2005) text – includes biosecurity and biosafety considerations within its "prevention" core element.[16] Here, the JEE guidelines discuss the storage and transportation of pathogenic explicitly, defining "Desired Impact" as "Implementation of a comprehensive, sustainable and legally embedded national oversight program for biosafety and biosecurity, including the safe and secure use, storage, disposal, and containment of pathogens found in laboratories and a minimal number of holdings across the country, including research, diagnostic and biotechnology facilities. ... The transport of infectious substances will also be taken into account."[17] In light of this, the JEE process holds the potential to improve the safety and security of pathogenic samples, despite the absence of such explicit considerations in the IHR (2005) themselves. However, even as the JEE has raised the awareness around IHR (2005) compliance, many countries still lack the core capacities for public health security required under the regulations.[18] Figure 6.1 shows the level of global capacity for biosafety and biosecurity as measured by the countries that have completed the JEE at the time of writing.[19]

The objectives of the IHR are well aligned with international regulatory law aimed at reducing risks from materials related to biological weapons (e.g., highly pathogenic samples). The Biological and Toxin Weapons Convention (BWC), which entered into force in 1975, is a multilateral treaty which obligates the countries that are party to the convention to prohibit the development, production,

---

[14] Lawrence Gostin and Rebecca Katz, *The International Health Regulations: The Governing Framework for Global Health Security*, 94 THE MILBANK QUARTERLY (2016).

[15] Feng-Jen Tsai and Rebecca Katz, *Measuring Global Health Security: Comparison of Self- and External Evaluations for IHR Core Capacity*, 16 HEALTH SECURITY 304–10 (2018).

[16] Kadiatou Dao and Dana Perkins, *Opportunities for Strengthening Biosafety and Biosecurity Oversight through International Cooperation and Compliance with International Obligations: A Perspective from Mali*, 11 1540 COMPASS ARTICLES 24–30 (2016).

[17] WORLD HEALTH ORGANIZATION, *Joint External Evaluation tool (JEE tool), first edition*, at 21 www .who.int/ihr/publications/WHO_HSE_GCR_2016_2/en/ (last visited Feb. 18, 2020).

[18] Vin Gupta et al., *Analysis of results from the Joint External Evaluation: examining its strength and assessing for trends among participating countries*, 8 J GLOB HEALTH, www.ncbi.nlm.nih.gov/pmc/ articles/PMC6204750/ (last visited Jul. 23, 2019).

[19] Rebecca Katz et al., *Tracking the Flow of Funds in Global Health Security*, EcoHEALTH (2019), link .springer.com/article/10.1007/s10393-019-01402-w (last visited Feb. 18, 2020).

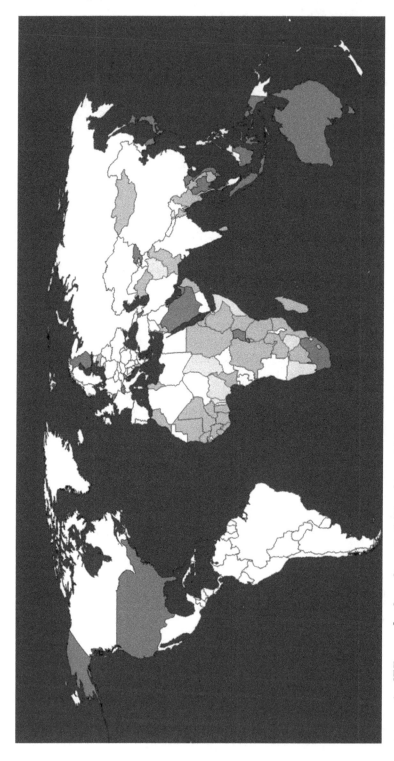

FIGURE 6.1 JEE score for Core Capacity 6: Biosafety and biosecurity by country. Shading represents JEE score, with light gray representing scores from 0 to 1, mid gray being 2 to 3; and dark gray being 4 to 5. Source: Georgetown Infectious Disease Atlas.

acquisition, and stockpiling of biological weapons.[20] The Eighth Review Conference of the BWC reaffirmed the commitment of state parties to "ensure the safety and security of microbial or other biological agents or toxins in laboratories, facilities, and during transportation, to prevent unauthorized access to and removal of such agents or toxins."[21]

The United Nations Security Council Resolution 1540 (UNSCR 1540) – adopted unanimously in 2004[22] and since reaffirmed with the adoption of Resolution 2325 in 2016[23] – requires countries to develop and maintain effective measures to prevent non-state actors from acquiring materials related to biological weapons. This includes measures to account for, secure, and physically protect biological materials as well as measures to prevent illicit trafficking and export of these materials. Notably, the UNSCR 1540 establishes a mechanism for overseeing implementation on the national scale. Under paragraph 4 of the UNSCR 1540, a Committee is charged with overseeing and reporting on national implementation of the resolution.

These binding international agreements are complemented by initiatives aimed at strengthening global health security. The Global Health Security Agenda, launched in February 2014, is a consortium of more than sixty countries that have committed voluntarily to strengthening their capacity to "prevent, detect, and respond to infectious diseases threats whether naturally occurring, deliberate, or accidental."[24] The GHSA directly addresses the issue of biosafety and biosecurity for dangerous pathogen samples. Among its eleven Action Packages, one of them (Prevent-3) addresses biosafety and biosecurity specifically, and recommends as a five-year national target that "a whole-of-government national biosafety and biosecurity system is in place, ensuring that especially dangerous pathogens are identified, held, secured and monitored in a minimal number of facilities according to best practices."[25]

While international regulations and legal agreements are vital, the challenge of inadequate compliance highlights the necessary role of national legislation in ensuring the safety and security of dangerous biological materials. Moreover, as discussed elsewhere in this volume, national legislation can help countries as they seek to prevent the unwanted export of pathogen samples to foreign sites. Given the

---

[20] The Biological and Toxin Weapons Convention does not explicitly prohibit the use of biological weapons. Instead, in the preamble, it refers to the Geneva Protocol of 1925, which does prohibit use of such weapons.

[21] BIOLOGICAL WEAPONS CONVENTION, *Final Document of the Eighth Review Conference*, BWC/CONF. VIII/4 at 11 (2016).

[22] UNITED NATIONS SECURITY COUNCIL, *UNSCR Resolution 1540*, S/RES/1540 (2004).

[23] UNITED NATIONS SECURITY COUNCIL, *UNSCR Resolution 2325*, S/RES/2325 (2016).

[24] Global Health Security Agenda – About, www.ghsagenda.org/about (last visited Feb. 18, 2020).

[25] GLOBAL HEALTH SECURITY AGENDA, *Global Health Security Agenda: Action Packages* at 8 (2014), www .cdc.gov/globalhealth/security/pdf/ghsa-action-packages_24-september-2014.pdf (last visited Feb. 18, 2020).

essential role of national legislation, several steps should be taken in order to achieve public health security objectives.[26]

First, governments should consider creating legislation aimed at ensuring the safety and security of dangerous biological materials, as is called for in the GHSA (Action Package Prevent-3).[27] VERTIC, for example, has provided guidance for countries through its "Sample Act for National Implementation of the 1972 BWC and Related Requirements of UN Security Council Resolution 1540."[28] In addition, the Danish Centre for Biosecurity and Biopreparedness has created a manual for creating national biosecurity laws, based on Denmark's experience with enacting a comprehensive biosecurity law in 2008.[29] Furthermore, the UN Recommendations on the Transport of Dangerous Goods can inform national regulations.[30] While they are not legally binding, the Recommendations form the basis for biosecurity regulation regarding the transportation of infectious substances in many countries.

Second, an exhaustive repository of national level laws and regulations is needed to highlight gaps in national legislation and allow for the dissemination of legislative best practices. Fundamentally, strong regulatory systems are essential for safe and secure pathogen management. However, as the following section shows, regulatory capacity is not the only area in need of strengthening to prevent, detect, and respond to risks associated with dangerous pathogens.

6.3 STRENGTHENING THE GLOBAL CAPACITY FOR SAFE AND SECURE PATHOGEN MANAGEMENT

As the US biosafety and biosecurity incidents presented in the introduction illustrate, the challenges associated with dangerous pathogen management are faced by public health communities even in high-income countries. However, while biosafety and biosecurity concerns may be ubiquitous, there is significant variation in the capacity of countries to address them. This section outlines some of the distinct difficulties associated with managing pathogens in resource-limited settings. It demonstrates how significant investments are needed to strengthen the ability of low- and middle-income countries (LMICs) to safely and securely manage

---

[26] Abayomi et al., *supra* note 3.

[27] GLOBAL HEALTH SECURITY AGENDA, *supra* note 26.

[28] VERTIC, *Sample Act for National Implementation of the 1972 Biological and Toxin Weapons Convention and Related Requirements of UN Security Council Resolution 1540* (2012), www .vertic.org/media/assets/nim_docs/NIM%20Tools%20(Model%20Laws)/BWC/BTWC%20Sample% 20Act_EN_14feb2012.pdf (last visited Feb. 18, 2020).

[29] CENTRE FOR BIOSECURITY AND BIOPREPAREDNESS, *An efficient and practical approach to biosecurity* 276 (2015), www.biosecurity.dk/fileadmin/user_upload/PDF_FILER/Biosecurity_book/ An_efficient_and_Practical_approach_to_Biosecurity_web1.pdf (last visited Feb. 18, 2020).

[30] United Nations, *UN Recommendations on the Transport of Dangerous Goods – Model Regulations, twentieth revised edition* (2017), www.unece.org/trans/danger/publi/unrec/rev20/20files_e.html (last visited Feb. 18, 2020).

dangerous pathogens.[31] In particular, it discusses the need for expanding biobanking capacity in LMICs. While the section has a particular focus on West Africa and the 2014–16 Ebola outbreak, its key points are relevant to many other geographic and epidemic contexts.

An alarming inverse relationship between disease endemicity and health system capacity characterizes the global landscape of health security.[32] Countries with fewer resources and less capacity often face the largest, severest epidemic risks, while wealthier countries with more robust health systems face lighter infectious disease burdens. The 2014–16 Ebola outbreak in West Africa embodied this relationship, as Guinea, Liberia, and Sierra Leone had extremely fragile health systems. According to the most recently available data from the WHO, the three countries rank 175th, 189th, and 190th, respectively, among 193 countries with respect to doctors per capita, while the Democratic Republic of Congo, the epicenter of the 2018–19 Ebola outbreak, ranks 172nd.[33] It is well documented that health system weakness has exacerbated the severity of the two outbreaks by complicating effective surveillance, diagnosis, and response. For instance, a 2015 survey of national health systems concluded that "[t]here is general agreement that the [2014–16] Ebola crisis was not quickly contained in Guinea, Liberia, and Sierra Leone because their national health systems were dangerously under-resourced, understaffed, and poorly equipped."[34] Moreover, limited resources and capacity complicate public health research efforts during outbreaks.[35] It is worth noting that the challenges faced by LMICs are not only caused by physical or monetary constraints: Lacking regulatory capacity can also complicate aspects of epidemic response efforts, such as medical countermeasure distribution.[36]

Beyond these general complications, resource limitations also lead to distinct challenges from biosafety and biosecurity perspectives. In terms of biosafety, the lack of adequately equipped research facilities in resource-poor areas of the world has

---

[31] Rahim Moloo and Alex Khachaturian, *The Compliance with the Law Requirement in International Investment Law*, 34 FORDHAM INT'L. L.J. 1473 (2011).

[32] Petra Dickmann, Heather Sheeley and Nigel Lightfoot, *Biosafety and Biosecurity: A Relative Risk-Based Framework for Safer, More Secure, and Sustainable Laboratory Capacity Building*, 3 FRONT. PUBLIC HEALTH (2015), www.frontiersin.org/articles/10.3389/fpubh.2015.00241/full (last visited Feb. 18, 2020).

[33] World Health Organization, *Health workforce: Density of physicians (total number per 1,000 population)* (2019), www.who.int/gho/health_workforce/physicians_density/en/ (last visited Jul. 19, 2019).

[34] SIMON WRIGHT, LUISA HANNA AND MATHILDE MAILFERT, *A Wake-Up Call: Lessons from Ebola for the World's Health Systems* 40 (2015), www.savethechildren.org.uk/content/dam/global/reports/health-and-nutrition/a-wake-up-call.pdf (last visited Jul. 16, 2019).

[35] NATIONAL ACADEMIES OF SCIENCES, ENGINEERING, AND MEDICINE ET AL., INTEGRATING CLINICAL RESEARCH INTO EPIDEMIC RESPONSE (2017), www.ncbi.nlm.nih.gov/books/NBK441679/ (last visited Jul. 11, 2019).

[36] Sam F. Halabi and John Monahan, Chapter 6 – *Regulatory Capacity in Low – and Middle-Income Countries: Lessons from the H1N1 Influenza Pandemic*, in FOOD AND DRUG REGULATION IN AN ERA OF GLOBALIZED MARKETS 63–76 (Sam F. Halabi ed., 2015), www.sciencedirect.com/science/article/pii/B9780128023112000060 (last visited Feb. 18, 2020).

long been identified as a problem. At the time of the 2014–16 West Africa epidemic, there were only two BSL-4 laboratories on the African continent,[37] each of which were located about 2,900 and 6,000 kilometers from the suspected ground zero of the outbreak in Guinea. Since then, construction has begun for another maximum biocontainment laboratory in Cote d'Ivoire,[38] and there are several examples of successful constructions of BSL-3 laboratories in resource-limited countries.[39] Still, it remains the case that highly advanced biocontainment units are scarcer in low- and middle-income countries than in higher-income countries[40] and, more generally, that lacking infrastructure and equipment constrain laboratories in LMICs to a greater extent.[41] For instance, a 2009 assessment of biosafety precautions in 190 diagnostic laboratories of Khartoum state, Sudan, found that very few of the surveyed laboratories had access to equipment such as biosafety cabinets, autoclaves, incinerators, and waste containers for chemical and radioactive materials.[42] Similarly, a 2013 review of eighty diagnostic laboratories in Nigeria found marked deficiencies concerning biosafety equipment, devices, and measures;[43] as did an inspection of dozens of laboratories across the Asia-Pacific region.[44]

In addition to the biosafety risks associated with the handling of pathogens in ill-equipped laboratories, the scarcity of well-equipped facilities also poses distinct challenges from a biosecurity perspective. One such challenge arises when a large volume of highly pathogenic samples is concentrated within a few laboratories without adequate capacity in place. Until additional laboratory facilities were established in early 2015, all Sierra Leonean Ebola samples were sent to the Kenema Viral Haemorrhagic Fever Laboratory in the far east of the country, as this was the only facility in the country with the ability to diagnose Ebola.[45] The resulting stress on the laboratory meant that documentation of samples was poor and

---

[37]	NATIONAL ACADEMY OF SCIENCES, BIOSECURITY CHALLENGES OF THE GLOBAL EXPANSION OF HIGH-CONTAINMENT BIOLOGICAL LABORATORIES (2011), www.ncbi.nlm.nih.gov/books/NBK196156/ (last visited Jul. 16, 2019).

[38]	WORLD HEALTH ORGANIZATION, *WHO Consultative Meeting on High/Maximum Containment (Biosafety Level 4) Laboratories Networking* (2017), https://apps.who.int/iris/bitstream/handle/10665/311625/WHO-WHE-CPI-2018.40-eng.pdf (last visited Feb. 18, 2020).

[39]	C. N. Paramasivan et al., *Experience Establishing Tuberculosis Laboratory Capacity in a Developing Country Setting*, 14 THE INTERNATIONAL JOURNAL OF TUBERCULOSIS AND LUNG DISEASE 59–64 (2010); Willy Ssengooba et al., *Feasibility of Establishing a Biosafety Level 3 Tuberculosis Culture Laboratory of Acceptable Quality Standards in a Resource-Limited Setting: an Experience from Uganda*, 13 HEALTH RESEARCH POLICY AND SYSTEMS 4 (2015).

[40]	Aftab Ahmad, Sadia Ashraf and Shoji Komai, *Are Developing Countries Prepared to Face Ebola-Like Outbreaks?*, 30 VIROL SIN 234–37 (2015).

[41]	Robert A. Heckert et al., *International Biosafety and Biosecurity Challenges: Suggestions for Developing Sustainable Capacity in Low-resource Countries*, 16 APPL BIOSAF. 223–30 (2011).

[42]	Adel Hussein Elduma, *Assessment of Biosafety Precautions in Khartoum State Diagnostic Laboratories, Sudan*, 11 PAN AFR MED J 19 (2012).

[43]	Bankole Henry Oladeinde et al., *Biorisk Assessment of Medical Diagnostic Laboratories in Nigeria*, 4 SAFETY AND HEALTH AT WORK 100–04 (2013).

[44]	Ewen Callaway, *Biosafety Concerns for Labs in the Developing World*, 485 NATURE NEWS 425 (2012).

[45]	Abayomi et al., *supra* note 3.

heightened biosecurity risks. These risks remained present long after the outbreak concluded, as samples were scattered across the country.[46]

Given these challenges, it is apparent that considerable investment in strengthening LMIC biosafety and biosecurity capacity is urgently needed. Such investments should focus on bolstering general capabilities such as diagnostics and surveillance with relevance for a wide variety of pathogens and conditions.[47] On the African continent, they can support the objectives of the Africa Centres for Disease Control and Prevention's (Africa CDC) Initiative to Strengthen Biosecurity and Biosafety.[48] The initiative, which was launched in May 2019 at the second Global Biosecurity Dialogue in Addis Ababa, Ethiopia, aims to "to develop and implement strategies for addressing capacity gaps at both the national and regional levels to measurably advance achievement of WHO [JEE] biosafety and biosecurity targets across Africa."[49] It emphasizes the importance of building training programs on biosafety and biosecurity as well as broad health infrastructure improvements.

In addition to broader health security investments, funders should consider directing resources towards the specific goal of strengthening the global capacity for safely and securely storing pathogens used for research. One way of strengthening this capacity is by building repositories for biological samples, also known as biobanks. Researchers and public health professionals have long been calling for the development of national and regional biobanks across the African continent,[50] and this need became all the more apparent in the wake of the 2014–16 West African outbreak.[51] In response to the epidemic, multiple stakeholders undertook efforts to build biobanks, including in Abidjan, Côte d'Ivoire,[52] and Kinshasa, Democratic Republic of Congo (DRC).[53] These projects were launched with the specific purpose of improving the regional capacity for storing infectious pathogens, and will complement the biobanks already operating on the continent, such as the Gambian National DNA Bank, which was established for the study of

---

[46] *Id.*

[47] Gostin and Katz, *supra* note 15.

[48] African Union, *Social affairs commissioner launches Africa CDC initiative to protect Africa against dangerous pathogens* (2019), https://au.int/en/pressreleases/20190508/social-affairs-commissioner-launches-africa-cdc-initiative-protect-africa (last visited Feb. 18, 2020).

[49] SOUTHERN AFRICA REGIONAL COLLABORATING CENTRE, *Report of the first meeting of the Africa CDC Initiative to Strengthen Biosecurity and Biosafety* at 3 (2019).

[50] Akin Abayomi et al., *Challenges of Biobanking in South Africa to Facilitate Indigenous Research in an Environment Burdened with Human Immunodeficiency Virus, Tuberculosis, and Emerging Noncommunicable Diseases*, 11 BIOPRESERV BIOBANK 347–54 (2013).

[51] Hayden, *supra* note 11.

[52] Institut Pasteur, *We have achieved some of our dreams to advance science in Africa* (2017), www.pasteur.fr/en/institut-pasteur/institut-pasteur-throughout-world/news/we-have-achieved-some-our-dreams-advance-science-africa (last visited Feb. 18, 2020).

[53] Amy Maxmen, *Science under fire: Ebola researchers fight to test drugs and vaccines in a war zone*, NATURE (2019), www.nature.com/articles/d41586-019-02258-4 (last visited Feb. 18, 2020).

infectious disease genetics.[54] However, considerable investments are needed in order to develop and sustain such biobanking projects.

There are various viable models for financing the development of biobanks in LMICs. One such model is bilateral arrangements between governmental public health agencies. After the 2014–16 West Africa outbreak, the government of Canada supported Sierra Leone's capacity-building efforts, in part by committing 8.5 million CAD towards the provision of a new biobank.[55] Similarly, the Japanese government has been funding the National Institute for Biomedical Research in the DRC to establish a biobank in Kinshasa.[56] While bilateral agreements can be effective, the importance of multilateral or regional approaches to global health security capacity-building is increasingly recognized;[57] for example, the second WHO consultation on biobanking, held in Sierra Leone in August 2015, discussed the viability of a regional biobank in West Africa.[58] Commercial investments provide another potential avenue for financing biobank development. In July 2019, the Lagos-based genomics company 54gene secured seed-funding to establish the first Pan-African biobank.[59] Notably, however, the organization is initially focusing on obtaining samples for noncommunicable – as opposed to infectious – diseases.

6.4 MANAGING DANGEROUS PATHOGENS IN RESOURCE-LIMITED SETTINGS

The previous section highlighted the various resource limitations facing health systems around the world. These constraints create discrepancies between the quality of local resources and facilities available in many countries and the biosafety and biosecurity standards found in official guidelines. As noted, these discrepancies should be minimized through sustained investments in global health security capacity. However, the lack of resources and facilities in many LMICs has another critical implication. Specifically, it is ill-advised to apply one-size-fits-all prescriptions across the wide variety of circumstances in which pathogens are handled. This section introduces and discusses a context-sensitive approach to biosafety and biosecurity, focusing primarily on the framework presented in the landmark forthcoming edition of the WHO laboratory biosafety manual.

---

[54]   Giorgio Sirugo et al., *A National DNA Bank in The Gambia, West Africa, and Genomic Research in Developing Countries*, 36 NATURE GENETICS 785 (2004).

[55]   Government of Canada, *Canada–Sierra Leone Relations*, GAC (2019), www.canadainternational.gc .ca/ghana/bilateral_relations_bilaterales/canada_sierraleone.aspx?lang=eng (last visited Feb. 18, 2020).

[56]   Maxmen, *supra* note 54.

[57]   Rebecca Katz and Claire J. Standley, *Regional Approaches for Enhancing Global Health Security*, 19 BMC PUBLIC HEALTH 473 (2019).

[58]   WORLD HEALTH ORGANIZATION, *Report on the 2nd WHO Consultation on Biobanking: Focus on West Africa* (2015), www.who.int/medicines/ebola-treatment/meetings/2nd_who_biobaking-consultation /en/ (last visited Feb. 18, 2020).

[59]   Paul Adepoju, *Africa's First Biobank Start-Up Receives Seed Funding*, 394 THE LANCET 108 (2019).

Historically, many best-practice standards and guidelines have been conceived in the context of high-income health systems and have primarily intended to inform decision-making in resource rich settings.[60] While it is of utmost importance that biosafety and biosecurity be a top priority anywhere that dangerous pathogens are handled, it is impractical to expect the same approach to be applied everywhere. For one thing, guidelines that mandate the utilization of complex facilities, which are simply beyond the assets available in some contexts, fail to achieve adequate levels of compliance. Moreover, an excessive emphasis on reaching specific, prescribed standards sometimes leads to cost-ineffective priorities in policymaking and laboratory construction. In response to these issues, the global biosafety and biosecurity communities are increasingly recognizing that efforts to reduce biological risks must be "context-sensitive."

For instance, a 2014 research paper from the Chatham House Centre on Global Health Security observes that "it is unclear whether it is imperative for global health protection that all countries reach the standards demanded in the most developed countries and whether such an approach is sustainable, or whether sufficient biosafety and biosecurity levels can be reached with a more context-sensitive approach and smarter use of existing resources."[61] Echoing this message, Dr. Xavier Abad, head of the biocontainment unit at the Animal Health Research Center in Barcelona, noted in 2018 that "there is no 'one size fits all' approach" and that biocontainment standards must recognize the circumstances on the ground in low-income countries.[62] Similarly, the conclusions from the first technical workshop of the Africa CDC Initiative to Strengthen Biosecurity and Biosafety emphasized that "[t]here is a need for contextualised [biosafety and biosecurity] guidelines and standards that are practical and fitting for the African environment."[63]

The clearest sign that this approach is taking hold in the international biosafety community is found in the forthcoming fourth edition of the WHO's *Laboratory Biosafety Manual* (*LBM*), currently under revision.[64] The *LBM*, which was first published in 1983[65] and most recently in 2004,[66] has long defined the thinking on biosafety internationally, informing both policymaking and laboratory construction. However, over the past decades, various advances in the understanding of what makes for cost-effective biosafety have created the foundation for an updated approach. In an essay published in *Science* during the revision stage for the new *LBM*, Dr. Kazunobu Kojima and other key contributors describe how earlier editions of the manual were more "precautionary and prescriptive" and how the

[60]   Dickmann, Sheeley, and Lightfoot, *supra* note 33.
[61]   PETRA DICKMANN ET AL., *Safe and Secure Biomaterials – A Risk-Based Alternative Approach* at 2 (2014).
[62]   Xavier Abad, *Biocontainment in Low Income Countries: A Short Discussion*, 07 MEDICAL SAFETY & GLOBAL HEALTH 2 (2018).
[63]   SOUTHERN AFRICA REGIONAL COLLABORATING CENTRE, *supra* note 50 at 11.
[64]   WORLD HEALTH ORGANIZATION, *Laboratory Biosafety Manual, fourth edition* (forthcoming).
[65]   WORLD HEALTH ORGANIZATION, *Laboratory Biosafety Manual, first edition* (1983).
[66]   WORLD HEALTH ORGANIZATION, *Laboratory Biosafety Manual, third edition* (2004).

new edition is "part of a broader initiative to globalize biosafety, emphasizing principles and approaches that are accessible to countries spanning a broad range of financial, technical, and regulatory resources."[67] At the time of writing, this theme is front-and-center in the draft text for the *LBM*. For instance, the foreword of the manual states that its approach will "enable countries to implement economically feasible and sustainable laboratory biosafety and biosecurity policies and practices that are relevant to their individual circumstances and priorities,"[68] while the section on risk assessment describes a good risk control strategy as one that will "be achievable using the available resources in the context of the local conditions."[69] Similar considerations are emphasized in the section on national and international biosafety oversight, which cautions against the simplistic application of one national regulatory framework in another, dissimilar setting, stating that "[g]iven the challenges countries might face because of limited resources on the one hand and emerging diseases and the (mis)use of advanced technologies on the other, controlling biological risks at the national level may require context-specific consideration to devise the most appropriate approach for a country."[70] Furthermore, the manual advises that regulatory frameworks remain flexible and capable of adjusting to changing circumstances and knowledge.

While recognizing the variation in the resources and capacity of health systems across the world is important in its own right, the real value of the revised *LBM* – and the general approach it represents – lies with its actionable recommendations. Far from implying that biosafety and biosecurity can be deprioritized because of resource limitations, the approach advocates maximizing biosafety and biosecurity within given resource and capacity constraints. Specifically, the fourth edition of the *LBM* recognizes the central role of human behavior for biosafety and focuses on procedural modifications accordingly.

Among the key findings underpinning the evidence-based approach of the new *LBM* is a better understanding of the causes of biosafety incidents, such as laboratory-associated infections (LAIs). Recent reviews have shown that LAIs are more often caused by human errors than by malfunction of engineering controls.[71] Consequently, laboratory managers and researchers can often achieve the necessary level biosafety by focusing on procedural factors, such as staff training and the use of standard operating procedures, even when resource constraints may prohibit investment in costly and complex facilities.[72] In light of these findings, the fourth *LBM*

---

[67] Kazunobu Kojima et al., *Risk-Based Reboot for Global Lab Biosafety*, 360 SCIENCE at 262 (2018).

[68] WORLD HEALTH ORGANIZATION, *supra* note 65 at VII.

[69] *Id.* at 15.

[70] *Id.* at 84.

[71] N. Wurtz et al., *Survey of Laboratory-Acquired Infections around the World in Biosafety Level 3 and 4 Laboratories*, 35 EUR. J. CLIN. MICROBIOL. INFECT. DIS. 1247–58 (2016); A. Bienek, M. Heisz, and M. Su, *Surveillance of Laboratory Exposures to Human Pathogens and Toxins: Canada 2016*, 43 CAN. COMMUN. DIS. REP. 228–35 (2017).

[72] Kojima et al., *supra* note 68 at 262.

places greater emphasis on the procedural and human components of biosafety than earlier editions have done. As Kojima et al. note, the previous emphasis on strict engineering controls led some readers to prioritize complex structural systems that are cost-ineffective in resource-limited settings;[73] a point which has been increasingly recognized in the biosafety community over the past decade.[74] In a word, the *LBM* aims to provide a "technology-neutral" approach to biosafety.[75] This is not to say that the manual in any way fails to recognize the essential role that technology can play in laboratory biosafety. Instead, it offers a critical approach to risk assessment that allows decision-makers to determine when and if costly engineering solutions are required to achieve biosafety.

While the new *LBM* and similar context-sensitive frameworks represent essential progress towards more cost-effective approaches to biosafety and biosecurity, key steps remain in the effort to globalize health security. First, actors on the national and global stage must expound upon context-sensitive frameworks in the realm of biosecurity. As an example of such work, David Harper and colleagues at the Chatham House Centre on Global Health Security have published a tool intended to facilitate sustainable laboratory development, which includes extensive considerations of biosecurity.[76]

Second, this new approach should be popularized and applied to pathogens in specific circumstances across the world. This has already been done in the context of tuberculosis laboratory safety,[77] for which the WHO published a special biosafety laboratory manual in 2012.[78] Crucially, conclusions regarding specific diseases and contexts should rely on evidence-based analysis, as has recently been conducted in the domain of typhus-related laboratory activities.[79]

6.5 BALANCING BIOSAFETY AND BIOSECURITY WITH EFFECTIVE RESEARCH PRACTICES

While the focus of this chapter so far has been on the difficulties associated with managing dangerous pathogens in resource-limited settings, many biosecurity and biosafety challenges arise in any environment – even those with abundant resources.

---

[73] *Id.* at 261.

[74] Heckert et al., *supra* note 42 at 228; Thomas M. Shinnick and Christopher Gilpin, *A Risk Assessment-Based Approach to Defining Minimum Biosafety Precautions for Tuberculosis Laboratories in Resource-Limited Settings*, 17 APPL BIOSAF. at 7 (2012); Abad, *supra* note 63 at 2.

[75] Kojima et al., *supra* note 68 at 260; WORLD HEALTH ORGANIZATION, *supra* note 65 at 2.

[76] DAVID R HARPER, EMMA ROSS & BEN WAKEFIELD, *The Chatham House Sustainable Laboratories Initiative. Prior assessment tool* (2019).

[77] Shinnick and Gilpin, *supra* note 75.

[78] WORLD HEALTH ORGANIZATION, *Tuberculosis laboratory biosafety manual* (2012), www.who.int/tb/publications/2012/tb_biosafety/en/ (last visited Feb. 18, 2020).

[79] Stuart D. Blacksell et al., *Laboratory-Acquired Scrub Typhus and Murine Typhus Infections: The Argument for a Risk-Based Approach to Biosafety Requirements for* Orientia tsutsugamushi *and* Rickettsia typhi *Laboratory Activities*, 68 CLIN INFECT DIS 1413–19 (2019).

Measures designed to improve the safety and security of biological research may limit the actions available to researchers. As a result, the Danish Centre for Biosecurity and Biopreparedness observes that "finding the right balance between biosecurity needs and legitimate scientific freedom is key to the success of [biosecurity] legislation."[80] The following section investigates the challenge of reducing risks to an acceptable level while at the same time avoiding excessive obstacles to investigation. We begin by discussing the case of gain-of-function research with highly pathogenic influenza virus strains, showing how safety and security concerns loom large concerning both the conduct and dissemination of such research. Then, we discuss how this challenge applies to sample collection and storage. Finally, we consider the relevance of biosafety and biosecurity for countries' decisions about whether to share biological materials for public health research.

The challenge of ensuring adequate biosafety and biosecurity while allowing for effective research is present whenever studies are conducted using potentially pandemic pathogens. A prime example of this challenge occurs in the context of gain-of-function research into highly pathogenic avian influenza (HPAI). The consequences of a biosafety incident involving the accidental release or exposure to HPAI – especially a genetically modified strain of the virus – could be disastrous. For this reason, researchers should take extreme caution when investigating HPAI.[81] At the same time, however, this kind of research has the potential to generate vital new insights with implications for epidemic surveillance as well as the development of novel diagnostics tests, vaccines, and antiviral drugs. Since precautionary measures can limit the scope of possible research projects,[82] biosafety and research communities strive to strike the appropriate balance between reducing risks while facilitating effective research.

In addition to the risks associated with conducting research, there are pronounced risks concerning the dissemination of results and methodologies. In the fall of 2011, these risks provoked one of the most famous biosecurity controversies in recent years. Two research groups independently submitted work on gain-of-function mutations of an H5N1 avian influenza strain to the journals *Science* and *Nature*. Before the work could be published, however, the US National Science Advisory Board for Biosecurity (NSABB) recommended that the manuscript should omit particular sections. The NSABB judged that the publication of detailed methodology posed a distinct biosecurity threat, as "certain information obtained through such studies has the potential to be misused for harmful purposes."[83] At the same time, some

[80] CENTRE FOR BIOSECURITY AND BIOPREPAREDNESS, *supra* note 30 at 40.
[81] L. CASEY CHOSEWOOD AND DEBORA E. WILSON, BIOSAFETY IN MICROBIOLOGICAL AND BIOMEDICAL LABORATORIES (BMBL) (5th ed. 2009) at 213.
[82] Amy C. Shurtleff et al., *The Impact of Regulations, Safety Considerations and Physical Limitations on Research Progress at Maximum Biocontainment*, 4 VIRUSES 3932–51 (2012).
[83] National Institutes of Health (NIH), *Press Statement on the NSABB Review of H5N1 Research* (2011), www.nih.gov/news-events/news-releases/press-statement-nsabb-review-h5n1-research (last visited Feb. 18, 2020).

researchers argued that the benefits of publishing the full methodology would allow for vital research on the area and outweighed the countervailing considerations.[84] The NSABB recommendation became the beginning of a sustained discussion in scientific and biosecurity communities,[85] involving a research moratorium,[86] an extraordinary WHO consultation,[87] and intensive media coverage.[88]

Ultimately, the NSABB issued a new recommendation in March 2012, supporting the publication of newly revised versions of the manuscripts.[89] The intensity of the H5N1 controversy illustrates the remarkable challenge of balancing necessary biosecurity and biosafety measures with conditions that allow for vital research progress.

Striking this balance is especially critical for public health research during an active epidemic outbreak. During the 2014–16 Ebola outbreak, local researchers working in the affected West African countries reported that the need to conduct biocontainment training in addition to other research responsibilities put them under increased pressure.[90] In this case, the biocontainment training was an indispensable measure that should not be compromised for the sake of expediency. However, the experience exemplifies how biosafety can interact with the practice of research and underscores the importance of recognizing the potential dilemmas that can arise as a result.

This dilemma also presents itself when collecting and storing dangerous pathogen samples. Many biosafety and biosecurity challenges and risks scale directly with the number of live pathogen samples that are being stored or transported at any given moment. For this reason, public health communities must identify the appropriate number of samples to preserve for research. It may be prudent to keep samples for further research, even when they were initially obtained for diagnostic purposes, as the study of live pathogens is necessary for efforts to understand, track, and respond

---

[84] Ron A. M. Fouchier, Sander Herfst and Albert D. M. E. Osterhaus, *Restricted Data on Influenza H5N1.Virus Transmission*, 335 SCIENCE 662–63 (2012); Ron A. M. Fouchier, comments made at the *American Society for Microbiology Biodefense and Emerging Diseases Research Meeting* (2012), www.youtube.com/watch?v=900P2ez8l4k&t=930s (last visited Feb. 18, 2020).

[85] COMMITTEE ON SCIENCE, TECHNOLOGY, AND LAW ET AL., PERSPECTIVES ON RESEARCH WITH H5N1 AVIAN INFLUENZA: SCIENTIFIC INQUIRY, COMMUNICATION, CONTROVERSY: SUMMARY OF A WORKSHOP (2013), www.ncbi.nlm.nih.gov/books/NBK206987/ (last visited Feb. 18, 2020).

[86] National Institutes of Health (NIH), *NIH Statement on H5N1* (2012), www.nih.gov/about-nih/who-we -are/nih-director/statements/nih-statement-h5n1 (last visited Feb. 18, 2020).

[87] World Health Organization, *Technical consultation on H5N1 research issues – consensus points*, WHO (2012), www.who.int/influenza/human_animal_interface/consensus_points/en/ (last visited Jul. 10, 2019).

[88] Denise Grady and Donald G. McNeil Jr, *Debate Persists on Deadly Flu Made Airborne*, THE NEW YORK TIMES, December 26, 2011, www.nytimes.com/2011/12/27/science/debate-persists-on-deadly-flu-made-airborne.html (last visited Feb. 18, 2020).

[89] National Institutes of Health (NIH), *Statement on NSABB's March 30, 2012 Recommendations to NIH on H5N1 Research* (2012), www.nih.gov/about-nih/who-we-are/nih-director/statements/statement-nsabbs-march-302012-recommendations-nih-h5n1-research (last visited Feb. 18, 2020).

[90] ENGINEERING NATIONAL ACADEMIES OF SCIENCES ET AL., STRENGTHENING CAPACITY FOR RESPONSE AND RESEARCH (2017), www.ncbi.nlm.nih.gov/books/NBK441672/ (last visited Jul. 11, 2019).

to an outbreak. Additionally, the fragility of human pathogen samples means that there are benefits to collecting and storing as many samples as possible.[91]

However, it may be advisable to destroy samples after their diagnostic purpose has been met, especially in settings where adequate safety standards are missing, to avoid the accidental release or loss of live pathogens.[92] In essence, there is both an efficiency argument for keeping as many samples as possible, and a safety and security argument for keeping the stock of samples to a manageable minimum.

The most well-known example of this dilemma concerns samples of variola virus, the pathogen which causes smallpox. Since the eradication of smallpox in the late 1970s, the scientific community has debated the fate of remaining vials of the live virus. Those calling for the destruction of remaining stockpiles argue that the continued existence of live variola samples poses a biosecurity threat that jeopardizes the successful eradication of smallpox.[93] These concerns were raised by experts such as D. A. Henderson[94] – who directed the international effort to eradicate smallpox, and were amplified in June of 2014 when six vials of forgotten variola virus were found in an unused portion of a cold storage at a US Food and Drug Administration laboratory.[95] Others insisted that the existing vials should be preserved, as they continue to have important applications for viral research and the development of medical countermeasures: Unknown samples of the virus might still exist outside of licensed laboratories.[96]

Even after sustained discussions at the World Health Assembly over the past two decades,[97] the issue remains a point of contention in the scientific community. In light of this controversy, there is a need for guidelines to support researchers and public health workers in deciding the fate of collected samples, allowing them to strike the correct balance between biosafety, biosecurity, and research efficiency in the context of sample storage.[98] Such guidelines must account for the fact that potential risks and benefits to sample storage vary considerably between pathogens.

---

[91] Claire Standley, *Safety, Security, and Sovereignty: The Need for Global Guidelines for Sample Collection during Outbreaks.* Unpublished manuscript (no date) at 2.

[92] *Id.* at 3.

[93] J. Michael Lane and Gregory A. Poland, *Why Not Destroy the Remaining Smallpox Virus Stocks?*, 29 Vaccine 2823–24 (2011).

[94] D. A. Henderson, *Smallpox Virus Destruction and the Implications of a New Vaccine,* 9 Biosecur Bioterror 163–68 (2011).

[95] Henry Fountain, *Six Vials of Smallpox Discovered in Laboratory Near Washington,* The New York Times, July 8, 2014, www.nytimes.com/2014/07/09/science/six-vials-of-smallpox-discovered-in-laboratory-near-washington.html (last visited Feb. 18, 2020).

[96] Inger K. Damon, Clarissa R. Damaso and Grant McFadden, *Are We There Yet? The Smallpox Research Agenda Using Variola Virus,* 10 PLOS Pathogens e1004108 (2014); Jean-Vivien Mombouli and Stephen M. Ostroff, *The Remaining Smallpox Stocks: The Healthiest Outcome,* 379 The Lancet 10–12 (2012).

[97] World Health Organization, *Smallpox eradication: destruction of variola virus stocks – Report by the Director-General for provisional agenda item 12.6 at the 72nd World Health Assembly* (2019), http://apps.who.int/gb/ebwha/pdf_files/WHA72/A72_28-en.pdf (last visited Feb. 18, 2020).

[98] Standley, *supra* note 92.

The tension between biosafety and security, and research efficiency, also emerges in the domain of material transfer. Transferring samples between different institutions can facilitate effective surveillance, diagnostics, and research. However, concerns over biosafety and biosecurity often affect the transportation of biological materials when dangerous pathogens are involved. In July 2014, the National IHR Focal Point for Nigeria confirmed the first probable case of Ebola virus disease in the country. When a sample from the patient was supposed to be sent to the Institute Pasteur in Dakar, Senegal, courier companies refused to transport it.[99] The following month, the WHO similarly reported difficulties arising from airlines refusing to transport personal protective equipment.[100] In October of the same year, the diagnosis of a suspected Ebola patient from Canada was delayed for more than twenty-four hours, in part because an Air Canada pilot refused to fly with a blood specimen[101] (the patient ultimately tested negative for Ebola), and US military and UN planes reportedly made similar refusals.[102] Such incidents can complicate research efforts during and after an outbreak: The strict protocols associated with the transport of live samples affected the efforts of American institutions to obtain EBOV samples for research during the same outbreak.[103,104]

It is important to recognize that the actors in these situations may have had legitimate concerns about the safety and security of transporting or transferring pathogenic samples. The research applications of dangerous pathogens should not be used to justify a reduction of necessary biosafety and biosecurity standards. At the same time, however, these cases highlight the need for safety measures and guidelines that allow for effective and flexible transfer of materials, both within and between countries, when such transfer is necessary for diagnosis and research.

6.6 CONCLUSION AND RECOMMENDATIONS

Managing dangerous pathogens involves inherent dangers, not only to those directly handling biological materials but also to local and global communities vulnerable to an outbreak. To mitigate these dangers, it is necessary to place matters of biosafety

[99] World Health Organization, *WHO Disease outbreak news – Ebola virus disease, West Africa*, 31 July 2014, WHO (2014), www.who.int/csr/don/2014_07_31_ebola/en/ (last visited Feb. 18, 2020).

[100] World Health Organization, *WHO Ebola situation assessment, August 11 2014*, WHO (2014), www.who.int/mediacentre/news/ebola/overview-august-2014/en/ (last visited Feb. 18, 2020).

[101] CBC News & 2014, *Air Canada refuses to transport blood sample for Ebola test, delaying diagnosis*, CBC, October 17, 2014, www.cbc.ca/news/canada/edmonton/ebola-diagnosis-delayed-after-air-canada-refuses-to-transport-blood-sample-1.2803879 (last visited Feb. 18, 2020).

[102] Associated Press, *supra* note 5.

[103] Julie Steenhuysen, *U.S. Ebola researchers plead for access to virus samples*, REUTERS, November 5, 2014, at 1–5.

[104] Security concerns have not only been raised in the context of transporting samples. In the aftermath of the 2014–16 Ebola outbreak, several countries outside West Africa cited "biosafety and biosecurity concerns" or even reasons of "national security" as justifications for not disclosing information about their holdings of EBOV samples. See Freudenthal, *supra* note 4, as well as Hayden, *supra* note 11.

and biosecurity front and center in public health research. This task is incumbent on researchers, health workers, policymakers, and other stakeholders, who must address it in conjunction with the ethical, legal, and scientific issues that arise with all public health research. In this chapter, we have provided an overview of central biosafety and biosecurity issues relating to each stage of dangerous pathogen management, including the collection, storage, transfer, and use of potentially pathogenic samples. Our discussion has elucidated several steps that relevant stakeholders must take to promote safe and secure pathogen management.

While international agreements play an essential role in safeguarding global health security, they must be complemented by national regulations governing the management of dangerous pathogens. Countries without existing regulations should consider drafting and adopting comprehensive legislation concerning issues of both biosafety and biosecurity. Not only will such legislation be crucial to achieve biosafety and biosecurity objectives, but it will also give countries leverage in safeguarding their viral sovereignty. Interested parties should undertake an extensive review of existing legislative best practices to facilitate the creation of such legislation.

Resource constraints significantly hinder the ability of many countries to implement the International Health Regulations (2005) and other international laws with similar objectives. Notwithstanding existing initiatives like the World Bank's Regional Disease Surveillance Systems Enhancement project, there remains a need for robust financing mechanisms to strengthen the global capacity for preventing disease outbreaks before they occur. Importantly, funders must direct resources towards "horizontal" capacity-building, in addition to the prevalent "vertical" programs which address particular diseases. Furthermore, investments must focus on supporting sustainable initiatives and facilities that local stakeholders can maintain within the bounds of available technical capacity and resources.

Building robust health systems and research facilities in resource-limited settings is a costly and complicated process that cannot be accomplished overnight. Consequently, many public health research communities are bound to continue operating under severe resource constraints in the short-term. Policymakers and researchers must recognize that the task of managing dangerous pathogens should not be approached uniformly across the unique circumstances under which they exist. Instead, stakeholders must adopt a context-sensitive approach to reducing biosafety and biosecurity risks. By using evidence-based risk assessments and adapting solutions to the resources available, it is possible to manage pathogens cost effectively without compromising biosafety and biosecurity. Policymakers, academics, and health professionals are increasingly recognizing the importance of this approach, a fact which is reflected in the forthcoming WHO laboratory biosafety manual as well as other publications and projects. However, more work is needed to popularize the framework and to extend it to the domain of biosecurity.

In addition to being locally feasible, biosafety and biosecurity strategies must also be compatible with effective research practices. Although research into dangerous pathogens can yield vital insights for epidemic preparedness, these benefits should not be pursued at the expense of keeping biosecurity and biosafety risks at an acceptable level. As the history of H5N1 research and the smallpox virus retention debate show, striking this balance is both essential and complex. It involves developing guidelines for deliberate sample collection to ensure that enough samples are collected and retained for research applications without creating unnecessary biosafety and biosecurity risks. In the domain of biological material transfer, biosafety and biosecurity cannot be compromised when countries or couriers are justifiably concerned about shipping biological materials. At the same time, unwarranted apprehensions should not hinder the flexible exchange of samples for surveillance, diagnosis, and research.

Whenever dangerous biological materials are stored, transferred, or used for research, there exists a pronounced risk of accidental or deliberate spread of pathogens. To adequately reduce this risk, biosecurity and biosafety measures must be integrated into policy and research efforts before, during, and after epidemic outbreaks.[105]

---

[105]   Olivier De Schutter, *The Right of Everyone to Enjoy the Benefits of Scientific Progress and the Right to Food: From Conflict to Complementarity*, 33 HUMAN RIGHTS Q. 304, 311 (2011).

7

Human Rights Implications of Pathogen Sharing and Technology Transfer

Alexandra Phelan

7.1 INTRODUCTION

Both the rapid and comprehensive sharing of pathogens and the fair and equitable sharing of benefits arising from their use are central to the protection of global public health. As a result, international access and benefit sharing regimes pose significant challenges, and opportunities, for global public health, human rights, and justice. There is a broad array of human rights that may be implicated in pathogen sharing for individuals, including issues arising during the taking of samples, the use of experimental treatments during emergencies, informed consent, as well as fundamental issues relating to the rights of indigenous peoples and biodiversity. This chapter however takes a more conceptual view, focusing on pathogen sharing as it relates to the nature of state obligations under international law and how a human rights-based approach – in particular using the right to health as well as the right to science – may inform government policymaking in implementing or responding to the Nagoya Protocol.

This chapter briefly sets out the relevant international legal landscape for pathogen sharing, before taking an in-depth examination of the right to health. The chapter then examines the role of the right to health in access to pathogens and the sharing of benefits arising from their use, while considering the role that the right to science may also play in shaping state obligations. Finally, the chapter examines these issues within the broader colonial histories of both global health and international law and recommends contextualizing both access to pathogens and the sharing of benefits within human rights obligations of states in a manner that is cohesive, and non-fragmented, with other international agreements.

7.2 THE INTERNATIONAL LEGAL LANDSCAPE FOR PATHOGEN SHARING

Despite the centrality of pathogen and associated benefits sharing to global health, the protection of global public health is not the main objective of all access and benefit sharing regimes that apply to pathogens under international law. Entering into force in 2014, the Nagoya Protocol on Access to Genetic Resources and the Fair and Equitable Sharing of Benefits Arising from their Utilization to the Convention on Biological Diversity (Nagoya Protocol) expands on the recognition of viral sovereignty under the Convention on Biological Diversity and establishes an access and benefit sharing regime for genetic resources. The Nagoya Protocol is broadly, but not unanimously, considered to apply to human pathogens, posing challenges and opportunities for global public health.[1]

The Nagoya Protocol expressly links access to genetic resources with the sharing of benefits, facilitated, typically, by material transfer agreements. However, where there is a specialized international instrument for a specific genetic resource, consistent with the goals of the protocol, the Nagoya Protocol will not apply.[2] This allows for the adoption of specialized regimes that may operate on multilateral access to resources and benefit sharing, rather than bilateral arrangements, with material transfer agreements negotiated on a case by case basis. The express linkage between the sharing of pathogens as a genetic resource with global public health goods as benefits occurred in one of the more significant events for global health and pathogen sharing, when Indonesia withheld avian influenza A H5N1 samples from the global influenza surveillance network in 2007.[3] While this virus only demonstrated clustered and non-sustained transmission in humans, it was highly virulent in birds, raising concerns that it was a potential precursor to a human pandemic influenza. Indonesia based its decision on a claim of sovereignty over genetic resources found within its territory under Article 15 of the Convention on Biological Diversity.[4] Indonesia argued that

> Disease affected countries, which are usually developing countries, provide information and share biological specimens/virus with the WHO system; then PHARMACEUTICAL industries of developed countries obtain free access to this information and specimens, produce and patent the products (diagnostics, vaccines, therapeutics or other technologies), and sell them back to the developing countries at unaffordable prices.[5]

In response, in 2011, the World Health Assembly adopted the Pandemic Influenza Preparedness (PIP) Framework, which establishes an access and benefits sharing regime for the multilateral sharing of human influenza viruses with pandemic potential, and the equitable sharing of benefits, such as pandemic influenza vaccines. While the process for formal recognition under the Nagoya Protocol is still

---

[1] World Health Organization, *Implementation of the Nagoya Protocol and Pathogen Sharing: Public Health Implications. Study by the Secretariat* (2016).
[2] The Nagoya Protocol on Access and Benefit-Sharing (2010), Article 4(4).
[3] Endang R. Sedyaningsih et al., *Towards Mutual Trust, Transparency and Equity in Virus Sharing Mechanism: The Avian Influenza Case of Indonesia*, 37 ANN. ACAD. MED. SINGAP. 482 (2008).
[4] *Id.* at 485.
[5] *Id.* at 486.

ongoing, the PIP Framework is likely a specialized international instrument, carving pandemic influenza pathogens from the application of the Nagoya Protocol.

For non-influenza human pathogens, there is currently no specialized international instrument, meaning that where states implement the Nagoya Protocol domestically and, expressly or impliedly, include pathogens within their domestic legislation, it still applies to govern access and benefit sharing. This has implications for other international treaties that states are likely party to.

Under the International Health Regulations (2005) (IHR), states have obligations to prevent, detect, respond, and control the spread of international public health threats, including obligations to provide international assistance and cooperation. Similarly, under a range of international human rights treaties, in particular, the International Covenant on Economic, Social, and Cultural Rights, states have obligations to realize the right to health. States must be particularly cognizant of how these obligations are relevant to the operation of the Nagoya Protocol. The right to health provides a framework for accountability for these issues: Framing both the facilitation of access to pathogens and the sharing of benefits arising from their use as right to health issues.

7.3 THE INTERSECTION OF HUMAN RIGHTS AND PATHOGEN SHARING: THE RIGHT TO HEALTH

A common goal between access to pathogens and the sharing of benefits arising from their use is to improve global health through the prevention, detection, and control of infectious disease. The right to health, articulated under a number of international legal instruments, recognizes the right of everyone to the highest attainable standard of health, and the obligation on states to take measures to prevent and control infectious diseases. The right to health provides a framework for a mechanism for holding states accountable for these obligations, which include facilitating access to pathogens and the sharing of benefits arising from their use.

7.3.1 *The Origins of the Right to Health*

The earliest expression of a right to health in an international treaty is within the preamble of the WHO Constitution, providing that "[t]he enjoyment of the highest attainable standard of health is one of the fundamental rights of every human being without distinction of race, religion, political belief, economic or social condition."[6] While the WHO Constitution is a legally binding treaty on Member States, this expression of the right to health guides the interpretation and application of the organization's constitutive document as a principle rather than an explicit declaration of a directly actionable right. Two years after the adoption of the WHO

---

[6] World Health Organization, WHO Constitution, 2 OFF. REC. WLD HLTH ORG 100 (1948), preamble.

Constitution, the right to health was included in the Universal Declaration of Human Rights (UDHR).[7] While a non-binding resolution of the UN General Assembly, the UDHR is normatively influential and serves as the foundational instrument for international human rights law. Some scholars argue that the UDHR – in its entirety or part, including the right to health – has the status of customary international law, and is thus binding on all States.[8] However, the right to health is expressed in a number of international and regional human rights treaties, imposing binding legal human rights obligations on relevant States Parties.

7.3.2 *The Right to Health and Nature of State Obligations*

The most notable legal source for the right to health is Article 12 of the International Covenant on Economic, Social and Cultural Rights (ICESCR). Under Article 12, States Parties "recognize the right of everyone to the enjoyment of the highest attainable standard of physical and mental health."[9] The right to health under ICESCR is an inclusive right that is broader than the provision of health care, extending to the underlying determinants of health,[10] and expressly includes the prevention, treatment and control of epidemic and endemic diseases.[11]

The recognition of the right to health is coupled with a series of specific legal obligations that states respect, protect, and fulfill this right. In 2000, the UN Committee on Economic, Social and Cultural Rights (ESCR Committee), the treaty body for ICESCR, adopted General Comment 14, to assist with interpretive guidance for the content of these obligations as they pertain to the right to health.[12] Respecting the right to health requires states to refrain from denying or limiting access to health care services, products, and information, or unlawfully contributing to environmental threats to health.[13] This obligation would also include states refraining from directly or indirectly denying or limiting the availability, accessibility, acceptability, and quality of public health functions and goods necessary to prevent and respond to an infectious disease outbreak. The obligation to protect the right to health requires that states adopt laws or other measures that ensure third parties do not engage in practices that limit or deny the availability, accessibility, acceptability, and quality of health services and goods.[14] The duty on states to fulfill

---

[7] United Nations General Assembly, Universal Declaration of Human Rights, 302 UNGA RESOLUTION 217 A (III), Art. 25.

[8] Eiba Reidel, *The Human Right to Health: Conceptual Foundations, in* 3 MARY ROBINSON & ANDREW CLAPHAM, REALIZING THE RIGHT TO HEALTH 21, 22 (2009).

[9] International Covenant on Economic, Social and Cultural Rights, 993 U.N.T.S. 3 (1976), Article 12(1).

[10] Committee on Economic, Social and Cultural Rights, General Comment No. 14: The Right to the Highest Attainable Standard of Health (Art. 12), UN Doc. No. E/C.12/2000/4 (2000).

[11] International Covenant on Economic, Social and Cultural Rights, *supra* note 9, Article 12(2)(c).

[12] Committee on Economic, Social and Cultural Rights, *supra* note 10.

[13] *Id.* para. 34.

[14] *Id.* para. 35.

the right to health obliges states to take positive steps, such as through legislation and policies, to facilitate the enjoyment of the right to health.[15] In 2013, the Optional Protocol to ICESCR entered into force, providing individuals with a path for procedural justice and remedy for State Party violations of the right to health.[16]

Beyond ICESCR, a number of additional international human rights treaties establish obligations relating to the right to health. Addressing the particular vulnerabilities of children to violations of their rights, the Convention on the Rights of the Child recognizes children's right to health.[17] The right to health is further recognized under the Convention on the Elimination of all Forms of Racial Discrimination,[18] the Convention on the Elimination of Discrimination Against Women,[19] and the Convention on the Rights of Persons with Disabilities.[20] As a result of this broad recognition of the right to health under international law, every state on earth is a State Party to one or more treaties which contain the right to health.[21]

A number of regional human rights treaties, including the African Charter on Human and Peoples' Rights,[22] and the European Social Charter,[23] contain protections for the right to health. Beyond the international and regional legal sphere, the right to health is expressly recognized in more than seventy national constitutions,[24] either directly or indirectly through interpretation of other rights such as the right to life. This recognizes that the right to health is intrinsically interconnected upon the realization of human rights, including rights to life, nondiscrimination, the prohibition against torture, food, education, and science.[25]

7.3.3 *The Right to Health and the Global Challenge of Infectious Diseases*

As part of the right to health, states have an express obligation to take steps to prevent, treat, and control epidemic and endemic diseases.[26] This includes having capacities

---

[15] *Id.* para. 36.

[16] United Nations General Assembly, Optional Protocol to the International Covenant on Economic, Social and Cultural Rights, A/RES/63/117 (2013).

[17] United Nations General Assembly, Convention on the Rights of the Child, 1577 U.N.T.S. 3 (1990), Article 24.

[18] United Nations General Assembly, Convention on the Elimination of All Forms of Racial Discrimination, 660 U.N.T.S. 195 (1969), Article 5(e)(iv).

[19] United Nations General Assembly, Convention on the Elimination of All Forms of Discrimination Against Women, 1249 U.N.T.S. 13, Articles 11(1)(f) and 12.

[20] United Nations General Assembly, Convention on the Rights of Persons with Disabilities, A/RES/61/106, Article 25.

[21] Paul Hunt, *Interpreting the International Right to Health in a Human Rights-Based Approach to Health*, 18 HEALTH HUM RIGHTS 109, 111 (2016).

[22] Organization of African Unity, African Charter on Human and Peoples' Rights ("Banjul Charter"), OAU Doc. CAB/LEG/67/3 REV. 5, 21 I.L.M. 58 (1982) (1986), Article 16.

[23] Council of Europe, European Social Charter, 35 ETS (1965), Article 11.

[24] Jody Heymann et al., *Constitutional Rights to Health, Public Health and Medical Care: The Status of Health Protections in 191 Countries*, 8 GLOBAL PUBLIC HEALTH 639 (2013).

[25] Committee on Economic, Social and Cultural Rights, *supra* note 10, para. 3.

[26] International Covenant on Economic, Social and Cultural Rights, *supra* note 9, Article 12(1), 12(2)(c).

to conduct surveillance, laboratory capacity for detection, implementing control strategies, including deployment of preventative and responsive vaccinations and treatments.[27] Under General Comment 14, the ESCR Committee provides that the control of infectious diseases under the right to health includes "States' individual and joint efforts" in making relevant technologies available, and "using and improving epidemiological surveillance and data collection."[28] Each of these steps are dependent upon, and intertwined with, the sharing of pathogens, both domestically – to be able to meet these capacity obligations – and, in many cases, internationally – to fulfill the right to health through surveillance and the development of vaccines, diagnostics, and treatments.

There are also parallel international legal obligations requiring states to develop similar capacities to prevent, detect, and respond to infectious diseases. Under the IHR, States Parties must develop core capacities for a range of public health functions including surveillance, reporting, notification, verification, and response, and must implement these capacities with full respect for the dignity, human rights, and fundamental freedoms of persons.[29] These obligations are legally binding and immediately realizable, however States Parties' financial, technical, and political capacity to implement these obligations has meant that implementation of these core capacities globally is an ongoing process.

Under ICESCR, the principle of progressive realization means that states are required to take steps, to the maximum of available resources, to meet their obligations and progressively achieve the full realization of rights under the treaty.[30] However, certain obligations are immediately binding on states, such as ensuring nondiscrimination in guaranteeing rights under ICESCR,[31] as well as a states having minimum core obligations to ensure the satisfaction of "minimum essential levels" of rights under ICESCR.[32] The ESCR Committee has defined minimum core obligations under ICESCR to include access to health goods and services on a nondiscriminatory basis, access to sanitation and essential medicines, and equitable distribution of health goods and services.[33] The ESCR Committee further notes that taking measures to prevent, treat, and control epidemic and endemic diseases are of comparable priority with ensuring reproductive, maternal, and child health care, and providing immunization, education, and health care workforce

---

[27]   Gian Luca Burci & Riikka Koskenmäki, *Human Rights Implications of Governance Responses to Public Health Emergencies: The Case of Major Infectious Disease Outbreaks.*, in 3 ANDREW CLAPHAM & MARY ROBINSON, REALIZING THE RIGHT TO HEALTH 249, 517 (2009).

[28]   Committee on Economic, Social and Cultural Rights, *supra* note 10, para. 16.

[29]   World Health Organization, IHR 2005, 3rd edition RESOLUTION WHA 58.3 (2016), Article 3(1), 5, 6, 13, and Annex 1.

[30]   International Covenant on Economic, Social and Cultural Rights, *supra* note 9, art. 2(1).

[31]   *Id.*, art. 2(2).

[32]   Committee on Economic, Social and Cultural Rights, General Comment No. 3: The Nature of States Parties' Obligations (Art. 2, Para. 1, of the Covenant) UN Doc. No. E/1991/23 ¶ 10 (1990); Committee on Economic, Social and Cultural Rights, *supra* note 10, para. 43.

[33]   Committee on Economic, Social and Cultural Rights, *supra* note 10, para. 43.

training.[34] However, minimum core obligations and comparable obligations are limited in their capacity to provide sufficient guidance as to what steps states must take to implement these obligations.[35] Furthermore, while General Comment 14 emphasizes that it is "particularly incumbent" on wealthy States Parties to provide international assistance and cooperation to enable developing countries to fulfill their minimum core obligations and comparable obligations,[36] there is no process or "burden-sharing mechanism for managing this shared responsibility," potentially placing "financially unrealistic obligations on poorer countries."[37] This echoes similar issues with the IHR's Article 44 collaboration and assistance obligations, which lack clear processes for obtaining international assistance to meet core capacities and distributing the costs of capacity-building that benefit all.

Full realization of the right to health globally is highly dependent on international cooperation. As recognized in the Declaration of Alma-Ata, "existing gross inequality in the health status of people particularly between developed and developing countries as well as within countries is politically, socially and economically unacceptable and is, therefore, of common concern to all countries."[38] The obligation for international assistance and cooperation in realizing the right to health under ICESCR is particularly relevant for infectious diseases "given that some diseases are easily transmissible beyond the borders of a State" and as a result "the international community has a collective responsibility to address this problem," with "economically developed States parties hav[ing] a special responsibility and interest to assist the poorer developing States in this regard."[39] This highlights the rationale underpinning claims to a right to health, which are fundamentally "about the way power is distributed in society,"[40] and are in effect, "a claim to a distribution of power as a matter of entitlement."[41] As a result, while individuals may be the primary actors holding states to account for violations, framing issues through a human rights lens is not necessarily "espousing radical ethical individualism but rather as essential for the promotion of the common good."[42] There perhaps is no greater example of a common good than health: An individual's health being subject to influence by social, economic, and political determinants and systems, as well as the collective health of others locally, nationally, and globally. The collective endeavor required to ensure that goods and services for public health are available, accessible, acceptable,

---

[34] *Id.* para. 44.

[35] John Tobin, The Right to Health in International Law 240 (2012).

[36] Committee on Economic, Social and Cultural Rights, *supra* note 10, para. 45.

[37] Lisa Forman et al., *What Do Core Obligations under the Right to Health Bring to Universal Health Coverage?*, 18 Health Hum Rights 23, 29 (2016).

[38] Declaration of Alma-Ata International Conference on Primary Health Care, Alma-Ata, International Conference on Primary Health Care, Alma-Ata, USSR, Article II.

[39] Committee on Economic, Social and Cultural Rights, *supra* note 10, para. 40.

[40] J. Eekelaar, Family Law and Personal Life 30 (2017).

[41] J. Eekelaar, Family Law and Personal Life 137 (2006).

[42] Christopher McCrudden, *Human Dignity and Judicial Interpretation of Human Rights*, 19 Eur J Int Law 655, 662 (2008); as cited by Tobin, *supra* note 35, at 58.

and of sufficient quality further underpins the intertwining and interdependent elements of realizing the right to health.

7.4 REALIZATION OF THE RIGHT TO HEALTH AND ACCESS AND BENEFIT SHARING

Like the realization of the right to health, preparing and responding to global infectious disease threats are dependent on international cooperation, including both the global sharing of pathogen samples for a range of public health reasons, and the global sharing of public health goods, such as vaccines. As a number of public health goods are developed from the use of pathogen samples, such goods may be conceived of as benefits that arise from the utilization of genetic resources, bringing these issues into the realm of access and benefit sharing. This part examines the role of both accessing pathogen samples and benefits sharing in realizing the right to health, as well as the potential application of a right to science.

7.4.1 *The Right to Health and Access to Pathogens in Outbreak Preparedness and Response*

Applying a human rights lens to pathogen sharing illuminates the importance of access to pathogen samples across all stages of outbreak preparedness and response. Preventing infectious disease outbreaks relies on continuous surveillance to detect new cases of a disease. Surveillance requires continuous and comprehensive sample sharing. This includes taking clinical samples from unwell individuals that may confirm the presence of a known pathogen, a known pathogen that has mutated or developed resistance, or a previously unknown pathogen. This may be done routinely at the local level, with information communicated to subnational and national levels. Alternatively, if resources and capacities are limited or domestic laws or policies require certain pathogens be both notified and verified at higher levels, pathogen samples may be shared with other laboratories and institutions within a country. If a country does not have domestic resources or capacities to identify a pathogen, its subtype, or to conduct more complex analyses, including genetic sequencing, then pathogen samples may be sent to laboratories in the region or internationally. During health emergencies or outbreaks in low-resource settings, international response teams that have been brought in to assist in the response may collect and conduct initial testing of clinical and pathogen samples. In practice, responders may send the data, clinical, or pathogen samples back to their own country or to other institutions. As technology develops and reduces in cost, this may also include conducting advanced analyses in the field such as genetic sequencing, which in turn helps inform risk assessments. While building national capacities and technological advancements may reduce sending physical samples internationally, pathogen samples are still necessary for a range of other outbreak preparedness and response activities.

Access to pathogen samples is fundamental to the development, testing, and manufacturing of medical countermeasures such as vaccines, treatments, and diagnostics.[43] Typically, vaccines require access to a pathogen sample to obtain an attenuated virus or to obtain the necessary antigens for while there have been advancements in the potential for synthetic vaccines,[44] they still rely on pathogen samples within the process to obtain genetic sequence data, are not yet approved in any market, and mass production is not yet demonstrated. While these are not insurmountable issues, pathogen samples are still generally necessary for continuous assessment of the efficacy of countermeasures in response to inherent tendency to mutate or the development of resistance.

7.4.2 *Benefit Sharing and the Realization of Human Rights*

While access to pathogen samples has significant implications for global public health, and in turn the realization of the right to health, so too does the fair and equitable sharing of benefits that arise from the use of these pathogens. As described above, pathogen samples are used for the development of a range of potential benefits relevant to global public health, including risk assessments, vaccines, diagnostics, and other treatments, such as antivirals. However, there are indirect benefits that arise from the use of pathogens that go beyond tangible public health goods, including royalties and intellectual property from products developed, recognition or acknowledgment in publications, grants, or other academic forums, technology transfer (including both know how and hard technology), and other forms of capacity building.[45]

The Nagoya Protocol, facilitated in practice by the use of material transfer agreements, directly links sample sharing to benefits sharing and provider to recipient. This process does not necessarily ensure guarantee of the right to health, or fulfilment of international assistance obligations under the IHR or ICESCR. The PIP Framework seeks to address benefit sharing on a needs basis, with benefits – including pandemic vaccines and antivirals – to be expressly distributed on a "public health risk and needs" basis, particularly for developing or affected countries that do not have their own domestic capacities to produce vaccines, antivirals, and diagnostics.[46] This decouples the directly transactional relationship,

---

[43] Sam Halabi and Saad Omer, *Evidence, Strategies, and Challenges for Assuring Vaccine Availability, Efficacy, and Safety*, in GLOBAL MANAGEMENT OF INFECTIOUS DISEASE AFTER EBOLA (Sam Halabi, Lawrence Gostin, & Jeffrey Crowley eds., 2016).

[44] P. R. Dormitzer et al., *Synthetic Generation of Influenza Vaccine Viruses for Rapid Response to Pandemics*, 5 SCIENCE TRANSLATIONAL MEDICINE 185ra68 (2013).

[45] The Nagoya Protocol on Access and Benefit-sharing, *supra* note 2, Article 5(4), Annex.

[46] WHA, Pandemic Influenza Preparedness Framework for the Sharing of Influenza Viruses and Access to Vaccines and Other Benefits (2018), Article 6.0.2.

for an approach that prioritizes global health and conceptualizes access and benefits as intrinsically linked through a right to health lens.

However, in the absence of a specialized international instrument for non-pandemic influenza pathogens, the Nagoya Protocol still largely applies. In examining benefits sharing for non-pandemic influenza pathogens, other applicable human rights may help guide the development of an access and benefits sharing regime that may be recognized as a specialized international instrument.

Despite being relatively unexamined in the literature and by treaty bodies,[47] the Right to Enjoy the Benefits of Scientific Progress and its Applications (known as REBSPA or the right to science) is slowly gaining prominence. The right to science is expressly set out under the UDHR (Article 27) and the ICESCR (Article 15(1)(b)) however the ESCR Committee has not yet produced a General Comment or similar instrument providing interpretive guidance on the right's scope or application.[48] The United Nations Special Rapporteur in the Field of Cultural Rights, Farida Shaheed, has proposed that the right to science includes access to all of the benefits of science by all, without discrimination, opportunities to contribute to scientific enterprise and the freedoms necessary for that goal by all, participatory decision-making, and an enabling environment for scientific development and diffusion.[49] The intersection between the right to science and benefits sharing has been broadly discussed and recognized within the context of the environment, biodiversity, and climate change,[50] however human health, and benefits sharing and the right to health, are also particularly intertwined. While not expressly recognized in the text itself as a right to health issue, this is implicit in the operation of the PIP Framework. The PIP Framework operates as not simply an access and benefits sharing regime but a governance instrument for international assistance and cooperation; intertwining the realization of the right to health through pandemic influenza preparedness and response, the right to science, and benefits-sharing.

There is significant potential, as a result, for "cross-fertilization" between human rights, including the right to health and the right to science, and benefits-sharing for non-pandemic influenza pathogens under the Nagoya Protocol.[51] While not

---

[47] Audrey R. Chapman, *Towards an Understanding of the Right to Enjoy the Benefits of Scientific Progress and Its Applications*, 8 JOURNAL OF HUMAN RIGHTS 1, 1 (2009). Chapman notes "this right is so obscure and its interpretation so neglected that the overwhelming majority of human rights advocates, governments, and international human rights bodies appear to be oblivious to its existence."

[48] The ESCR Committee has noted the potential for a future General Comment on the right to science.

[49] United Nations Human Rights Council, Report of the Special Rapporteur in the Field of Cultural Rights: The Right to Enjoy the Benefits of Scientific Progress and Its Applications. UN Doc A/HRC/20/26 ¶ 25 (2012).

[50] *Id.* para. 67; See also: Elisa Morgera, *Fair and Equitable Benefit-Sharing at the Cross-Roads of the Human Right to Science and International Biodiversity Law*, 4 LAWS 803 (2015); and Alexandra Phelan, *Climate Change and Human Rights: Intellectual Property Challenges and Opportunities*, in INTELLECTUAL PROPERTY AND CLEAN ENERGY (Rimmer ed., 2018).

[51] For a discussion of this intersection between the right to science and international biodiversity laws, see: Morgera, *supra* note 50.

binding, the UN Special Rapporteur formulation of the right to science describes a right to "access" the benefits of science, however *sharing* the benefits of science, describes a more active, participatory, engagement in science and its benefits for all, not simply scientists or those directly receiving pathogen samples.[52] This interpretation is also consistent with the language of the UDHR and the preparatory materials for the drafters of the ICECSR.[53] Interpreting of the content of the right to science in a manner that informs the nature of benefits sharing under the Nagoya Protocol, may not only serve to reduce potential fragmentation between fields of international law and ensure coherence between international human rights law and international environmental laws, but also reinforce realization of the right to health.

7.4.3 *Moving Beyond Access and Benefit Sharing Tensions: Capacity Building As Synergy with Human Rights*

Capacities and resources to use pathogen samples for prevention, detection, and response vary significantly between states. Consequentially, states rely on the rapid and comprehensive sharing of pathogen samples regionally and internationally to adequately achieve each of these goals. Realization of the right to health, within a state and in other states, is dependent on pathogens being shared, while withholding pathogen samples, with the knowledge of, or deliberate blindness to, the potential global health implications of such action, risks undermining the global realization of the right to health. As with any other resource a state may have sovereignty over, a human rights-based approach requires that states respect, protect, and fulfill the right to health in the governance of such resources. This is held in conjunction with a state's obligation to respect, protect, and fulfill the right to health in relation to the benefits that arise from the use of such resources.

Respecting the right to health requires that states do not withhold pathogen samples where sharing is necessary to conduct public health preparedness and response activities, such as surveillance and vaccine development. However, it is possible that such samples do not need to be shared internationally to achieve these goals where a state domestically has the capacity to adequately conduct these activities and produce goods. Where a state does have such capacities, realizing the right to health requires the sharing of these benefits internationally, even if an access and benefits sharing regime is focused on more narrow obligations between provider and recipient. Where a state does not have domestic capacities due to resource constraints that prevent it from fulfilling its obligations under the right to health and IHR, it is incumbent on other states, through their parallel obligations under ICESCR and the IHR, to provide international assistance and cooperation to build these capacities.

---

[52] *Id.* sec. 4.1.
[53] Chapman, *supra* note 47, at 5–6.

As historical examples have demonstrated, like state obligations related to the right to health, focus is often on the obligations of developing countries to provide access to samples, and not on the equal obligations on developed countries to provide financial and technical international assistance and cooperation, and benefit sharing. For both human rights and access and benefit sharing regimes, these counterweighing obligations need to be conceived as equally important for advancing global health equity and justice.

7.5 CONCEPTUAL FRAMING OF GLOBAL HEALTH THROUGH VIRAL SOVEREIGNTY AND HUMAN RIGHTS

Enumerating the human rights affected by pathogen sharing and benefits for their use, unpacks the obligations upon states to respect, protect, and fulfill these rights.[54] By defining these obligations within a human rights framework, states can then be more readily held accountable with meeting these standards. Accountability can be an equivocal term, indicating potential blame or associated punishment. This is reflected in Member States' hesitation to include it in the language of treaties during negotiations.[55] However, accountability is "the raison d'être of the rights-based approach."[56] Under international human rights law, this accountability is typically directed at states, being the primary duty-bearers. Similarly, states are typically conceived as holding a primary duty to the people within their borders. In practice, states draw a further distinction between the rights afforded to citizens compared with noncitizen residents, migrants, refugees, asylum seekers, temporary visitors, and undocumented individuals.[57] This is despite the principle of equality under international human rights law, which permits exceptional distinctions only where it serves a legitimate objective and is reasonable and proportionate to the achievement of that objective.[58]

---

[54] Committee on Economic, Social and Cultural Rights, *supra* note 10.
[55] For example, during the negotiations for a new international instrument on the conservation and sustainability of marine environments in areas beyond national jurisdiction, including consideration of an access and benefits sharing regime for marine genetic resources, the Australian delegates said: In relation to draft text, article 5 – general [principles] [and] [approaches], sub-article [(e) "Ensure accountability]," Australia intervened to add that "we support transparency but we would prefer for the principle to be embedded in the principles of the agreement, rather than be reflected as a general approach." When further clarity was sought by the Facilitator, Australia responded, "the accountability part was a question we had as to what that was intended to capture. Was it something more than transparency? What the principle was? ... For us the bottom line is that we don't think that it's a provision that needs to be reflected [in article 5]." [Authors notes as observer, 5.18PM, 28 August 2019, United Nations New York, Committee Room 4.]
[56] Malcolm Langford, *Claiming the Millennium Development Goals: A Human Rights Approach* (United Nations, Office of the High Commissioner for Human Rights 2008) 15; as cited, and reinforced by, Alicia Ely Yamin, Power, Suffering, and the Struggle for Dignity: Human Rights Frameworks for Health and Why They Matter 133 (2015).
[57] David Weissbrodt, *The Rights of Non-Citizens* (United Nations, Office of the High Commissioner for Human Rights 2006) 7.
[58] HRC, CCPR General Comment No. 18: Non-Discrimination ¶ 13 (1989).

Beyond this domestic inequality, international inequities have been embedded in the structures of both global health and international law. Conceptually, access and benefit sharing regimes echo the rationales that underpin claims to a right to health, which similarly seek to address the way power is distributed within global society, through a claim to sovereignty over resources, rather than a claim to an individual's rights.

Both global health and human rights have been at the forefront of demonstrating the limits of state sovereignty under international law. Both have particular relevance for pathogen access and benefits sharing. The revision of the International Health Regulations in 2005 has been described as the beginnings of a "new public health world order."[59] While the revised IHR broadened the scope beyond historical regulations that focused on a specific set of diseases to an "all-hazards" approach, the IHR also had significant implications for state sovereignty. Under the revised IHR, the WHO is empowered to receive reports of potential public health emergencies of international concern from unaffected states and non-state sources.[60] The WHO is also empowered to seek verification of these reports from potentially affected states,[61] and, in specific circumstances, the WHO Director-General is empowered to declare a public health emergency of international concern.[62] Unlike previous iterations of the IHR which gave primacy to state sovereignty in limiting the WHO's action to state-reported events, the acceptance by WHO Member States of this new regime demonstrated "a subtle but undeniable dilution of sovereign control" over the global governance of threats to global public health.[63] In 2019, the extent of acceptance of this dynamic was tested when Tanzania refused to share clinical samples with the WHO to demonstrate the absence of Ebola cases in that country.[64] However, this public callout highlighted the significant shift in perceptions of sovereignty over potential domestic health threats that have global implications.

Similarly, international human rights law is often framed as being in direct tension with state sovereignty requiring reconciliation.[65] While international human rights law seeks to govern the relations between a state and individuals

[59] The Lancet Infectious Diseases, *A New Public Health World Order*, 4 THE LANCET INFECTIOUS DISEASES 475 (2004).
[60] World Health Organization, *supra* note 29, Articles 6 and 9.
[61] *Id.*, Article 10.
[62] *Id.*, Article 12.
[63] *Id.*, Article 18.
[64] WHO accuses Tanzania of withholding information about suspected Ebola cases – The Washington Post, www.washingtonpost.com/world/tanzanias-refusal-to-acknowledge-possible-ebola-casesrepresents-a-challenge-who/2019/09/22/70bf9a80-dd19-11e9-be96-6adb81821e90_story.html.
[65] Hélène Ruiz Fabri, *Human Rights and State Sovereignty: Have the Boundaries Been Significantly Redrawn?*, in HUMAN RIGHTS, INTERVENTION, AND THE USE OF FORCE 33, 33 (Philip Alston & Euan Macdonald eds., 2008).

within its territory, sovereignty may be used to justify excluding the international community from oversight from a state's actions.[66] However, the sovereignty of a state is central to the provision of the conditions that enable the protection and fulfilment of human rights, granting the state authority over third parties.[67] Claims to state sovereignty have also been an element in the process of the realization of human rights, such as self-determination.

In the first generation of the Third World approaches to international law (TWAIL) movement, sovereignty was a goal that marked independence and autonomy from colonialism. The movement critiqued international law's role in facilitating colonialism and the justification for the exploitation of developing countries' natural resources, by colonial powers and other developed nations.[68] This recognized the way in which colonizers wielded international law to legitimize subjugation of peoples in Third World countries and the movement in turn sought to use core principles of international law to achieve self-determination and justice.[69] This was largely done through engagement with the United Nations' system and its principles of the "sovereign equality of all its Members."[70] As S. K. Agrawala reflected in 1977, developing countries recognized during the emergence of TWAIL that "their newly-won independence can become meaningful only when the benefits of [progress in science and technology] are shared equitably by them ensuring them an existence with dignity."[71]

The applicability of these issues for pathogen sharing means that claims to sovereignty over genetic resources must be made in a manner consistent with state obligations under international human rights law: Both for facilitating access to pathogens for global health, and in the fair and equitable distribution of benefits arising from their use. The interconnection and interdependence of global health go beyond the capacities of individual states, requiring international assistance and cooperation *in all directions*: Recognizing that when it comes to infectious diseases, we already live in a global society. Conceptualizing this global society "on the principles of human rights and the logic of health interdependence"[72] can occur while also upholding the crucial role of the sovereign state as the primary duty bearer in guaranteeing the right to health, especially against third parties, and as a bulwark against neocolonialism in global health.

---

[66] *Id.* at 34.
[67] Wim De Ceukelaire & Marc Johan Botenga, *On Global Health: Stick to Sovereignty*, 383 THE LANCET 951 (2014); cf Julio Frenk et al., *From Sovereignty to Solidarity: A Renewed Concept of Global Health for an Era of Complex Interdependence*, 383 THE LANCET 94 (2014).
[68] Andrea Bianchi, *Third World Approaches, in* INTERNATIONAL LAW THEORIES 211 (2016).
[69] Antony Anghie & B. S. Chimni, *Third World Approaches to International Law and Individual Responsibility in Internal Conflicts*, 2 CHINESE JOURNAL OF INTERNATIONAL LAW 77, 80 (2003).
[70] United Nations, UN Charter, 1 UNTS XVI (1945), Art. 2(1).
[71] S. K. Agrawala, *The Emerging International Economic Order*, 17 INDIAN JOURNAL OF INTERNATIONAL LAW 261, 261 (1977).
[72] Frenk et al., *supra* note 67.

7.6 CONCLUSION: A HUMAN RIGHTS-BASED APPROACH TO FACILITATING ACCESS TO PATHOGENS AND BENEFIT SHARING

Decoupling access to pathogens from the sharing of benefits may go towards removing the transactional nature of current access and benefit sharing regimes. In the absence of novel, concerted multilateral commitments to ensure fair and equitable distribution of global public health goods, such as vaccines, diagnostics, and treatments, there is a risk that access to these goods reverts to charity. Moving beyond charity to empowerment and accountability can be facilitated by the right to health, which provides a framework for a mechanism for holding all states accountable for their obligations, including both facilitating access to pathogens and the sharing of benefits arising from their use. This accountability is further found in the obligations under ICESCR, the IHR, and the Nagoya Protocol's benefits sharing options, to provide international assistance and cooperation to empower and build capacities to meet international obligations. Going forward, a multilateral instrument for non-influenza pathogens will likely be necessary to ensure global health security and the right to health. Such an instrument should be recognized as a specialized international instrument under the Nagoya Protocol, expressly cognizant of obligations under the IHR, and grounded in the right of all persons to the highest attainable standard of health.

Using a human rights framework to examine health is to call for us each to imagine a different, more just, world.[73] While access and benefits sharing seek to achieve this, a human rights-based approach to pathogen sharing obligations, in particular one grounded in the right to health and the right to science, may provide a more cohesive, more comprehensive, pathway to global health with justice.[74]

---

[73] YAMIN, *supra* note 56, at 231.
[74] www.industrydocumentslibrary.ucsf.edu/tobacco/docs/#id=lhxcoo39 and www.wipo.int/edocs/mdocs/copyright/en/sccr_18/sccr_18_5.pdf.

PART III

Solutions: Standard Material Transfer Agreements, Repositories, and Specialized International Instruments

8

Material Transfer Agreements and the Regulation of the Collaborative Environment

Sherry Brett-Major

Sharing data, samples, and cooperatively pursuing analysis among researchers from different institutions is increasingly normal practice. The notion of a solitary researcher in a paper-filled office working on a problem for years has been replaced by a vision of a team of vibrant and inquiring specialists who share ideas, expertise, and materials. Indeed, if collaboration is important to new discovery, then continuing to facilitate these collaborative efforts is critical. Undertaking projects with the expectation of a beneficial end product requires a carefully defined course where details are explained and good working relationships are fostered. Whether cooperating in one's own country or internationally, it is of particular importance to fully define the expectations of the entire program cycle – this includes the responsibilities of each party from the beginning of the project through to the end of the project. Who supplies materials? Who has ownership and bears the responsibility of liability for those materials? Who controls publication and timing? Who controls the methods of intellectual property documentation and at what stage? What monetary benefits are expected in return for what supplies? All of these questions should be answered from the outset of a course of research. Internationally, and sometimes within a country spanning distinct provinces, differences in customs, expectations, and laws should be noted so that all parties are clear in their understanding. Documents such as material transfer agreements (MTAs) serve to define the expectations of all who embark in a program of cooperative study. In this capacity, they can encourage proactive sharing, and also protect a researcher in a strained relationship. Although this chapter focuses on Material Transfer Agreements (MTA) between research entities, the actuality is that these agreements may occur when the parties are ministries, governmental agencies, nongovernmental organizations, research institutions, private industry, or a lone scientist requesting materials while on a quest to solve a problem. The characteristic provisions of MTAs may occur in a variety of documents such as a Collaborative Agreement or License to Use Unpatented Technology, but regardless of the name, the same options for managing expectations apply.

A Material Transfer Agreement (MTA) is a contract where material is supplied to another entity – usually a researcher or

| MTA is a form of contract. |

institution. Occasionally, such sharing is treated by institutions as a simple transaction, but increasingly longer-term arrangements are sought, similar to those established under cooperative agreements. These agreements should be signed by someone with authority to bind an institution to the agreement, and all provisions in the agreement should be understood by relevant parties before the material is transferred. If the ethos of contracting is transparency, then MTAs serve as a reminder of what the parties intended from the outset of a project, and internationally this may serve to resolve arguments before they become more serious. For example, in 2012, as Middle East respiratory syndrome coronavirus (MERS-CoV) became a high profile infectious disease threat, the use of an MTA by Erasmus University in an attempt to direct the way that specimens from Saudi Arabia were employed drew controversy. Viewed from the lens of cooperation and transparency, the MTA may have served its purpose. The intent of Erasmus was clear, and Saudi Arabia had an opportunity to intervene.[1] The documentation surrounding each action included not only an MTA but also a clear paper trail that enabled the subsequent dispute to be resolved in the courts; thus bringing the matter to a quick resolution and avoiding a more serious international incident. As MTAs become more common in research, it is tempting to view them as perfunctory and nearly meaningless with boilerplate language that can be disregarded; to the contrary, as one judge put in a decision on a case regarding the importance of an MTA to a researcher's claim, "Plaintiffs contend this was just a boilerplate document used to transfer two programs to a joint research project … however, the language on the face of the document speaks for itself."[2] Each of the provisions in these agreements has an important meaning that should be understood by the parties involved, because agreeing to the terms of these contracts means that a continuing relationship has been formed. This makes the act of signing an MTA very different from making a purchase from a supply house. After a sale, further dealings between the parties are not necessarily expected and certain consumer laws apply, whereas a transfer of material under an MTA forms a relationship between the parties where the terms of the MTA control.

8.1 MATERIAL TRANSFER AGREEMENTS ARE CONTRACTS

An MTA is an agreement and a contract (all contracts are agreements, but generally under the law of US states and the US federal government, not all agreements are contracts). A valid contract requires an offer, an acceptance of that offer,

---

[1] Laurie Garrett, Council on Foreign Relations, *Why a Saudi Virus Is Spreading Alarm* (ForeignAffairs .com May 29, 2013), available at www.cfr.org/expert-brief/why-saudi-virus-spreading-alarm.

[2] Rouse v. Walter & Associates, L.L.C., 513 F.Supp.2d 1041 (S.D. Iowa, 2007) at 1070.

consideration, and an intent to be bound. In legal terms, an offer presents an option. Acceptance is agreeing to that option. Consideration is something of value that is bargained for; it is a motivator in an exchange; it may be a promise; it may be an action. Intent to be bound means that all parties to the agreement will fully execute their promise made under the terms of the bargain; it is also referred to as a meeting of the minds. A good contract is a recorded version of the expectations of the parties, consequently, transparency and mutual understanding are very important.

MTAs are sometimes considered to be a type of contract known as a bailment, where the physical possession of an object transfers from one entity to another but the title or ownership does not transfer with it. MTAs are sometimes considered to be a license whereby an entity is granted permission to do something that might otherwise be a violation of the original owner's rights. Whether you consider an MTA to be a bailment, a license, or something in between . . . without it, you have a gift, and with it you have use of material with expectations defined by the document.

The MTA is likely not the only legal document involved in a research project. In order to avoid discord, an MTA should work harmoniously with other documents such as an employment contract, cooperative research agreement (CRA/CRADA), memorandum of understanding (MOU), memorandum of agreement (MOA), and other guiding documents. Use of these documents is advised because relationships are tricky. Even gifts can result in arguments and litigation, so using MTAs can serve to explain in advance the parties' expectations and maintain good working relationships.

8.2 DISPUTING MATERIAL TRANSFER AGREEMENTS UNDER US LAW

Sometimes relationships break down, and parties are surprised when their expectations are not met. While there are several steps

> Violation of expectations results in litigation.

parties may take if their expectations are not fulfilled (including negotiation, mediation, conciliation, and arbitration), one solution is to assert their legal rights in court – litigation. In US litigation, the first step is to establish jurisdiction, because in order for a court to rule on a controversy in the US, they must first have the authority to bind the litigants to a decision. If the case involves interpretation of patent claims, the case may be decided by a patent trial and appeal board. In other cases, federal court is proper if the suit involves federal law, intellectual property, or involves citizens of different states with a controversy in excess of $75,000.

In some cases, both federal and state law apply, allowing the parties to choose where the case is heard. A party to the case may request summary judgment which allows a judge to rule on an issue where there is no question of material fact, and the petitioner to the judge (movant) may prevail as a matter of law. This procedure allows a case (or portions of a case in partial summary judgment) to be decided quickly and without a trial. If the judge denies summary judgment, then the case may proceed further into what most people think of as a court action or trial. None of this is unique to the US justice system. However, the laws themselves, the ways that judicial and extra-judicial processes (like patent appeal boards in the US) interact, and the extent of judicial discretion will differ. Going to litigation means that control of the outcome no longer rests with the parties, but rather in the hands of a judicial official or some other panel or jury. So, just as an MTA may provide a remedy to a breakdown in trust by guiding the outcome of litigation, it also serves to enable proactive discourse between parties because everyone has a vested interest in resolving the dispute on their terms.

8.3 MTA COMPLAINTS AND SOLUTIONS

The most common criticisms of MTAs are that (1) the legal approval process takes too long, (2) the reach-through provisions are onerous and daunting, and (3) the parties and researchers are not really sure what they are agreeing will happen to the material.

To keep research and commercial collaborators out of litigation and maintain good working relationships, commonly used agreement templates have been refined over time. However, there remain some complaints about the use of MTAs, and positions vary widely by agency and entity. The National Research Council in the United States holds the position that MTAs take too long to evaluate and are an unnecessary drain on resources.[3]Other institutions take a different approach and advocate use of a single document with little variation. The National Institutes of Health produced a template that is widely used – the Uniform Biological Material Transfer Agreement, which is detailed more thoroughly in Chapter 10.[4] It can be used as is, but it is designed for institutions to agree on terms in advance of a research project, and for all participating institutions to use the same agreement. Underlying this idea was the notion that when all parties know what to expect in an arrangement, there is minimal legal processing and the turnaround time for approval is brief.[5]

[3]   Commission on Life Sciences, National Research Council, Finding the Path issues of access to research sources chapter 3 (National Academy Press 1999), available at www.nap.edu/read/9629/chapter/3$5; AUTM, Material Transfer Agreements (MTAs) in Research, https://autm.net/surveys-and-tools/agreements/material-transfer-agreements.

[4]   AUTM, Uniform Biological Material Transfer Agreement, https://autm.net/surveys-and-tools/agreements/material-transfer-agreements/mta-toolkit/uniform-biological-material-transfer-agreement.

[5]   United States Public Health Service, United States Public Health Service Technology Transfer Policy Manual, chapter 502 (2012), available at www.ott.nih.gov/sites/default/files/documents/policy/pdfs/502-Policy.pdf.

International organizations have been more circumspect in their approach to MTAs. The World Intellectual Property Organization (WIPO) may reference MTAs with other contracts and cooperative agreements, and has several options for topics to include in an MTA. In addition, they have MTA templates for specific circumstances and to reflect inputs of the various stakeholders who contributed to the final version.[6] The World Health Organization (WHO) has several MTA templates that are not uniform, but are considered to guide a basic agreement that should be altered according to the parties involved and the research project under consideration. The WHO provides an MTA tool for general use, but also has specific forms for particular research areas such as can be found in the malaria material request form, Pandemic Influenza Preparedness Framework (PIP Framework) MTA, SMTA 1, and SMTA 2 (S is for standard and contains the basic provisions for customizing agreements).[7]

Reach-through provisions confer benefits to the provider of material when the recipient realizes value. Such benefits include either royalties on future product sales or an exclusive license in pro-

---

Common MTA pitfalls
- Takes too long
- Onerous reach-through provisions
- No mutual understanding

---

ducts developed using the subject material of the MTA. These provisions have come under scrutiny, yet remain common in MTAs. Researchers tend to be less concerned about these provisions from the outset of a project; however, they are the source of delays within institutional offices of technology transfer as interests and their necessary details must be aligned before a project can move forward.

As a reach-through provision, licensing can take several forms. An exclusive license grants to a single entity the right to practice an invention in a specific field of use. Difficulty arises when multiple suppliers request exclusive licenses and do not agree to anything less. At that point, a researcher must either choose among materials or attempt yet another round of negotiations. A nonexclusive license grants to multiple entities the right to use an invention. Allowing multiple parties into the operational landscape makes some institutions hesitant because so many participants might dilute the brand or make the product less attractive for manufacture. Further, some parties, investors, or funders to a project demand exclusive licenses and are

---

[6] World Intellectual Property Organization, Standard Material Transfer Agreement: International Treaty for Plant Genetic Resources for Food and Agriculture (ITPGRFA), available at www .wipo.int/tk/en/databases/contracts/texts/smta.html.
[7] World Health Organization, www.who.int/ (last accessed April 2019).

discouraged by the possibility of not controlling their market share of a potential product.

The alternative to licensing is royalty payments. This may seem an attractive option for an invention in a high-risk market. As a reach-through provision, it assumes that a marketable product will result and guarantees payment to a provider of raw material if there is a downstream sale. Difficulty arises when the addition of reach-through royalties begins to stack from several contributions to an eventual product, resulting in significantly increased prices or even claims of interfering with market competition. In Europe, there is a possibility of such structures running afoul of Article 81 of the Treaty of Rome.[8] While in Australia, there is some academic discussion of reach-through provisions and their impact on section 51 of the Trade Practices Act.[9] Despite arguments, currently they are a valid provision in contracts and are commonly agreed to.

Despite the disadvantages and concerns discussed above, reach-through provisions can be used as a cost-shifting device for a research institution. Instead of immediately charging an institution to use a research tool (the subject of the MTA), a reach-through provision provides that payment will be made through a return on future products resulting from use of the supplied material. So, with reach-through provisions, the initial cost of a research project is lower, and if the research results in a small product with modest return, the cost of the supplied material was a license or downstream royalty – a cost that many research institutions are willing to grant.

Another common concern among researchers who encounter MTAs is that they may not fully understand what they are signing. International issues, differences in language and custom, as well as a lack of knowledge of local applicable laws, can be overcome but it requires extensive preparation. It is incumbent on all parties to an agreement to take the time to fully understand the document to which they will be bound. Knowledge of laws and treaties is essential and adequate translation may be desired for a satisfactory outcome and complete understanding on the part of all entities involved. Often, negotiation of the details of these agreements are performed at an administrative level and not by individual researchers; however, that process should not result in a perfunctory or cavalier perception on the part of the researcher. Individual researchers should care about details from the outset of defining the bounds of a project in an MTA if they expect to invoke those rights at the end of a project.

International negotiations can be complicated by unmentioned expectations. For example, the Nagoya Protocol stipulates guidelines for actions and access to

---

[8]   Bristows, *Reach-Through Licensing in Europe* (September 7, 2001) available at www.bristows.com /news-and-publications/articles/reach-through-licensing-in-europe/.

[9]   Jane Nielsen, *Reach-Through Rights in Biomedical Patent Licensing: A Comparative Analysis of their Anti-Competitive Reach*, 8 FedLawRw (2004); 32(2) Federal Law Review 169 (2004) (Austl) available at http://classic.austlii.edu.au/au/journals/FedLawRw/2004/8.html.

resources;[10] although benefits sharing is not a required component of an MTA, assurances recorded in a formal document may provide a better understanding of the intent of each party from the outset of a project.[11] Explanation of terms and benefits also provides understanding of expectations from countries that may not be signatories to the Convention on Biological Diversity.

In finding a solution to common pitfalls, entities have evaluated MTAs and recommended core elements for making these agreements effective.

8.4 CORE ELEMENTS OF AN EFFECTIVE MTA

Legal documents should have a clearly stated purpose with important details that are worded simply but balanced with complete intent. In drafting agreements, many attorneys and contracts specialists are trained to use few sentences but many words in an attempt to predict and solve every possible scenario that might apply to the use of the materials and projects that may be performed in the future. The result is tortured phrases and lengthy provisions that require multiple readings to understand, but sometimes the most useful provision is *communication*. Communication avoids the violation of expectation that surprises bring. When an entity is essentially the caretaker for another's material – when they are allowed to use but not abuse their rights as possessor – simple and complete agreements may be preferable. The MTA does not necessarily represent a singular opportunity to communicate, so state the intent clearly, modify minor statements as necessary, and abide by the terms that were agreed upon. Long documents with complex provisions actually decrease readability, so simplicity can at times be advantageous as shorter documents are easier to track.[12]

CORE ELEMENTS OF AN EFFECTIVE MTA

   I. Parties to the agreement
     a. Ensure that material is specified
  II. Definition section
 III. Use of the material. Property and rights
     a. Custodianship of the original material
     b. Ownership of data
     c. Requirements to obtain permission to distribute
     d. Sharing of information – permission

---

[10]   United Nations, Convention on Biological Diversity, *Text of the Nagoya Protocol*, available at www .cbd.int/abs/text/ (last accessed April 2019).
[11]   Research Council of Norway, SEA-EU-NET, EU FP7 Contract 311784, Material Transfer Agreements: a Multipurpose Tool for International Cooperation (2014), page 8.
[12]   Tania Bubela et al., *Use and Misuse of Material Transfer Agreements: Lessons in Proportionality from Research, Repositories, and Litigation*, PLoS Biol. (Feb 3, 2015), DOI:10.1371/journal.pbio.1002060.

(*CONT.*)

     e. Restrictions on use
        i. Only by the person specified
        ii. Use only for the research specified
        iii. Human use restrictions
     f. Cost recovery for storage and transportation
IV. Liability
     a. Safety warnings if material is hazardous
     b. Warranty
     c. Information privacy protection
V. Adherence to applicable laws
     a. Including data protection
     b. Local laws
     c. International requirements
     d. Administrative requirements
VI. Confidentiality
VII. Intellectual property
     a. Patenting
     b. Licensing rights
     c. Publications
        i. Timing
        ii. Notice
        iii. Acknowledgment of contribution
VIII. Governing law/dispute resolution
IX. Duration
X. Signatures/authority

Some standard, but very important pieces of information that an MTA should contain include the name of the parties to the agreement, and the signatures of those with authority to bind parties to the agreement.[13] A section that includes definitions constructed by the parties serves to clarify terms with inherent ambiguity. Sometimes the material to be transferred is specifically defined in this section; otherwise this information should be listed in another provision of the document.

---

[13] Sample MTA of the European Commission, Directorate General, Joint Research Centre, available at 160703-model-mta-final-m.doc (May 2018); Paolo de Paoli et al., *Drafting Biological Material Transfer Agreement: A Ready-to-Sign Model for Biobanks and Biorepositories*. INT J BIOL MARKERS 31(2):e211–e217 (2016)' ASTP-Proton, *Checklist for Revising and Amending Material Transfer Agreements*, available at https://www.astp-proton.eu/checklist-for-revising-and-amending-material-transfer-agreements/;ASTP-Proton, *Guidelines for Reviewing MTAs*, available at http://www.astp-proton.eu/downloads/BPL/BP_95__guidelines_MTA.pdf.

The section of MTAs that is a common source of complaints and sometimes litigation involves use of the material. In this section, the parties state their intentions regarding use of the material and boundaries that describe activities not intended for the material. It answers such questions as who is responsible for maintaining the material, and what are the expectations if the material is somehow damaged. It outlines the conditions under which information may be shared, any circumstances under which the parties should consult each other to obtain permission for activities that involve the material itself, as well as circumstances under which use of the material is not intended. With great flexibility, the parties can agree to confine use of the material to a specific laboratory or even to a specific person. The parties can also agree that the material will not be used in human research or be tested on primates, and they can agree if they wish that the material may only be used in pre-clinical investigations. Delving into even greater detail, some MTAs outline which parties pay for which costs in specifying who pays for storage and under what conditions, as well as who pays to transport the material at the beginning and the end of a project.

There is often a section that limits the liability of the supplier of the material. If the material is hazardous, there is a safety warning letting users know that safe handling is required. If information is being transmitted that is covered by privacy laws, then compliance by the sender is assured in the MTA, thereby limiting the sender's liability if the receiver mishandles the material or information.

Similarly, a section on applicable laws informs the receiver of material that the sender has complied with the law and expects the receiver to do so as well. If there is a particular set of laws or administrative requirements that may be unusual for the circumstances, those should be listed in the MTA.

Defining expectations for confidentiality is of paramount importance. A poorly timed publication can destroy the ability to protect intellectual property. Likewise, providing information to a business competitor can ruin the parties' working relationship and even leave them vulnerable to lawsuit. Therefore, it is important to set reasonable terms that define what is considered confidential information, how it is marked, and when restrictions are lifted so as to balance confidentiality with eventual publicity of research results.

The MTA section concerning intellectual property usually receives the most attention. It is in this section that the parties define their expectations for patenting, licensing, and publications. Parties can agree that the supplier of material receive a portion of proceeds through royalties or be granted a license to practice an invention created from the supplied material. This section also outlines expectations with respect to publications. If the supplied material has not yet been granted a patent, notice of publication is important to allow the parties sufficient time to protect their intellectual property. It is also important in maintaining a good working relationship to notify parties in advance of publication and acknowledge their contributions.

Despite best efforts, sometimes relationships break down. it is advisable from the outset of a project to agree to a procedure to follow should the parties be unable to resolve any dispute among themselves. Such information should include whether adjudication in a court or alternative dispute resolution (e.g., mediation or arbitration) will take place, as well as the location of the decision-maker and the selection of law that will govern the agreement. The parties can decide that the laws of one location will govern the terms of the contract, but a body in another location will decide the dispute. This is more commonly found in international agreements where the terms of the contract are governed by one location's set of laws with adjudication taking place in a location equidistant between the parties.

Duration is a brief section that allows the agreement to automatically expire on a certain date or upon occurrence of a specific event. The agreement can remain in force for a brief period of time, but they commonly remain in effect for several years. Agreements can usually be modified if the parties consent, and such a modification should either be memorialized in writing and attached to the original MTA, or incorporated into a new MTA.

8.5 CASES: WHERE DO THINGS GO WRONG?

Litigation occurs in the absence of an MTA, and it occurs in the presence of an MTA.[14] These agreements do not imply that the parties expect litigation – of the thousands of MTAs that have been signed, very few result in the parties arguing in court. In cases where the MTA plays a central role in litigation, it is plain to see where things go wrong and where expectations are not met between the parties. Litigation involving MTAs can be separated into a few basic categories: International litigation, instances where the MTA is not executed properly (signatory authority), contention over ownership of intellectual property, and instances where the MTA conflicts with other documents governing a relationship.

> Litigation involving MTAs.

8.6 INTERNATIONAL ASPECTS OF MATERIAL TRANSFER AGREEMENTS

Details and differences in customs vary between countries. Occasionally this brings surprises with respect to patent law and procedure, contract law, notions of ownership, and expectations of methods of compliance. Therefore, contracts involving entities from different countries may require more detail in a contract enabling the parties to fully understand what they are expected to do and when.[15] Of great importance in clarity when an international document is involved is the need for a precise and complete translation including an explanation for the rationale behind some of the provisions. For example, with respect to publication permission, the European Patent Office has a requirement of absolute novelty; under those laws, publication in advance of patent

---

[14]   Yeda Research and Devel. Co. Ltd., v. Imclone Systems Inc., 443 F.Supp.2d 570 (S.D. N.Y., 2006).
[15]   Bavarian Nordic A/S v. Acambis Inc., 486 F.Supp.2d 354 (D. Del., 2007).

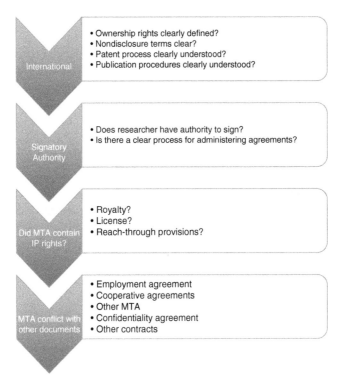

FIGURE 8.1 Categories of litigation involving MTAs.

filing can damage the ability to protect intellectual property. Data Protection and privacy laws differ among countries, and those laws may need to be fully explained so that researchers and institutions understand the necessity of their compliance and the gravity of nonadherence. For example, the European Union General Data Protection Regulation (GDPR) extends its reach to protect the privacy of European citizens' information globally.[16] It may be important to remind all parties to an international agreement the ways in which laws of one jurisdiction have an impact.[17]

8.7 SIGNATORY AUTHORITY

The capacity to bind an institution to a contract may be different from the signature of a recipient of material. A researcher may be requested to sign an MTA, but the

---

[16] EU GDPR.org, The EU General Data Protection Regulation Is the Most Important Change in Data Privacy Regulation in 20 Years, available at https://eugdpr.org/ (last accessed April 2019), referring to European Commission, 2018 Reform of EU Data Protection Rules, available at https://ec.europa.eu/commission/priorities/justice-and-fundamental-rights/data-protection/2018-reform-eu-data-protection-rules_en (last accessed April 2019).

[17] U.S. v. Kurtz, No. 04-CR- 0155A (W.D.N.Y. Apr. 21, 2008).

document must also be authorized by a technology transfer office, an office of research administration, or another office that has the official capacity to sign legal documents for the entire organization.[18] A researcher may request material and sign an MTA as the recipient (not as the person authorizing the contract), and upon signing, the researcher is expected to be aware of the rights and responsibilities contained in the document, comply with applicable law, and ensure that requirements for notice (such as notifying the material supplier before publication) are satisfied.[19]

8.8 INTELLECTUAL PROPERTY RIGHTS

The most commonly encountered issue in litigation over an MTA in its essence is an argument over ownership of patentable ideas. This may be an unavoidable consequence of people working together or it may be misunderstanding from the outset of the parties' expectations. In several notable cases, a suit was brought forward claiming breach of the MTA, but the essence of the case involved interpretation over the question of how much of a modification is required for an invention to be distinct from the original material.[20]

Reach-through provisions granting IP rights in a downstream invention that was created through use of material supplied by another are scrutinized if they extend too far. For example, in one court case, a judge sided with a small entity researcher stating "nearly all scientific work is inspired by or based on information or ideas from other scientists. It cannot be that [this company] is entitled to a license to every invention ever made which is inspired by a discovery made during [their] funded research project."[21] They remain a common complaint among researchers because of potential limitations on ownership and commercialization of an invention. Institutions sending materials and samples require an MTA to clarify ownership rights over the original sample and define expectations to preserve their ability to perform research collaboratively.[22]

8.9 CONFLICTS BETWEEN MTAS AND OTHER DOCUMENTS

Usually, the MTA is not the only document defining rights and responsibilities in a project. It is important to adhere to the terms as agreed and ensure uniformity of terms across multiple documents (see Table 8.1). Failure to verify that the terms of

---

[18] Davidson v. Cao, 211 F.Supp.2d 264 (D.Mass., 2002).

[19] *Matter of* United Univ. Professions v. State of New York, slip op. 50084 (New York State Law Reporting Bureau)(Supreme Court, Albany County decided Jan. 7 2013).

[20] Ariz. Bd. of Regents v. Seattle Genetics Inc. (D. Ariz., 2013); Univ. of Penn. v. St. Jude Children's Research, 982 F.Supp2d 518 (E.D. Pennsylvania, 2013); Dana-Farber Cancer Institute, Inc. v. Gatekeeper Pharmaceuticals, Inc. (D.Mass., 2012); Ibio, Inc. v. Fraunhoffer USA, Inc. (Del. Ch., 2016); W.L. Gore & Assocs. Inc. v. GI Dynamics, Inc. (D. Ariz., 2010), *motion granted in part*, 872 F.Supp.2d 883 (2012).

[21] Dana-Farber Cancer Institute, Inc. v. Gatekeeper Pharmaceuticals, Inc. (D.Mass., 2012).

[22] Washington University v. Catalona, 437 F.Supp.2d 985 (E.D. Mo., 2006); Yeshiva University v. Greenberg, 644 N.Y.S.2d 313, 228 A.D.2d 494 (N.Y. App. Div., 1996), aff'd, 681 N.Y.S.2d 71, 255 A. D.2d 576 (1998).

TABLE 8.1 *Relevant US precedent on Material Transfer Agreements*

Case name	Category MTA Use	Case in brief
	MTA Use	
Arizona Board of Regents v. Seattle Genetics	**IP Rights** MTA to assert jurisdiction MTA breach	In 1999, Arizona licensed a compound to Seattle Genetics. 2002, the compounds were deemed unsuitable for its purposes by Seattle Genetics and they independently developed new compounds. In 2003, Seattle Genetics signed an MTA for two compounds from Arizona. Seattle Genetics subsequently patented a compound. Arizona claims breach of the MTA and unjust enrichment from Seattle Genetics' improper use of materials and information. Question before the court: Is the modification enough to be its own invention or is this infringement on Arizona's patent?
Bavarian Nordic v. Acambis	International, IP rights – Ownership MTA as Evidence of ownership	Bavarian Nordic is headquartered in Denmark. Acambis is headquartered in the UK with its principal place of business in the US. A research consultant for Bavarian Nordic gave a stock of virus he had to the company and signed an MTA. The former research assistant for this consultant also had a stock of the virus, and brought it when he was a researcher with NIH and Acambis. Question before the court: Did the research assistant steal the virus? The court held that neither researcher had stolen the virus, but neither owned as much as they asserted. The case involved questions of ownership under German customs and laws.
Cancer Genetics v. Kreatech Technology	International, IP rights, Conflicting documents MTA to assert jurisdiction MTA expired, MTA breach	In 2001 Cancer Genetics (CG), a US company, signed a license and supply agreement with Kreatech, a Dutch company wherein Kreatech would label CG's probes and allow them to sell the combined product. In 2004, the agreement expired, but the companies continued with their business as usual. In 2006, Master Diagnostica, a Spanish company, signed an MTA with the parties to distribute the labeled probes in Europe. CG defaulted on payments to Kreatech and claimed breach of contract arising from the MTA. CG asserts that Kreatech kept the product, and copied and sold the product without permission. Before deciding on those merits, the court first decided where the case will be heard. The MTA contained a provision that New York law governs interpretation of the agreement; therefore, jurisdiction of the dispute was transferred to New York.

(continued)

TABLE 8.1 (continued)

Case name	Category MTA Use	
	MTA Use	Case in brief
Dana-Farber Cancer Institute v. Gatekeeper Pharmaceuticals	IP rights MTA breach	Gatekeeper researchers who were employed by Dana-Farber but maintained consulting contracts with Novartis discovered a new therapeutic kinase inhibitor. An MTA was signed containing a provision that prohibited transfer to third parties and gave them rights to inventions if the materials were used for other studies or if transfer occurred. The researcher did not distribute the physical material, in compliance with the MTA; however, information regarding the structure of the compound was shared. Novartis asserted this sharing of knowledge gave them rights to subsequent inventions based on the material they supplied. The court found that the researcher did not violate the terms of the MTA; therefore, Novartis was not entitled to IP rights in the kinase inhibitor.
Davidson v. Cao	Signatory authority, Conflicting documents No MTA signed	A researcher required more material for his laboratory and made a request to a researcher at another facility. The material was provided initially without an MTA. A year later, the material provider offered to send more if a confidentiality agreement with IP provisions was signed. The researcher signed the document without reading it and forwarded a copy to the university technology transfer office. The university objected to the terms of the confidentiality agreement and instead offered a Uniform Biological Materials Transfer Agreement. No agreement was signed by a person with authority to bind the university and no terms were agreed to or finalized by the institution. The researchers continued to share material, however, and the result was confusion. A patent was filed on an invention resulting from the research, and the parties litigated their rights in court.
DSM Research v. Verenium	IP Rights MTA to assert jurisdiction MTA expired	The parties had an MTA that expired. Further negotiations resulted in an impasse and no agreement was finalized. DSM developed the strain at the focus of the controversy and began to commercialize a product. The case at hand argued jurisdiction however, the issues at the heart of the controversy were later settled out of court.
Gilead v. Merck	IP rights, Conflicting documents MTA breach	Pharmasset (acquired by Gilead) gave Merck a product and signed an MTA. The terms provided that Merck would only evaluate the product and not discern its chemical composition. Merck asked for more information and set up a firewall to protect confidential information. The firewall was breached by a Merck employee, and the subsequent patent was held unenforceable.

Case	Issues	Description
Ibio v. *Fraunhoffer USA*	IP rights; MTA breach	The parties differed over their interpretations of the same MTA provision. 27 agreements over an 11 year period were signed, but the dispute focused on ownership of an invention. The court, after carefully examining all provisions in the pertinent MTAs ruled that the plaintiff owned the inventions created while their technology transfer agreement was in place, but the defendant owned the improvements on the invention made after the agreement expired.
Immunomedics v. *Roger Williams Med. Ctr.*	IP rights; MTA to assert jurisdiction; MTA breach	Three MTAs were at issue for inventions involving three antibodies. The plaintiff (a Delaware company) claimed the defendant (a Rhode Island company) knowingly violated provisions of the MTAs. The case was dismissed for lack of jurisdiction but could be litigated where jurisdiction is proper.
Massachusetts Eye and Ear v. *Qlt Phototherapeutics*	IP rights; Conflicting documents; MTA breach	QLT had a patent on a compound and asked a researcher at MEEI to find a use for that compound. Following a series of MTAs and a confidentiality agreement, MEEI developed clinical trials eventually resulting in a therapeutic product. However, while the product was still in clinical trials, QLT violated confidentiality when they approached a large pharmaceutical company about a potential partnership and commercialization. QLT's actions were found to have diminished MEEI's bargaining power, unjustly enriching themselves at MEEI's expense.
Roquette Frères v. *Solazyme*	Conflicting documents; MTA to assert jurisdiction	Arbitration was conducted to resolve a dispute under a joint venture operating agreement (JVOA). Plaintiff claims the arbitration exceeded its powers when it did not confine its decision to the JVOA and decided issues related to an MTA with a separate dispute resolution procedure. The court held that the arbitration was conducted properly, the MTA was part of an overarching agreement which specified arbitration, in addition the decision regarding the MTA was surplusage and would have had no bearing on the outcome.
Rouse v. *Walter & Assocs*	IP rights; Conflicting documents; MTA evidences ownership	An Employee Handbook and Employment Agreement assigned ownership of products to Iowa State University. An MTA referred to the computer program at issue as belonging to Iowa State. Rouse developed software (LAIPS) and assigned the copyright to Iowa State. He continued to refine the program and created USOFT. However, USOFT incorporated a segment of programming with a license for non-commercial use only. An MTA and license was signed and asserted USOFT was the property of Iowa State, which then licensed the program to Walter & Associates. Rouse asserts that Iowa State did not own the USOFT program. The court held that Iowa State owned the computer program under the *work for hire* doctrine.
Stanford University v.	IP rights – Ownership; Conflicting documents	A researcher signed an employment agreement with Stanford promising to assign IP rights to the university. The researcher visited Cetus (succeeded in interest by Roche) to learn PCR work and

(continued)

TABLE 8.1 (continued)

Case name	Category MTA Use	
	MTA Use	Case in brief
Roche Molecular Systems	MTA evidence of ownership	signed several MTAs and a confidentiality agreement with an assignment clause stating he "does hereby assign" rights to inventions. In determining ownership of a subsequent invention, the court ruled that the present tense in the confidentiality agreement gives the document priority over the employment agreement wherein the researcher "agrees to assign" (implying a future possibility).
Unigen Pharmaceuticals v. Colgate-Palmolive	IP rights MTA to assert jurisdiction MTA breach	An MTA and a confidentiality agreement were signed and materials were transferred from the plaintiff to the defendant. A patent application was subsequently filed. The plaintiff claims the subject of patent is based on information and material it received through the MTA. The subsequent lawsuit claims breach of contract, misappropriation of trade secret, and unjust enrichment. The defendant attempted to have the case heard in federal court, but the court decided jurisdiction was proper at the state level as the claims arose from breach of contract.
United University Professions v. State of New York	Signatory authority MTA breach	A researcher owned a side company selling laboratory mice. The researcher sold the mice and charged a state grant for shipping costs in violation of the MTA.
University of Pennsylvania v. St. Jude Children's Research	IP rights MTA breach	An MTA transferred material from St. Jude to the University of Pennsylvania. The MTA covered a specific "cell receptor construct, including any progeny, portions, unmodified derivatives and any accompanying know-how or data . . . to be used in pre-clinical studies." The University of Pennsylvania researcher modified the material's genetic sequence to make it suitable for a lentiviral vector and planned to conduct clinical trials. The question over breach of the MTA involved the definition of whether the material was "contained" or if it was "incorporated." St. Jude alleged the construct contained the material and would be subject to patent infringement while the University of Pennsylvania alleged the construct incorporated the material and was therefore derivative and able to be independently patented. The parties settled out of court with Novartis and the University of Pennsylvania paying $12.25 million and royalties to St. Jude (and its licensee) in exchange for a license to continue research and commercialization of the product.
UPM-Kymmene v. Renmatics	International, Conflicting documents	This case involved multiple MTAs, confidentiality agreements, and joint development agreements (a bilateral agreement, and a trilateral agreement). An MTA was signed by UPM (a Finnish company) and Renmatics (a US company) that provided disputes would be arbitrated by the International

Case	Topic	Description
	MTA to assert jurisdiction	Chamber of Commerce with proceedings conducted in English in Toronto, Canada. However, a subsequent Tri-lateral agreement contained a provision that disputes would be resolved using the American Arbitration Association. The court held that the later document received priority, so its terms prevailed.
US v. Kurtz	International, Signatory authority, Conflicting documents; MTA breach	Kurtz attempted to circumvent restrictions on distribution of products. An MTA, preventing distribution to third parties, accompanied each sale of the restricted product. Plaintiffs referenced violation of the MTA but did not use this argument in their complaint as filed, so the indictment was dismissed.
W.L. Gore & Assocs v. GI Dynamics	IP rights, Conflicting documents; MTA as evidence of activity, MTA breach	The relationship between the parties spanned two years, several contracts, two confidentiality agreements and a supply agreement. GI Dynamics supplied their products to Gore for sale, but soon Gore developed a competing product. The parties dispute interpretations of the use and licensing provisions of the various agreements including the MTA. Additionally, GI Dynamics claims misappropriation of confidential information and theft of trade secret. The court held that some claimed trade secrets were generally known but others were not; therefore, the undecided issues of the case may proceed to another trial.
Washington University v. Catalona	IP rights – Ownership; MTA as evidence of ownership	A researcher enrolled participants in a study while at Washington University. The researcher moved to another university and wanted to take study samples with him. Several MTAs were used as evidence for the claim that Washington University was owner of the material. The court held that the samples were a gift to Washington University to be maintained in their repository.
Yeda Research and Devel. v. Imclone Systems	No MTA	The case was brought forward to determine inventorship among a group of collaborating scientists. The parties expressed surprise that there was no MTA to assist with clarification of ownership issues, because the document was standard procedure for them.
Yeshiva University v. Greenberg	IP rights – Ownership; MTA as evidence of activity	A researcher worked for a university and developed an antibody and cell line. The researcher left and took samples of the material to a new position. University policy allowed this as long as the material was used for continued academic research; furthermore, they distributed to third parties under an MTA. The defendant distributed the materials to a commercial entity, and a lawsuit over ownership commenced. The court held that the materials belong to the university under a work for hire doctrine.

all documents are satisfactory and do not conflict with each other can result in consequences that are unpleasant.[23]

8.10 THE RESOLUTION OF MTA DISPUTES

Cases resolve in several ways. Questions over patentability may be answered before the Patent Trial and Appeal Board. Some disputes end when the parties settle out of court, and other disputes end when one party to the suit purchases the other party thereby extinguishing the justiciable controversy.[24]

Lessons drawn from cases litigating an MTA reflect questions and controversies in contract law, property law, patents, and employment. Courts have held that when documents conflict, generally the latest document governs interpretation of terms, as it is the latest in time the court expects that it reflects the intention of the parties as a project moved forward. In a conflict involving employment agreements, the term "hereby assigns" has priority over a document with the term "will assign." Additionally, in the absence of an assignment, ownership of intellectual property remains with the researcher if they are hired under a general employment contract. If, however, they were hired to specifically work on a project, then ownership remains with the research institution under a "work for hire" or "corporate authorship" doctrine.

Ownership of unmodified samples usually remains with the institution where they were initially donated. Ownership of modifications to material transferred to another entity under an MTA depends on the amount and quality of transformation.

Requesting material for research under an MTA is unlike purchasing supplies. It creates a collaboration, and parties to this kind of group work carry with them certain expectations which when not met lead to disparate perceptions of value, which can lead to court so that an adjudicative body can determine the value.[25]

---

[23] Rouse v. Walter & Associates, L.L.C., 513 F.Supp.2d 1041 (S.D. Iowa, 2007); Stanford Univ. v. Roche Molecular Systems, Inc. 563 U.S. 776 (2011); Massachusetts Eye and Ear v. Qlt Phototherapeutics, 412 F.3d 215 (1st Cir., 2005), aff'd 552 F.3d 47 (2009); UPM-Kymmene Corp., v. Renmatics, Inc. (Del. Ch., 2017); Gilead Scis., Inc. v. Merck & Co. (N.D. Cal. 2016), aff'd, 888 F.3d 1231 (Fed. Cir., 2018); Roquette Freres, S.A. v. Solazyme, Inc., 154 F.Supp3d 68 (D. Del., 2015), aff'd (3rd Cir., 2016).

[24] DSM Research, B.V. v. Verenium Corp., 686 F.Supp.2d 159 (D. Mass., 2010).
The case at hand argued jurisdiction however, the issues at the heart of the controversy were later settled out of court when Verenium purchased DSM. DSM press releases, *DSM Acquires Food Enzymes business and Key Technology from Verenium,* available at www.dsm.com/corporate/media/information center-news/2012/03/04–12-dsm-acquires-food-enzymes-business-and-key-technology-from-verenium.html (published March 26, 2012); Ibio, Inc. v. Fraunhoffer USA, Inc. (Del. Ch., 2016).

[25] Suerie Moon et al., *Will Ebola Change the Game? Ten Essential Reforms Before the Next Pandemic. The Report of the Harvard-LSHTM Independent Panel on the Global Response to Ebola,* www .thelancet.com (Nov. 22, 2015), www.who.int/about/who_reform/emergency-capacities/advisory-group/Report-Harvard-LSHTM.pdf.

9

Sharing of Biological Samples during Public Health Emergencies

Challenges and Opportunities for National and International Action

Maria Julia Marinissen, Ruvani Chandrasekera, John Simpson,
Theodore Kuschak, and Lauren Barna[*]

9.1 INTRODUCTION

Public health emergencies caused by outbreaks of emerging and reemerging infectious diseases, including the accidental or intentional release of biological agents, can have serious long-lasting health, socioeconomic, and political consequences in the affected country. Moreover, the interconnectedness of today's world makes the likelihood of diseases and pathogens spreading across borders more impactful than ever. Responding to such events requires prompt action at the national level, and as seen in many recent disease outbreaks, international collaboration to implement effective preparedness and response measures. Rapid outbreak investigation is a critical first step in detecting, preventing the spread, and/or responding to these impending or actual emergencies, and typically requires access to biological samples. These samples may include the causative pathogen as well as clinical material (e.g., blood and tissue) from patients, suspected cases, contacts of patients or suspected cases; animal reservoirs; or the environment. Information obtained from these samples is critical to conducting basic research to identify and/or characterize the pathogen, conducting epidemiological research, performing risk assessments, developing and testing medical countermeasures (diagnostics, therapeutics, and vaccines), and for evaluating the applicability of potential non-pharmaceutical, public health interventions.

[*] The findings and conclusions in this chapter are those of the author(s) and do not necessarily represent the views of the US Department of Health and Human Services, Public Health Agency of Canada, Public Health England, or their components, neither of those entities mentioned in the document.
We thank Susan Sherman and Joseph Foster from the Office of the General Counsel at HHS for their helpful review of the chapter and their insight over the years to provide legal advice on sample sharing matters. We also thank the members of the GHSI Sample Sharing Task Group and members of the US Sample Sharing Working Group for the work over the years to address sample sharing challenges during public health emergencies.

However, ensuring timely access to samples to prepare for or respond to a public health emergency has proven to be a challenging and complex multistep process, particularly when samples need to be shared among international partners (beyond the routine mechanisms used to share samples among laboratories for research purposes). While the International Health Regulations (2005) call on signatory World Health Organization (WHO) Member States to collaborate with each other "in the detection and assessment of, and response to, events" (Article 44), and to share information (Article 7), there are no explicit requirements for countries to share samples to prepare and/or respond to public health emergencies of international concern (PHEIC).[1] This issue received international attention in 2007 when the government of Indonesia conditionally withheld samples of H5N1 avian influenza virus citing "viral sovereignty" and the asserted need to receive fair benefits in exchange for those samples. This was apparently a reaction to an Australian company that had developed an influenza vaccine derived from a virus strain provided by Indonesia to the WHO. Indonesia asserted that pharmaceutical companies in developed countries obtained the samples for free and then developed and patented vaccines to which developing countries had neither access to, nor could they afford to pay for those products.[2] Based on these challenges, the WHO developed and is managing the implementation of the Pandemic Influenza Preparedness (PIP) Framework.[3] This global effort established an access and benefit sharing (ABS) system that includes an annual Partnership Contribution[4] to the WHO from manufacturers of influenza vaccine, diagnostics, and other pharmaceuticals, who have access to the WHO Global Influenza Surveillance and Response System (GISRS).[5] Manufacturers also commit to sharing some of the benefits arising from their access to these materials, such as pandemic influenza vaccines, antiviral medicines, and other pandemic related products or technologies, with the WHO.[6] The agreements among stakeholders are based on standard material transfer agreements (SMTAs) that establish the terms and conditions for ABS. Sample sharing through this framework facilitates pandemic risk assessment, the development of candidate vaccine viruses, updating of diagnostic reagents and test kits, and surveillance for resistance to antiviral medicines; all critical steps for pandemic preparedness and response. These activities

---

[1] World Health Organization, INTERNATIONAL HEALTH REGULATIONS (2005) available at www.who.int /ihr/9789241596664/en/.

[2] David P. Fidler, *Influenza Virus Samples, International Law, and Global Health Diplomacy*, 14 EMERGING INFECTIOUS DISEASES 88 (2008), available at wwwnc.cdc.gov/eid/article/14/ 1/07-0700_article.

[3] World Health Organization, PANDEMIC INFLUENZA PREPAREDNESS FRAMEWORK available at www .who.int/influenza/pip/en/.

[4] World Health Organization, PARTNERSHIP CONTRIBUTION, available at www.who.int/influenza/pip/ benefit_sharing/partnership_contribution/en/.

[5] World Health Organization, GLOBAL INFLUENZA SURVEILLANCE AND RESPONSE SYSTEM available at www .who.int/influenza/gisrs_laboratory/en/.

[6] World Health Organization, STANDARD MATERIAL TRANSFER AGREEMENT-2, available at www.who.int /influenza/pip/benefit_sharing/smta2/en/.

represent the benefits afforded to institutions that provide these samples and to the global community that are derived from this knowledge, along with access to the response tools developed should a pandemic occur.

The PIP Framework is an effective model for access to pandemic influenza samples based on financial contributions and benefits for providers and recipient of samples. However there is no equivalent guidance or framework for the sharing of non-influenza pathogens with the potential of causing public health emergencies or pandemics. This lack of guidance generated similar and other equally important sample sharing challenges during recent disease outbreaks such as the Middle East Respiratory Syndrome (MERS) caused by the MERS-Coronavirus (MERS-CoV),[7] during the Ebola virus outbreak in West Africa,[8] and the more recent PHEIC related to the Zika virus outbreak in the Americas.[9] Thus, this chapter describes some of the sample sharing challenges encountered or observed as well as the sample sharing preparedness and response coordination efforts undertaken by the US Department of Health and Human Services (HHS) officials and international partners to find opportunities to overcome them both at the national and international level. The chapter also describes how these preparedness and response coordination efforts were implemented during the response to the Zika virus outbreak to facilitate sample sharing and the lessons learned from them.

9.2 ISSUES WITH SHARING OF SAMPLES RELATED TO NON-INFLUENZA PATHOGENS WITH PANDEMIC POTENTIAL

The emergence of MERS-CoV in the Middle East exposed a number of critical sample sharing challenges when in 2012 officials from Saudi Arabia claimed that MERS-CoV samples were sent to the Erasmus University Medical Center in the Netherlands (Erasmus MC) in Rotterdam without government consent.[10] On September 15, 2012, a doctor in a hospital in Saudi Arabia reported the discovery of a novel coronavirus, which was sequenced by the Erasmus MC.[11] Shortly after on September 26, 2012, the United Kingdom's Department of Health and Social Care alerted national and international authorities of a novel coronavirus detected in a male Qatari national who was receiving treatment for severe respiratory illness

---

[7] U.S. Centers for Disease Control and Prevention, Middle East Respiratory Syndrome, available at www.cdc.gov/coronavirus/mers/index.html.

[8] U.S. Centers for Disease Control and Prevention, 2014–16 West Africa Ebola Outbreak, available at www.cdc.gov/vhf/ebola/history/2014–2016-outbreak/index.html.

[9] World Health Organization, Zika virus and complications: 2016 Public Health Emergency of International Concern, available at www.who.int/emergencies/zika-virus-tmp/en/.

[10] Laurie Garrett, *Why a Saudi Virus Is Spreading Alarm*, Council on Foreign Relations Expert Brief, May 29, 2013, available at www.cfr.org/expert-brief/why-saudi-virus-spreading-alarm.

[11] V. M. Corman et al., *Detection of a Novel Human Coronavirus by Real-Time Reverse-Transcription Polymerase Chain Reaction*, 17(39) Euro. Surveill. 20285 (2012), available at www.ncbi.nlm.nih.gov/pubmed/23041020/.

in London, and which was identical to that identified by Erasmus MC.[12] The emergence of MERS-CoV was alarming to the public health community due to its association with severe respiratory disease and renal failure and clinical presentation,[13] similar to severe acute respiratory syndrome (SARS), another coronavirus that emerged in 2003. SARS spread across the globe infecting over 8,000 individuals and causing over 900 deaths.[14] In particular, there were concerns about the impending mass-gathering event, the Hajj, attended in Mecca, Saudi Arabia, by approximately three million travelers annually. The WHO convened an Emergency Committee on MERS-CoV and although the outbreak was not declared a PHEIC, the committee made strong recommendations for countries to increase surveillance and enhance their diagnostic capacity to be able to test pilgrims returning to their home countries.[15]

To gain a better understanding of MERS-CoV and its transmission dynamics and to prepare for a potential international spread, the global public health community (including various scientific and public health institutions within the US government) requested samples from Saudi Arabia and the United Kingdom after the first reported cases. These negotiations proved to be lengthy and complex and impeded rapid preparedness actions. Without access to a sufficient number of virus samples there was no way to learn whether potential mutations could change its virulence, routes of transmission, etc.

Additionally, without access to serum samples from convalescent patients or the general population, it was extremely difficult to develop and validate serology tests and to conduct timely research to determine if the disease spread person-to-person, or if MERS-CoV-infected patients could be asymptomatic.[16] Developing serologic

[12] World Health Organization, *Novel Coronavirus Infection in the United Kingdom*, available at www.who.int/csr/don/2012_09_23/en/.

[13] U.S. Centers for Disease Control and Prevention, Severe Respiratory Illness Associated with a Novel Coronavirus – Saudi Arabia and Qatar (2012) available at www.cdc.gov/mmwr/preview/mmwrhtml/mm6140a5.htm.

[14] World Health Organization, *Summary of SARS Cases by Country*, available at www.who.int/csr/sars/country/2003_08_15/en/.

[15] Eryn Brown, *WHO raises concern about possible spread of MERS among Hajj pilgrims*, LA Times, Sept. 25, 2013, available at www.latimes.com/science/sciencenow/la-sci-sn-who-mers-hajj-20130925-story.html. ("The World Health Organization's emergency committee on the Middle East Respiratory Syndrome coronavirus, or MERS-CoV, met Wednesday. After hearing updates on the spread of the virus – which as of Sept. 20 had killed 58 of the 130 people confirmed to have contracted it, most in Saudi Arabia – the committee decided against calling the outbreak a 'Public Health Emergency of International Concern': a situation that requires a certain level of immediate, coordinated international action.")

[16] U.S. Centers for Disease Control and Prevention, *CDC Laboratory Testing for Middle East Respiratory Syndrome Coronavirus (MERS-CoV)*, available at www.cdc.gov/coronavirus/mers/lab/lab-testing.html. ("The success of rRT-PCR testing depends on several factors, including the experience and expertise of laboratory personnel, laboratory environment (e.g., avoidance of contamination), and the type and condition of specimens being tested. For this rRT-PCR assay, CDC recommends collecting multiple specimens, including lower (bronchalveolar lavage, sputum and tracheal aspirates) and upper (e.g., nasopharyngeal and oropharyngeal swabs) respiratory samples, serum, and stool specimens.")

testing was critically important because it allowed determination of previous infection by detecting MERS-CoV antibodies in people, and to determine vaccine efficacy. Finally, the lack of sample sharing impaired the rapid testing of existing medical countermeasures (vaccines and therapeutics) and the development of new therapeutic interventions.[17] Moreover, to the extent of our knowledge, validated serology tests for MERS-CoV still are not available in many parts of the world. When MERS-CoV appeared in South Korea in 2015 imported from the Middle East, the country was ill-prepared and 36 people died from a total of 186 cases. In addition to the loss of life, reports indicate that thousands of schools were closed and that there was economic fallout, including decreased sales and tourism.[18] Clearly, worldwide preparedness efforts could have been strengthened if the disease were better understood, as many countries were (and are) at risk of receiving cases imported from the Middle East. Some of the key challenges related to sample sharing are explained in this chapter based on experiences from the initial MERS-CoV outbreak as well as others encountered during the Zika virus outbreak in 2015–16 in the Americas, and the Ebola virus outbreak in West Africa in 2014–16.

9.3 OWNERSHIP OF SAMPLES AND THEIR DERIVATIVES

Concerning the ownership of samples, there has been an increasing alignment with the notion that countries have sovereignty over biological resources in their territory, as recognized under the Convention on Biological Diversity (CBD). While the CBD is geared toward conservation and enabling preservation and sustainable use of biodiversity, some argue that these biological resources include pathogens and have applied this interpretation to pathogen sharing for public health purposes. Similar to the case around avian influenza samples, the concept of "viral sovereignty" also was raised by Saudi Arabia officials in relation to MERS-CoV samples sent outside of Saudi Arabia to Erasmus MC for further testing. Saudi Arabia claimed that the virus had been sent out of the country without their permission and raised claims about Erasmus for filing a patent application apparently then on the virus and host receptor data shortly after the report of the novel

---

[17] Timothy Uyeki et al., *Development of Medical Countermeasures to Middle East Respiratory Syndrome Coronavirus*, 22(7) EMERGING INFECTIOUS DISEASES (2016) available at wwwnc.cdc.gov/eid/article/22/7/16-0022_article. ("Prospective controlled clinical trials (ideally randomized clinical trials) of potential MERS-CoV therapies and vaccines in humans are needed urgently; however, there is uncertainty in estimating timelines for the development of potential MERS-CoV medical countermeasures because of the need to further characterize existing and new animal models, the unpredictability of demonstrating a favorable risk–benefit outcome during preclinical testing, and competition for resources with other emerging infectious diseases.")

[18] BBC, *S. Korea Cuts Interest Rates to Record Lows amid MERS Concerns*, June 11, 2015, available at www.bbc.com/news/business-33089930. ("The move is seen an attempt to stem the economic fallout from the outbreak that has killed nine people in Asia's fourth largest economy since it was first reported last month.")

virus came out.,[19] Saudi Arabia also claimed that the patent and the material transfer agreement (MTA) that Erasmus was using to share the virus was hindering Saudi Arabia's ability to detect and mitigate spread of the virus. These claims were denied by Erasmus MC, which stated that "it should be clear that a virus cannot be patented, only specific applications related to it, like vaccines and medicines."[20] Later on, although Saudi Arabia shared samples of animal origin[21] with the United States, the country then entered into lengthy and complex negotiations with the US government to share serum samples from patients in which they intended to assert expansive rights for them as providers. They intended to assert expansive rights including restrictive conditions for recipient institutions regarding use of the sample and derivatives, onward sharing, and access to benefits obtained for the direct or indirect use of the samples. Before long, this combination of issues fostered an international debate about non-influenza pathogen sample ownership and what benefits can be claimed based on it.[22]

Depending on a country's policies or laws on sample ownership, the individual providing the sample also may be able assert ownership or other rights related to the sample. Similarly, the provider institution of a sample of human origin may be able to assert ownership or other rights based on permissions/consent from the individual who provided the sample. Based on this, MTAs include conditions established by institutions, investigators, or the patient on how samples and its derivatives can be further used. For example, some typical MTAs for transferring nonproprietary biological samples establish that samples can be used for "teaching and/or internal research purposes only," and exclude "any research that may involve an exclusive license to inventions containing the material or if the material is used in a commercial product."[23] This can prevent the sample from being used to develop diagnostic techniques, or from being used in any research that can be derived in the development of new, or testing of existing, medical countermeasures such as vaccines and therapeutics. This restriction can, in turn, delay the implementation of response measures. Another factor to consider is that in some countries, protocols to collect samples from patients need to be approved by Institutional Review Boards (IRB). If these protocols do not include patients' consent for the samples to be used for purposes other than research or clinical diagnostic testing, going back to get protocols reapproved or to get new patient consents revised and re-signed during an

[19] International patent application WO 2014/045254 A2, published 27 March 2014, available at https://patentimages.storage.googleapis.com/4a/48/3e/c84fe4ebeac669/WO2014045254A2.pdf.
[20] Robert Roos, *Saudis to send animal samples to US in MERS-CoV probe*, May 24, 2013 available at www.cidrap.umn.edu/news-perspective/2013/05/saudis-send-animal-samples-us-mers-cov-probe.
[21] AFP, *Saudi to Send Animal Samples to US in Coronavirus Probe*, AL-ARABIYA, May 24, 2013, available at http://english.alarabiya.net/en/News/middle-east/2013/05/24/Saudi-to-send-animal-samples-to-us-in-coronavirus-probe-.html.
[22] Laurie Garrett, *Why a Saudi Virus Is Spreading Alarm*, COUNCIL ON FOREIGN RELATIONS EXPERT BRIEF, May 29, 2013, available at www.cfr.org/expert-brief/why-saudi-virus-spreading-alarm.
[23] wwwn.cdc.gov/ARIsolateBank/Downloads/SLAforBacterialBank_508c_fillable.pdf.

emergency can be extremely time-consuming and also add delays to sample collection and of course, their use for response purposes.

A significant issue related to the lack of patient consent to use the samples for research (other than clinical diagnostic purposes) became apparent during the Ebola virus outbreak in West Africa in 2014. News articles reported that thousands of samples were taken from patients in the affected countries and exported to laboratories in the United Kingdom, the United States, South Africa, and France, apparently without patient consent. The article mentions that most patients did not know that their samples would be used for research and that some argued that the research and derivatives of commercial value benefited others but not the patients or affected countries themselves. For example, they claimed that "among the patients whose blood was exported without consent is a woman from Guinea whose sample is anonymized under the code C15" and that the Ebola virus isolated from her blood was for sale by European Virus Archive at a price "170 times the price of gold."[24] In the absence of this patient's consent, this led to controversial discussions about the intent, the ethics, and even the legality of the collection and use of these samples, and the fair distribution of benefits. When preparing for and/or responding to an outbreak that has the potential to turn into a public health emergency, an important consideration is that research and development priorities may change based on evolving information resulting from the outbreak investigation. As a result, the work for which the samples are needed may change. Thus, it is critical in these situations to include appropriate consents in the sample collection protocols, detailing how the samples are to be used and who can have access to them to develop response tools (i.e., researchers, public health institutions, private sector as deemed necessary). These complex topics cannot be addressed easily in the midst of responding to an emergency. Importantly, preparedness plans at all levels should include provisions for human sample collection, sharing, and use in ways that can maximize emergency response while taking into account the patient's rights but also the benefit to the community's health security.

9.4 DISTRIBUTION OF SAMPLES TO THIRD PARTIES

During an emergency response, multiple sectors (e.g., public health institutions, academia, industry, laboratories) require access to samples to develop the necessary response tools. MTAs may contain conditions to restrict recipients from distributing the sample to third parties or require that the recipients receive permission from the original provider to do so. As stated, the process of going back to get permission or negotiating new MTAs during emergency could result in delays in sharing material and, in turn, delays in gaining the needed knowledge and response tools. During the

[24] Emmanuel Freudenthal, *Ebola's lost blood: row over samples flown out of Africa as "big pharma" set to cash in*, THE TELEGRAPH, February 6, 2019, www.telegraph.co.uk/global-health/science-and-disease /ebolas-lost-blood-row-samples-flown-africa-big-pharma-set-cash/.

MERS-CoV outbreak, news articles quoted Saudi authorities stating that the "Erasmus lab patented the process for synthesizing the virus, meaning that anyone else who wanted to use their method to study it would have to pay the lab."[25] According to the same publication, this delayed the development of diagnostic kits and serologic tests since samples could not be shared rapidly with any third party that needed them. According to Saudi officials, "that should not happen." Interestingly, one of the issues that surfaced when different agencies in the US Department of Health and Human Services were trying to obtain MERS-CoV samples from Saudi Arabia and from the United Kingdom is that the recipient agency could not share samples and sample derivatives with other HHS agencies or other US government agencies.[26] Given that all these agencies have different roles in developing tools such as diagnostics, vaccines, and therapeutics, this inability to share samples among preparedness and response partners limited access to clinical samples and virus isolates and hindered the preclinical development of MERS-CoV medical countermeasures.[27] Thus, onward sample sharing also became a central issue within the national and international debate around non-influenza sample sharing.

9.5 NEGOTIATING ACCESS AND BENEFIT SHARING

As mentioned in this chapter, during the course of research using biological samples related to an outbreak investigation, new scientific and public health knowledge could be generated leading to new, not originally pursued publications, derivatives, technologies, and response tools. In some cases, these developments can result in financial or other benefits to the researchers, particularly if the information is used to develop products or technologies for which the developer is able to claim intellectual property rights and limit licensing and transfer of such technology to the private sector for further development and commercialization. These issues arose during the MERS-CoV outbreak in 2012 when Saudi authorities stated that "The patenting [of the virus] had delayed the development of diagnostic kits and serologic tests for the disease," in theory due to intellectual property rights claimed by Erasmus MC, which caused considerable confusion among the scientific community.[28] Dr. Margaret Chan, then WHO Director General, went on record emphasizing that "making deals between scientists because they want to take IP [intellectual property], because they want to be the world's first to publish in scientific journals, these are issues we need to address." She further stated that "No IP will stand in the

25 Tom Miles and Stephanie Nebehay, *WHO Warns Countries Not to Hoard Secrets of Coronavirus*, REUTERS, May 23, 2013, available at https://in.reuters.com/article/us-coronavirus-who/who-warns-countries-not-to-hoard-secrets-of-coronavirus-idINBRE94M0ZL20130523.
26 Robert Roos, *Saudis to send animal samples to US in MERS-CoV probe*, May 24, 2013, available at www.cidrap.umn.edu/news-perspective/2013/05/saudis-send-animal-samples-us-mers-cov-probe.
27 Uyeki et al., *supra* note 17.
28 Editorial, *MERS-CoV: A Global Challenge*, 381(98820) THE LANCET, June 8, 2013, available at www.thelancet.com/journals/lancet/article/PIIS0140-6736%2813%2961184-8/fulltext?rss=yes.

way of public health actions" and told health ministers "you are the boss" asking for them to take action to make sure that scientists shared their specimens with WHO's collaborating laboratories. Meanwhile, negotiations to share samples between Saudi Arabia and the US government turned extremely complex due to Saudi Arabia's intent to impose as part of an MTA, very restrictive use of the samples to ensure that the US government would not profit economically directly or indirectly from the use of the samples or their derivatives.

In many cases, MTAs designed for routine sample sharing include restrictions on publication rights, intellectual property rights, and benefits from the commercialization of the sample or its derivatives. Because of the financial and scientific benefits that could result from the use of the shared samples, some providing institutions or countries may require receipt of some of those or another form of benefits in exchange for the samples. Of note, the process of getting access to samples and sharing benefits from use of those samples is being institutionalized at the national level in some countries through legislation and/or policy measures. For example, the Nagoya Protocol on Access to Genetic Resources and the Fair and Equitable Sharing of Benefits Arising from their Utilization (Nagoya Protocol)[29] is a supplementary agreement to the CBD that entered into force in 2014 and currently has 116 signatory member parties. The agreement's goal is "the fair and equitable sharing of benefits arising from the utilization of genetic resources, thereby contributing to the conservation and sustainable use of biodiversity." The term "genetic resources" refers to genetic material (DNA, RNA) in plants, animals, microbes, and humans. Specifically, the Nagoya Protocol states that access to such genetic resources (except for the human genome) should be subject to case-by-case prior informed consent (unless otherwise determined by the Party holding the genetic resource), and that the sharing of benefits arising from the utilization of those resources be based upon case-by-case mutually agreed terms. Parties to the Nagoya Protocol are required to take legislative, administrative, or policy measures to implement their access obligations.

Based on the lengthy negotiation of MTAs in the context of preparing for and responding to public health emergencies, concerns grew about the implications that the Nagoya Protocol could have for viruses and other pathogen sharing if they became subject to ABS obligations.[30] Thus, in 2016, WHO published the results of a consultation with key stakeholders concerning this issue. Some participants expressed that the Nagoya Protocol, in the context of non-influenza pathogens, "provides an opportunity for Member States to establish clear, pre-arranged benefit-sharing expectations for access to pathogens that will contribute to the public health response to infectious disease outbreaks." Conversely, participants agreed that there were concerns about (1) uncertainty regarding the scope and implementation, (2)

---

[29]   Convention on Biological Diversity, The Nagoya Protocol, available at www.cbd.int/abs/about/.
[30]   Michelle Rourke, *Viruses for Sale: All Viruses Are Subject to Access and Benefit-Sharing Obligations under the Conventional on Biological Diversity*, 39 EUR. INTELL. PROP. REV. 79 (2017).

the high transactional cost of implementing a bilateral system for access and benefit sharing, and (3) the complexity of varying domestic access and benefit sharing legislations. They stated that together, these concerns showed the potential "impact on the comprehensiveness and speed of risk assessment as well as the timely development of vaccines, diagnostics and other medical countermeasures."[31] Until there is further clarification on the application of the Nagoya Protocol to sharing of non-influenza pathogens in the context of emergencies, there is a risk for lengthy negotiations, including at the highest political levels or even by other sectors, when samples need to be shared internationally. In turn, these potential lengthy negotiations could compromise fundamental elements of the response to a public health emergency.

9.6 TRANSPORTING SAMPLES

Mobilizing biological samples across borders, especially when dealing with select agents or novel pathogens, also proved to be a challenging process subjected to the regulations of the provider and recipient countries. While systems are in place for the routine import, export, and transport of samples, these normal regulatory and logistical pathways may be inadequate or inapplicable when a pathogen is unknown/dangerous, or when samples must be transported rapidly due to an emergency. Moreover, these regulations are not internationally harmonized, so understanding and navigating each country's system of permits in an emergency can delay the samples getting where they are needed. In addition, determining the relevant permits and licenses required can be extremely time-consuming. For example, in the United States, identifying these requirements and the government authority needed to issue a relevant permit depends on the composition of the sample, where it originated (i.e., organism, environment), what it may have been exposed to, and its intended end use, among other considerations. Failing to include all necessary permits may delay delivery and/or result in confiscation and/or destruction of the package by customs agencies at ports of entry. For example, for the US government to import MERS-CoV samples of animal origin, samples had to be sent to the US Department of Agriculture for quarantine and foot and mouth disease testing[32] as soon as they entered the country, and prior to being used by

---

[31] World Health Organization, IMPLEMENTATION OF THE NAGOYA PROTOCOL AND PATHOGEN SHARING: PUBLIC HEALTH IMPLICATIONS (2016) available at www.who.int/influenza/pip/2016-review /NagoyaStudyAdvanceCopy_full.pdf. ("As noted by respondents to this study, there are tools under the Nagoya Protocol that address these concerns. The manner in which the Nagoya Protocol is implemented –both collectively through the Protocol's Meeting of the Parties, and by individual Parties through their domestic legislation – will be vital to ensuring that the Nagoya Protocol supports public health.")

[32] USDA, Our Focus, available at www.aphis.usda.gov/aphis/ourfocus/animalhealth/animal-and-animal-product-import-information/import-live-animals/sa_cattle.

any other research institution. This was a necessary but time-consuming process that delayed the start of research studies needed to understand the disease. These requirements also exposed some coordination issues between the human and animal health sectors in terms of coordination of the sample sharing process for emergency preparedness and response purposes.

In addition, ensuring that couriers are willing and able to transport these materials may also be a challenge. Apprehension about the threat posed by such samples may limit the number of commercial shipping options, especially if companies or pilots refuse to transport the packages. For examples, news outlets reported that a pilot from a major Canadian airline refused to transport a blood sample from a suspected Ebola case in 2014 from Edmonton to the reference laboratory in Winnipeg.[33] Similarly, after live anthrax was shipped accidentally from an Army laboratory in 2015, a large courier announced that it would no longer transport potential bioterror pathogens. Such restrictions limit the number of commercial shipping options available, and may therefore limit the locations that can send or receive samples, and reduce the speed at which they can be shipped.

9.7 BIOSAFETY/BIOSECURITY

Another critical sample sharing issue is the biosafety and biosecurity capacity to store and manipulate samples. A few articles raised concern during and after the 2014–16 West African Ebola outbreak about the public health threat posed by stocks of virus samples stored in laboratories. The challenges include inadequate or limited safe storage capacity, challenges in tracking samples and related data, inability to create sample inventories, and a lack of plans in place to distribute/share/destroy the samples in a safe way and in accordance with appropriate guidance.[34] Some of these concerns became more evident when the outbreak started to wind down. The WHO convened a meeting in Freetown, Sierra Leone, to discuss the establishment of a biobank with "thousands of samples of blood, semen, urine and breast milk from

---

[33] Caitlin Hanson, *Ebola Diagnosis Delayed after Air Canada Refuses to Transport Blood Sample*, CBC NEWS, Oct. 17, 2014, available at www.cbc.ca/news/canada/edmonton/ebola-diagnosis-delayed-after-air-canada-refuses-to-transport-blood-sample-1.2803879.

[34] Akin Abayomi, Rebecca Katz, Scott Spence, Brian Conton and Sahr M. Gevao, *Managing Dangerous Pathogens: Challenges in the Wake of the Recent West African Ebola Outbreak*, 1(1) GLOBAL SECURITY: HEALTH, SCIENCE AND POLICY, 51–57 (2016) DOI:10.1080/23779497.2016.1228431 available at www .tandfonline.com/doi/pdf/10.1080/23779497.2016.1228431. ("Over the course of the outbreak, Ebola samples were subjected to one of the following: destruction, export out of the affected country through an official government agreement, export out of the affected country without an agreement or continued storage in country. The samples that remained in the region were often stored in facilities without adequate biosafety or biosecurity, that is, 'protection, control and accountability measures implemented to prevent the loss, theft, misuse, diversion or intentional release of biological agents and toxins and related resources as well as unauthorised access to, retention or transfer of such material'. Common practice for safe and secure handling of Ebola when conducting research is to operate within a Biosafety Level 4 (BSL4) laboratory. There are, however, only two BSL4 facilities in Africa, located in Gabon and South Africa.")

confirmed and suspected Ebola patients, as well as swabs taken from the bodies of people who died from the virus."[35] The notion of putting such a bank in place without sufficient biosafety and biosecurity capacity to facilitate storage, use, and shipping of the samples to other countries without sufficient control mechanisms, raised concerns about the potential for accidental release of virus and/or for the virus to end up in the hands of terrorist groups that could weaponize it.[36] This matter highlights a number of concerns about open sample sharing during an emergency: Who is receiving the samples? Do they have the right certification to work with the pathogen requested? Is their national certification process acceptable to the provider country in terms of biosafety and biosecurity? All of these questions in the absence of harmonized, agreed upon biobanking and sample sharing mechanisms system identify issues that can delay rapid access to samples significantly in emergencies.

9.8 THE US APPROACH: LAUNCHING NATIONAL EFFORTS AND COLLABORATING WITH INTERNATIONAL PARTNERS

As result of these experiences, the HHS convened an ad hoc, cross-sectoral sample sharing working group. The group was led by the Office of the Assistant Secretary for Preparedness and Response (ASPR) and the Centers for Disease Control and Prevention (CDC), whose membership comprises relevant agencies throughout the US government. Representatives focused on analyzing the barriers to sample sharing to improve access to limited samples (either of national or international origin) in the context of enhancing public health emergency preparedness and response capacities. This group also focused on developing a framework and process for US agencies to immediately determine sample needs, explore sources of samples, prioritize allocation to expedite response efforts, and ultimately share samples through a standard MTA denominated as a Simple Letter Agreement (SLA) that contained predetermined terms and conditions aimed at expediting response efforts. As part of the development of this process, the working group also focused on how to address the regulatory issues for import, export, and transport of samples. This discussion led to the creation of a team of experts from US government agencies

---

[35] Erika Check Hayden, *Proposed Ebola Biobank Would Strengthen African Science*, 524 NATURE 146–47 (2015), available at www.nature.com/news/proposed-ebola-biobank-would-strengthen-african-science -1.18158.

[36] Rose Gottemoeller, *Biosecurity in the Time of Ebola*, available at https://africsis.org/2015/03/press-releases-biosecurity-in-the-time-of-ebola/. ("We also completed a biosecurity assessment of the Malian high containment laboratory that processes Ebola samples, and will soon support this lab in bolstering its security measures. Working closely with our DoD threat reduction colleagues, we are also making sure that other labs in West Africa that store Ebola samples identify vulnerabilities and rapidly implement physical security measures. We put a premium on flexibility and speed so we could rapidly respond to developments in the outbreak. In November, when Mali experienced an unexpected uptick of Ebola cases, we responded to an urgent request to stand up an Emergency Operations Center in Bamako by quickly redirecting funds for this initiative. Within a week of the original request, the center's equipment was in place – lightning speed by government standards.")

with regulatory authority over biological specimens, who can be called upon during an emergency to help determine and obtain the necessary permits/licenses/approvals, to expedite the import/export process.

In addition to a national approach to the challenges of sample sharing, the working group also promoted international action in collaboration with partners of the Global Health Security Initiative (GHSI).[37] GHSI is an informal international partnership among Canada, the European Commission, France, Germany, Italy, Japan, Mexico, the United Kingdom, and the United States with the World Health Organization as an expert advisor. This partnership was launched in 2001 to address health security issues, including preparedness and response to biological threats.

Several GHSI members experienced challenges in trying to obtain MERS-CoV samples. To address these issues, members recognized "the importance of pathogen sample sharing in strengthening our capabilities to respond to emerging public health threats of international concern" during the 2013 GHSI ministerial meeting. At that time, GHSI ministers agreed upon their "intent to adhere to the principles, goals and spirit of the IHR in encouraging the timely sharing of samples and clinical information among GHSI member country laboratories when responding to non-influenza pathogens with pandemic potential," and they committed to "support open, transparent, and rapid sharing [of samples] to facilitate a timely public health response." They also instructed technical experts to create mechanisms to facilitate sample sharing among GHSI countries and to make the work available to the WHO in support of its continued global efforts to strengthen collective preparedness for public health threats with pandemic potential.[38]

Following this commitment, GHSI members established the GHSI Sample Sharing Task Group (SSTG) (chaired by the United Kingdom) which, in close collaboration with the GHSI Laboratory Network (chaired by Canada), analyzed case studies and conducted table-top exercises (at both the technical and ministerial levels) to document some of the major challenges encountered at various steps of the sample sharing process and to find solutions to address them. This was followed by the development of a framework to facilitate the rapid sharing of non-influenza biological materials among GHSI members during a potential or actual public health emergency of international concern. The framework is based on consensus for open, transparent, and rapid sharing to facilitate a timely public health response. This framework also provides a process for requesting/sending samples among the GHSI members, based on prioritization of sample distribution among countries when samples are limited, and based on which a GHSI member is able to advance collective public health preparedness and response efforts significantly for the wider group and the global community. Notably, GHSI members also developed

[37] Global Health Security Initiative, available at www.ghsi.ca/english/index.asp.
[38] Global Health Security Initiative, Ministerial Statement (2013) available at www.ghsi.ca/english/statementitaly2013.asp.

a template for an MTA based on the SLA to be used in emergency sample sharing situations, which sets expectations through agreed-upon terms and conditions around sample use, third party sharing, and other terms, during an emergency. In 2016, GHSI ministers committed to share these processes created for GHSI members with the WHO, members of the Global Health Security Agenda, and other international fora to help strengthen global public health capacity building for preparedness and response.[39]

9.9 TESTING THE APPROACH DURING ZIKA

While in the midst of developing the national and GHSI frameworks and template MTA, reports from Brazil[40] appeared to associate the Zika virus infections with a steep increase in the number of babies born with microcephaly (abnormally small heads and underdeveloped brains), and with a higher number of cases of Guillain-Barré syndrome, a neurological disorder characterized by temporary paralysis.[41] With widespread international concern, in particular in the Americas, the WHO declared the cluster of microcephaly cases and other neurological disorders reported in Brazil a PHEIC under the IHR (2005).[42]

Prior to the WHO PHEIC declaration, there was widespread interest in obtaining the virus to check whether mutations were the cause of the new symptoms the virus seemed to be causing, to better understand the disease, and to develop diagnostics for epidemiological investigation and clinical confirmation. Development of diagnostic tests was of crucial importance since apparently only 20 percent of the cases were symptomatic, meaning that pregnant women could have been unaware that they were infected. Although a reverse transcriptase polymerase chain reaction (RT-PCR) test was developed rapidly to detect Zika virus, the test was only able to detect the virus in symptomatic patients or during a very few days after the symptoms subsided. There was no validated serologic test to detect asymptomatic or convalescent patients. In addition, because of cross-reactivity among related chikungunya, dengue, yellow fever, and West Nile viruses, serological tests were difficult to develop, validate, and

---

[39] Global Health Security Initiative, Ministerial Statement (2016), available at www.ghsi.ca/english/ statementWashington2016.asp.
[40] Igor Paploski et al., *Time Lags between Exanthematous Illness Attributed to Zika Virus, Guillain-Barré Syndrome, and Microcephaly, Salvador, Brazil*, 22(8) EMERGING INFECTIOUS DISEASES 1438–44 (2016), available at www.ncbi.nlm.nih.gov/pmc/articles/PMC4982160/.
[41] E. E. Petersen, J. E. Staples, D. Meaney-Delman et al. *Interim Guidelines for Pregnant Women During a Zika Virus Outbreak – United States*, 65 MMWR MORB MORTAL WKLY REP (2016), available at http:// dx.doi.org/10.15585/mmwr.mm6502e1external icon.
[42] World Health Organization, WHO Statement on the First Meeting of the International Health Regulations (2005) Emergency Committee on Zika Virus and Observed Increase in Neurological Disorders www.who.int/news-room/detail/01-02-2016-who-statement-on-the-first-meeting-of-the-international-health-regulations-(2005)-(ihr-2005)-emergency-committee-on-zika-virus-and-observed-increase-in-neurological-disorders-and-neonatal-malformations.

interpret.[43] In addition, there was neither a specific antiviral treatment available for Zika virus nor a vaccine available to prevent Zika virus infection. Thus, the need for rapid and robust sharing of Zika materials such as Zika virus strains, serum samples, and quality control materials became essential. Once again, difficulties in international sample sharing became evident.

Brazil shared samples initially with the US CDC, which allowed the CDC to confirm the presence of the virus in the brain tissue of some babies who died with microcephaly.[44] Researchers from the United States and Europe largely had to work with samples from previous outbreaks. They agreed that without the virus currently circulating in Brazil – the epicenter of the Zika crisis in the Americas – laboratories were being forced to work with samples from previous outbreaks, not allowing experts to follow the evolution of the virus or to develop diagnostic tests, drugs, and vaccines.[45] Reportedly, the major reason for Brazil not sharing samples resided in their ABS legislation, which created special conditions and requirements for Brazilian researchers and institutions to be able to share genetic material (e.g., blood samples containing Zika and other viruses).[46] Press stated at the time that "the reluctance [to share samples] may stem from the uncertainty about how the samples would be used and in what way" by the end users. Brazil's new ABS legislation gave rise to considerable confusion within the country and abroad about how and when samples could be exported and shared. Although high-level discussions with intervention from WHO and ministers of health of some affected countries occurred, the flow of samples was impaired for months.

Before Zika cases were identified in the United States, and in the midst of trying to obtain samples from Brazil and other South American countries, the US sample sharing working group collaborated closely to implement some of the national protocols. They worked, first and foremost, to determine potential sources of

---

[43] T. Oduyebo, E. E. Petersen, S. A. Rasmussen et al. *Update: Interim Guidelines for Health Care Providers Caring for Pregnant Women and Women of Reproductive Age with Possible Zika Virus Exposure – United States*, 65 MMWR MORB MORTAL WKLY REP 122–27 (2016), available at www .cdc.gov/mmwr/volumes/65/wr/mm6505e2.htm.

[44] Sonja Rasmussen et al., *Zika Virus and Birth Defects – Reviewing the Evidence for Causality*, 374 NEW ENG. J. MED. 1981–87 (2016), available at www.nejm.org/doi/full/10.1056/NEJMsr1604338? query=featured_home.

[45] Associated Press, *Few Samples Are Being Shared by Brazil, Worrying International Researchers*, STATNEWS (Feb. 3, 2016) available at www.statnews.com/2016/02/03/zika-samples-brazil/; *Zika: When Research Goes off the Rails*, available at https://journosdiary.com/2016/02/07/zika-when-research-goes-off-the-rails/.

[46] Maria Cheng, Raphael Satter, and Joshua Goodman, *Few Zika Samples Being Shared by Brazil*, available at www.businessinsider.com/ap-health-officials-want-more-zika-samples-data-from-brazil -2016-2. ("U.N. and U.S. health officials tell The Associated Press that Brazil has yet to share enough samples and disease data needed to answer the most worrying question about the Zika outbreak: whether the virus is actually responsible for the increase in the number of babies born with abnormally small heads in Brazil. The lack of data is frustrating efforts to develop diagnostic tests, drugs and vaccines. Laboratories in the United States and Europe are relying on samples from previous outbreaks. Scientists say having so little to work with is hampering their ability to track the virus' evolution.")

samples (from foreign partners and for if/when cases appeared in the United States). The working group also developed and implemented a process to determine the specific needs for samples and to prioritize, through a consensus approach, access to the limited samples obtained. Priorities included the development of diagnostics tools. This encompassed initiatives such as the development and validation of serological diagnostics by the US CDC, development and validation of a test to determine blood supply safety, collaboration with the private sector to scale-up manufacturing of diagnostics at commercial scale for clinical diagnostics, and development or testing of medical countermeasures. As a result, and through concerted action by the working group and in close collaboration with Panama's Gorgas Memorial Institute, the first serum samples from convalescent patients arrived at the CDC. Soon after, cases appeared in Puerto Rico, and the CDC was able to isolate the virus from a sample sent to the CDC for confirmatory diagnostics.

Both sets of samples were obtained using the special MTA developed by the sample sharing working group, the Emergency Use Simple Letter Agreement (EUSLA). The EUSLA allowed the sample provider to authorize the recipient (in this case a US agency, in particular the CDC), to use the samples "for any legitimate purpose required to rapidly prevent, detect, prepare for and respond to the spread or transmission of Zika virus" and in addition, allowed for the samples to be "further distributed to other entities for this purpose." Based on the consent of the provider expressed through the EUSLA, samples were immediately shared with the US National Institutes of Health, which utilized existing infrastructure to amplify the material and make it available to the scientific and public health communities via the Biological and Emerging Infections Research Resources Repository (BEI Resources). Zika virus strains and genomic RNA from particular strains, the Zika MAC-ELISA diagnostic test, the CDC Trioplex rRT-PCR assay (which tests for Zika, dengue, and chikungunya infections) and other valuable Zika materials (i.e., reagents) were shared with academic institutions, companies, and public health agencies worldwide. BEI fulfilled 1,865 requests for Zika materials. Approximately 17 percent of the requests were for Zika materials provided by CDC's National Center for Emerging and Zoonotic Diseases (NCEZID). A total of 430 agreements were put in place to allow the shipments of Zika materials to 124 universities, hospitals, and research institutes, 43 biotech and pharma companies, 16 federal agencies and state public health departments, and 4 foreign governments. Materials were distributed to 35 US states, Puerto Rico, and 23 foreign countries.[47] By the end of July 2016 (approximately five months after WHO declared a PHEIC), the US Food and Drug Administration had issued Emergency Use Authorization (EUA) for seven molecular- and serology-based assays for Zika, which enabled greater public access to diagnostic testing. In recognition of the work done to

---

[47]   Data from the Technology Transfer and Intellectual Property Office (TTIPO) at the National Institute of Allergy and Infectious Diseases (NIAID), courtesy of Mukul Ranjan and Michael Mowatt.

facilitate rapid sharing of Zika virus specimens and related material, key members of the core sample sharing working group in the US Department of Health and Human Services received the Interagency Partnership Award from the Federal Laboratory Consortium for Technology Transfer in April 2018.[48]

In parallel to these actions, the GHSI Sample Sharing Task Group and the Global Health Security Action Group Laboratory Network implemented parallel and coordinated strategies to determine sample needs and prioritize distribution of scarce material among GHSI members, in addition to sharing scientific information and preparedness and response strategies. At the onset of the outbreak and when Zika was confirmed in Mexico, efforts focused on sharing their material. However, samples were not shared due to the need in Mexico to revise IRB-approved protocols to include new patient consents for sample collection and potential use of those samples beyond basic research and clinical diagnostics, as well as due to the lengthy and complex process to issue export permits. As a result of this combination of challenges, the samples were ultimately not shared.

Later, once the CDC isolated the virus from samples from Puerto Rico, the GHSI process was successful and Zika virus isolates were distributed using a template GHSI MTA. The MTA contained similar terms and conditions for sample sharing to ensure rapid, transparent sharing of the samples, allowed their use for any purposes related to preparedness for and response to the Zika outbreak, and with an agreement to share the knowledge obtained from the use of the samples in a way that could benefit the public health community worldwide. Clearly, in the absence of the years of work on sample sharing and without an agreed-upon set of guidelines to share samples during an emergency, the international sharing of samples among GHSI laboratories may have been additionally delayed. As agreed upon by the GHSI ministers, a key objective of this collaboration is to share these tools and the principles behind them with global organizations like the WHO, World Organisation for Animal Health (OIE), and Food and Agriculture Organization of the United Nations (FAO) so that they can be adapted and implemented, as desired, more broadly and cross-sectorally, to facilitate sample sharing during public health emergencies, including those where disease can be of zoonotic origin.

9.10 DISCUSSION

The examples provided show why the concept of "sample sharing preparedness and response coordination" is so critical in the context of public health emergencies and global health security. Having a pre-negotiated MTA that is based on an agreed-upon set of guidelines to share samples during an emergency enabled rapid sharing

[48] National Institute for Allergy and Infectious Diseases, *Zika Virus Material Sharing Earns NIAID, CDC, NIH, and HHS an Interagency Partnership Award* available at www.niaid.nih.gov/news-events /zika-virus-material-sharing-earns-niaid-cdc-nih-and-hhs-interagency-partnership-award.

of scarce samples in a way that fostered rapid response action both at national levels within and among a group of collaborating countries. However, much remains to be done, both for countries at the national level and at the international level.

In the United States, establishing capacities for sample sharing has been recognized as a national priority. Thus, the 2018 National Biodefense Strategy (NBS) calls for "appropriate needs for sharing – under both routine and crisis conditions – timely information (e.g., data and results), samples, and reagents among sectors including research, food security, emergency services, law enforcement and human, animal, and plant health." In addition, the NBS calls for the federal government to "seek to address impediments to the timely sharing of information, samples, and reagents among countries and international organizations under both routine and crisis conditions; and improve the end-to-end management of samples and specimens to minimize the potential of their accidental or intentional release."[49]

US government departments and agencies are addressing this issue under the post Joint External Evaluation's US National Health Security Plan,[50] to improve collaboration and coordination across all levels of government (i.e., federal, state, local, territorial, and tribal) so that samples can be collected quickly and efficiently, particularly at the onset of a potential public health emergency.

At the global level, efforts also continue. Following the 2014–16 Ebola outbreak and at the recommendation of a number of expert panels, the WHO Research & Development (R&D) Blueprint was developed to "create an enabling environment through which the R&D community, through increased funding, data sharing and partnerships, can drive change in the public health landscape to provide an elevated level of global impact."[51] As part of this initiative, the WHO has embarked on developing guidance and tools to frame collaborations and exchanges, including tools to aid with sample sharing and in 2017 made a call for public comments.[52] As a result of this process, the WHO developed a draft MTA building tool,[53] intended for use prior to a public health emergency. According to the WHO, this draft tool is "part of broader efforts to build capacity to manage sample sharing in a manner that ensures the full public health potential of valuable biological material is realized for rapid detection of, and response to public health emergencies." Although the tool establishes principles for sample sharing and helps guiding the potential user

[49] U.S. National Biodefense Strategy available at www.whitehouse.gov/wp-content/uploads/2018/09/National-Biodefense-Strategy.pdf.

[50] United States Health Security National Action Plan: Strengthening Implementation of the International Health Regulations based on the 2016 Joint External Evaluation (2016) available at www.phe.gov/Preparedness/international/Documents/jee-nap-508.pdf.

[51] World Health Organization, An R&D Blueprint for Action to Prevent Epidemics (2016) available at www.who.int/blueprint/what/improving-coordination/workstream_5_document_on_financing.pdf.

[52] World Health Organization, Public Consultation on Draft R&D Blueprint Tool available at www.who.int/blueprint/what/norms-standards/draft-mta-tool/en/.

[53] World Health Organization, Draft R&D Blueprint Tool available at http://apps.who.int/blueprint/mta-tool/.

through the typical content of an MTA, this tool still does not address the challenges for a potential lengthy negotiation about ABS outside of a bilateral negotiation in the context of an emergency.

The issue of ABS around sample sharing during emergencies remains a critical one. As noted in the WHO Director General's report to the 72nd World Health Assembly,[54] countries have started putting national ABS measures in place, including those implementing the Nagoya Protocol. This report reaffirms that "the Nagoya Protocol has public health implications, and that these implications include opportunities to advance both public health and principles of fair and equitable sharing of benefits." In addition, the report highlights that "issues are multidimensional, involving: diverse ministerial and stakeholder communities; developments in biotechnology, health technology and information technology; as well as questions of international and domestic policy, law and procedure." The report also recognizes that the implementation of the Nagoya Protocol at each country's national level requires involvement of many sectors and, importantly, that health sector action is critical to "ensuring that public health considerations are duly taken into account." Finally, the WHO committed to explore the issue further in a comprehensive, inclusive way that is aligned with the spirit of the IHR (2005).

The strong advocacy of GHSI members that started in 2013 and the work that followed were critical stepping stones in bringing this issue to the attention of the WHO along with the request to look at this from a global perspective. In summary, the ability to rapidly disseminate samples relevant to novel or reemerging threats is a critical link between detecting a threat to public health and mounting an effective response. Improved capacities and capabilities to detect threats will be limited if the global community cannot mutually share these samples and access the resulting information to develop needed response tools, whilst taking into account the stipulations of the IHR, CBD, and/or other international agreements, as appropriate. The international community must work across sectors at the national and international levels to raise awareness, discuss and develop policy and operational solutions to the challenges outlined here.

---

[54] World Health Organization, The Public Health Implications of Implementation of the Nagoya Protocol: Report of the Director-General, available at http://apps.who.int/gb/ebwha/pdf_files/ WHA72/A72_32-en.pdf.

10

Facilitating Material Transfer Agreements from a Practitioner's Perspective

Michael Mowatt and Mukul Ranjan

Two factors strongly influence the pace of innovation .... One is the level of resource deployment, how many resources are going into the process of innovation. The other is the speed of information flow in that process.

Robert Cook-Deegan, Director, National Cancer Policy Board, National Academy of Sciences, "Secrecy in Science: Exploring University, Industry and Government Relationships," 1999

Most scientists and observers of the biological sciences understand that the sharing of materials and samples is central to the natural sciences. Indeed, samples are representations of the natural world that science seeks to understand and the sharing of these is essential. In the normal progression of science, scientists share their discoveries with other scientists who then build on their work, this can only be done if the materials and information used to make the original discoveries are made available. Indeed, for science to function, the sharing, not just of ideas, but materials, data and procedures is essential.

This chapter will focus on the sharing of materials, that until recently occurred informally between scientists who knew each other or had heard about their work through publications or presentations. These transfers were collegial and would sometimes be documented in a letter, if at all.

For example, in June of 1736, Johan Frederik Gronovius, a Dutch botanist, wrote a letter to Carl Linnaeus in which he informs him that many of the seeds he received earlier have germinated. He gives an identification of some of these plants. He hopes that Linnaeus will bring with him a cutting of those plants in Dutch banker and naturalist Clifford's garden that have sprouted from Gronovius's seeds, when he will pay him a visit at Leiden. He informs him that by then Gronovius will have received another parcel from British botanist Mark Catesby containing some seeds from Florida. Gronovius states that he aims to share those plants that are completely unknown in Holland with Clifford exclusively, and asks that Linnaeus should bring with him a list of American plants that are growing in Clifford's garden.[1]

[1] Letter from Johan Frederik Gronovius to Carl Linnaeus (June 15, 1736). *See* http://urn.kb.se/resolve? urn=urn:nbn:se:alvin:portal:record-222924.

In August 1832, Charles Darwin wrote to John Stevens Henslow that he has

> sent home 4 bottles with animals in spirits I have three more, but would not send them till I had a fourth. – I shall be anxious to know how they fare. – I made an enormous collection of Arachnidæ at Rio. – Also a good many small beetles in pill-boxes; but it is not the best time of year for the latter. – As I have only 34 of a case of Diptera and I have not sent them.[2]

More recently, Arthur Kornberg wrote to R. K. Morton in Australia in November 1961, "First let me acknowledge with thanks your last two shipments of the yeast and cytochrome b2 DNA's. Each arrived frozen and we're impressed by the ingenuity of your packaging."[3]

As recently as the 1970s, Bruce Alberts describes a world when researchers participated in the free flow of ideas and subsequently materials at conferences such as the Cold Spring Harbor meetings during the heady early days of molecular biology.

> I was one of the early molecular biologists. I worked for 30 years with the bacteriophage T4 that Max Delbrück introduced as a model organism. The spirit that he promulgated in my field was one of complete sharing of ideas and resources, and at that time there were frequent Cold Spring Harbor meetings where everybody laid out their latest data and emptied their notebooks, with no idea that anybody would ever think to steal an idea or claim credit for something they didn't deserve. This was before the biotechnology revolution, before there was any idea that you could become wealthy or start a company and that there could be any major commercial value to what we were doing. We thought about it in terms of new developments for medicine and doing good for people.[4]

The examples cited above of a free exchange between scientists were the norm largely in the academic world. Scientists in industry operated very differently having long been used to contractual agreements for sharing materials.

For academic science, a shift started to take place in the mid-1970s as the molecular biology revolution occurred and both business and scientists saw its potential for new health interventions. The passage of seminal new legislation in the US in the 1980s further accelerated these trends. These factors, combined with changing standards of patenting, led to greatly increased interactions between commercial and academic science and the emergence of many biotechnology companies with strong ties to the academic world.[5] As a consequence, commercial practices and contractual arrangements entered the world of universities and the

---

[2] Letter from Charles Darwin to J. S. Henslow (July 3, 1832) (on file with the Darwin Correspondence Project). *See* www.darwinproject.ac.uk/letter/DCP-LETT-178.xml.

[3] Letter from Arthur Kornberg to Robert K. Morton (Nov. 16, 1961). *See* https://profiles.nlm.nih.gov/ps/access/WHBBCC.pdf.

[4] NAT'L RESEARCH COUNCIL, FINDING THE PATH: ISSUES OF ACCESS TO RESEARCH RESOURCES (1999).

[5] MEETING MINUTES OF THE NAT'L INST. HEALTH, WORKING GROUP ON RESEARCH TOOLS (June 4, 1998). *See* https://acd.od.nih.gov/documents/minutes/06041998minutes.html.

practice of documenting the exchange of research materials under Material Transfer Agreements (MTAs) commenced.[6]

The National Research Council report "Finding the Path" describes this changing climate:

> As recently as twenty years ago, universities played very little role in commercializing their own research. Typically, the government retained ownership of patentable inventions made with federal funds but rarely exercised its rights. Because scientists were, as they are today, free to publish the results of their research, advances in science quickly entered the public domain. This helped keep access to research resources open, in two complementary ways. First, any tools or materials that one university scientist developed were made available to all other scientists. There were, of course, always researchers who would keep the fruits of their work to themselves in order to maintain a competitive edge over their peers, but this was frowned upon. Sharing was the norm. Second, as long as university researchers were making their findings freely available to everyone, industry was generally willing to provide these basic scientists with research resources at little or no cost, on the theory that the results of the research would ultimately benefit industry. But the Bayh-Dole (Bayh-Dole) and Stevenson-Wydler Acts of 1980 and the (Federal) Technology Transfer Act of 1986 changed the rules, allowing universities to hold the rights to patents on innovations developed using federal funds. Universities have since plunged into the commercial world, licensing the research of their scientists to private companies.[7]

The report states further that post–Bayh-Dole there was increasing pressure on universities to generate revenue and a return on investment post–Bayh-Dole.

> And so it is that universities, in attempting to protect their interests, sometimes end up going down the same path as private industry, demanding restrictive MTAs on their most valuable technology. Or they sell or assign rights to the product of their research to a company – sometimes one started by the university scientists who performed the work; and that restricts access to the product."[8]

The National Institutes of Health (NIH) committee on research resources similarly notes that two substantial changes took place in the 1980s and 1990s that restricted how academic science operated: New legislation provided incentives for the increasing commercialization of academic science via newly established "technology transfer offices" (TTOs) at universities, and a new class of inventions relating to early stage discoveries has grown since then. This patenting of early stage technology led to the rise of spinoffs and the growth of the biotechnology industry.[9]

[6] NAT'L RESEARCH COUNCIL, SHARING LABORATORY RESOURCES: GENETICALLY ALTERED MICE (1994). *See* www.nap.edu/read/9156/chapter/1.
[7] NAT'L RESEARCH COUNCIL, *supra* note 4.
[8] *Id.*
[9] MEETING MINUTES OF THE NAT'L INST. HEALTH, WORKING GROUP ON RESEARCH TOOLS (June 4, 1998). *See* https://acd.od.nih.gov/documents/minutes/06041998minutes.html.

Eisenberg describes the new biotech sector as adding a complexity that had not hitherto been observed:

> These biotechnology firms differ from established pharmaceutical firms in important ways. Many of these firms have academic scientists as founders, retain strong scientific and financial ties to academic institutions, and rely on government grants for research funding. Lacking end products for sale to non-research consumers, some of these firms survive in the private sector by selling research tools and the research capabilities of their scientific personnel to other institutions, especially to major pharmaceutical firms.

Eisenberg points out that in this new environment institutions and some scientists also begin to view early stage technology and research tools as a means of revenue or by denying them to competitors as a means of maintaining a competitive advantage.[10]

The lines between academia and industry were also being blurred by increased funding and associated restrictions from industry to academia. Funding for science during this period also inverted from being largely publicly funded to being funded increasingly by the corporate sector.[11] Associated with this increase in corporate funding the university changed from being largely academic to having a more mixed academic-corporate view with associated changes in practice and perspective.

As universities began to work more closely with the commercial sector, they first began seeing MTAs when materials were received from companies. Soon universities became increasingly involved in the commercialization process itself and they began emulating many practices from the commercial world. One of these was valuing materials along with patents as assets that should be transferred under contractual agreements. Consequently, universities started sharing their own materials under MTAs. Thus, restrictions in MTAs that were first seen in agreements coming from companies before the 1980s became more widespread across all research sectors as university science increasingly embraced commercialization post–Bayh-Dole.

During the early years, some universities embraced their new role with enthusiasm. Some of the early problems with accessing platform technologies such as microarray technology, the OncoMouse and the polymerase chain reaction (PCR), were in fact because of academic licensing practices and not the use of MTAs.

Many university scientists began raising concerns by the late 1980s and into the early 1990s that this increase in assertion of proprietary rights (patents, MTAs, restrictive licenses) and the accompanying restriction of the free flow of ideas and materials in research was stifling research. Many complained about the delays

---

[10] Rebecca Eisenberg, *Bargaining over the Transfer of Research Tools: Is This Market Failing or Emerging?* in EXPANDING THE BOUNDARIES OF INTELLECTUAL PROPERTY: INNOVATION POLICY FOR THE KNOWLEDGE SOCIETY 223–49 (Dreyfuss, Zimmerman, and First, eds., 2001).

[11] *See* Figure 04.04 *in* Nat'l Science Foundation, *Science and Engineering Indicators* (2018), www.nsf.gov /statistics/2018/nsb20181/report.

caused by the use of MTAs and the curtailment of their ability to share reagents. With the growth of the biotechnology industry, there was also a broader division in the academic community into a few who embraced and benefitted from this new privatization and corporatization of science and the majority who did not and resented the erosion of broad academic freedoms that had characterized the academic life.

As these changes percolated through academic science, there was an early focus on MTAs as a problem: They were the most common form of agreement and affected many scientists. Often these agreements were simple contracts for an easily understood transaction, they were easy to count, and scientists were complaining about delays due to MTAs. In addition, the investment of resources required to process MTAs – largely managed by under-resourced technology transfer offices (TTOs) – created a convergence of interests, between both scientists and TTOs, to seek simpler solutions.

The NIH has played an important role in addressing concerns related to MTAs when they first appeared and in instituting practices at the NIH that reflect its policies promoting the free and rapid exchange of both materials and information. When concerns first appeared, NIH worked with the Association of University Technology Managers (AUTM) to develop the Uniform Biological Material Transfer Agreement (UBMTA), which was aimed at creating a standard set of terms and conditions for material transfers to which academic and government institutions could agree.[12] Later NIH convened a group to examine the problem and provide recommendations. This led to the development of the NIH research tools policy which was announced in 1999 along with an even simpler MTA, the Simple Letter Agreement (SLA), that is now used as the default at NIH intramural laboratories and which recipients of NIH funding are strongly encouraged to use.[13] Following this NIH developed a series of policies over the years that govern the sharing materials and data by recipients of NIH funding.[14]

The concern over material and data sharing continued to embroil the research community.[15] In October 2001, the National Academy of Sciences convened a committee on Responsibilities of Authorship in the Biological Sciences "to evaluate the responsibilities of authors of scientific papers in the life sciences to share data and materials referenced in their publications." The final report,

---

[12] Uniform Biological Material Transfer Agreement: Discussion of Public Comments Received; Publication of the Final Format of the Agreement, 60 Fed. Reg., 12771 (Mar. 8, 1995). *See* www .govinfo.gov/content/pkg/FR-1995-03-08/pdf/95-5644.pdf.

[13] Principles and Guidelines for Recipients of NIH Research Grants and Contracts on Obtaining and Disseminating Biomedical Research Resources, 64 Fed. Reg. 72090 (Dec. 23, 1999). *See* www.govinfo .gov/content/pkg/FR-1999-12-23/pdf/99-33292.pdf.

[14] Nat'l Inst. Health, *Sharing Policies and Related Guidance on NIH-Funded Research Resources. See* https://grants.nih.gov/policy/sharing.htm.

[15] Sam Halabi, Michelle Rourke, and Rebecca Katz, *The Law and Ethics of Data-Sharing during Infectious Disease Emergencies*, 8(4) J. HEALTHCARE L. & POL'Y, July 25, 2019.

sometimes referred to as the "Cech Report," was published in 2003.[16] The report stated that "common perceived problems are the ignoring or denial of requests for materials or data associated with a publication and long delays in honoring such requests. Increasingly, data and materials that are shared come with restrictions, such as material transfer agreements (MTAs) that limit how the resources may be used."

The committee concluded that

> community standards for sharing publication-related data and materials should flow from the general principle that the publication of scientific information is intended to move science forward. More specifically, the act of publishing is a quid pro quo in which authors receive credit and acknowledgment in exchange for disclosure of their scientific findings. An author's obligation is not only to release data and materials to enable others to verify or replicate published findings (as journals already implicitly or explicitly require) but also to provide them in a form on which other scientists can build with further research.

The report identified five principles, one of which deals explicitly with material transfers:

> Principle 4. Authors of scientific publications should anticipate which materials integral to their publications are likely to be requested and should state in the "Materials and Methods" section or elsewhere how to obtain them. Consistent with the spirit and principles of publication, materials described in a scientific paper should be shared in a way that permits other investigators to replicate the work described in the paper and to build on its findings. If a material transfer agreement (MTA) is required, the URL of a Web site where the MTA can be viewed should be provided.

The Cech Report also listed ten recommendations of which the following deal with MTAs and suggest: The use of a standard MTA to streamline the process and that the terms of the MTA should not create a barrier for sharing (Recommendation 4), avoiding giving exclusive licenses (Recommendation 3), complete negotiations within sixty days (Recommendation 5) and that recipients of materials should acknowledge the provider in publications (Recommendation 10).

In addition to its central importance to the proper functioning of science in general, material sharing during public health emergencies, especially those caused by infectious agents, is of vital importance. At a time of intense national and global pressure, when the identity of the pathogen is not certain nor are means to combat it, there is little appetite for lengthy negotiations or delays in accessing samples. We have seen increasing numbers of such epidemics recently and they are likely to be with us in the coming years.[17] The recent outbreak of Zika in South America was an

---

[16] Nat'l Research Council, Sharing Publication-Related Data and Materials: Responsibilities of Authorship in the Life Sciences (2003).

[17] David Morens, Gregory Folkers, and Anthony Fauci, *The Challenge of Emerging and Re-emerging Infectious Diseases*, 430 Nature 242–49 (2004)

example of a crisis in which samples were not easy to obtain.[18] Similar problems regarding access to samples manifested during the Ebola outbreak a few years earlier. These delays and sometimes the lack of a full range of relevant samples impaired the response activities by allowing uninformed speculation about the source of infection to spread, in limiting diagnostic capability and in slowing development of countermeasures to combat the infection.

In this context, we note that international transfers of materials are more complex and often take longer to complete. As science continues to become increasingly global, we anticipate seeing more of these transfers.

The US Department of Health and Human Services began working on a plan to share samples during public health emergencies of international concern in 2015 and has made substantial progress in this effort. More recently the World Health Organization has recognized the importance of sharing biological samples during an outbreak. These efforts are detailed in Chapter 9 of this volume.

Commercialization and difficult MTA negotiations are not the only reasons for reduced sharing. Increasing academic competition, scarce materials and cost of distribution especially for hard to make and ship materials such as genetically altered mice, difficult to purify proteins or hard to obtain microbial isolates are also contributing factors. Often these other factors may be playing a role when MTA negotiations fail. In the early days of making transgenic mice, the process took more than a year and was quite unpredictable. Understandably, laboratories were reluctant to share this resource to maintain a competitive advantage.[19] We have experienced MTA negotiations being dragged out because the investigator had informally told their TTO they are not ready to share until they themselves had published.

A 2002 survey of geneticists found that commercial interests are not the only reason for withholding data and materials. The geneticists surveyed by Campbell and his colleagues cited additional reasons for intentionally withholding information, data or materials related to their own published research. These reasons included the financial cost of providing the materials or information to others; the need to protect the ability of a graduate student, postdoctoral fellow or junior faculty member to publish follow-up papers; the need to protect one's own ability to publish follow-up papers; the cost of providing materials; the need to preserve patient confidentiality; and the likelihood that the recipient will never reciprocate. It is

---

[18] Maria Cheng, Raphael Satter, and Joshua Goodman, *Few Zika Samples Being Shared by Brazil*, available at https://apnews.com/2db2a3581d2a42a08f5b031419cb09ed. ("U.N. and U.S. health officials tell The Associated Press that Brazil has yet to share enough samples and disease data needed to answer the most worrying question about the Zika outbreak: whether the virus is actually responsible for the increase in the number of babies born with abnormally small heads in Brazil. The lack of data is frustrating efforts to develop diagnostic tests, drugs and vaccines. Laboratories in the United States and Europe are relying on samples from previous outbreaks. Scientists say having so little to work with is hampering their ability to track the virus' evolution.")

[19] Jon Cohen, *Share and Share Alike Is Not Always the Rule in Science*, 268 Science 1715–18 (1995).

not surprising that a reluctance to share is more common in fields in which scientific competitiveness is high.[20]

The NIH working group had noted earlier that "scientists ... may sometimes have hidden agendas of maintaining an edge in scientific competition as well as a desire for economic return. For example, despite norms (and often formal requirements) to distribute published research tools, some scientists use MTA clauses to delay or even block distribution to a competitor while maintaining a nominal willingness to cooperate."[21] As we can see from these examples, the reasons for not transferring materials can be complex, and MTAs and associated legal and policy concerns may not be the only reason that materials are not being shared but they do play a significant role.

WHAT IS AN MTA?

An MTA is a contract between two parties, the provider and the recipient, that lays out permissions, restrictions and obligations related to the receipt and use of the material. An MTA can address issues such as a description of the material being transferred, flow of information (publication), academic credit, liability, licenses or lack thereof to materials, derivatives or associated IP, ownership of new materials and inventions, permitted and non-permitted use of materials and importantly they provide a written record of the transfer (provenance). Typically, an MTA is a royalty-free, nonexclusive, nontransferable license for noncommercial research purposes. However, keeping in mind that contracts are very accommodating instruments, MTAs, depending on the language in them, can be quite variable and may include financial terms, be royalty-bearing and control yet-to-be developed intellectual property as well as have a host of controls over the research to be performed using the materials. Furthermore, MTAs are binding legal agreements and a breach of terms can lead to lawsuits. While there have been few lawsuits regarding MTAs it is suspected that more may have been settled out of court.

MTAs, like other contractual agreements that cross different sectors like academia, government or industry, must address the differing and sometimes conflicting objectives of each group. This often leads to negotiation and modification of the agreement to ensure that their goals are being met.

To alleviate concerns about MTAs, the NIH working group tried to make a distinction between materials that were primarily used for basic research ("research tools"), and materials that had commercial potential. While this was

---

[20]   Eric G. Campbell et al., *Data Withholding in Academic Genetics*, 287 JAMA 473–80 (2002).
[21]   MEETING MINUTES OF THE NAT'L INST. HEALTH, WORKING GROUP ON RESEARCH TOOLS (June 4, 1998). *See* https://acd.od.nih.gov/documents/minutes/06041998minutes.html.

easy to understand conceptually, in practice it became difficult to implement. This distinction is thought to be important for MTAs because two different kinds of MTAs could be used for these two categories: Standard ones without many restrictions that should not require much negotiation for the former and more complex ones for the materials with commercial potential. Thus, in theory, the majority of materials could be transferred rapidly under simpler nonnegotiable MTAs, and the negotiations would be limited to materials with commercial value where it made sense to spend more effort and time.

The NIH working Group also recognized at the same time a problem in defining "research tools" because depending on the use and definition the material could be both a tool for advancing research or a commercial product. For example, antibodies could be used in basic research to identify mechanisms of action for a biological pathway or they could be used in clinical diagnostics or even as a therapeutic product. If the provider and recipient do not agree on this, which is often the case, one can imagine that the terms they use for the transfer will differ, and standard nonnegotiable agreements will not be applicable. The final NIH guidelines stated:

> The definition of research tools is necessarily broad, and it is acknowledged that the same material can have different uses, being a research tool in some contexts and a product in others. In determining how an NIH funded resource that falls within the definition should be handled, Recipients should determine whether: (1) The Primary usefulness of the resource is as a tool for discovery rather than an FDA-approved product or integral component of such a product; (2) the resource is a broad, enabling invention that will be useful to many scientists (or multiple companies in developing multiple products), rather than a project or product-specific resource; and (3) the resource is readily useable or distributable as a tool rather than the situation where private sector involvement is necessary or the most expedient means for developing or distributing the resource.[22]

Closely tied to the issue of research tools is perceived value and the significance of the materials being transferred. This has been identified by many authors as being one of the reasons for extended negotiations and delays. One aspect that has not been addressed is that for most MTAs a majority of the TTO staff will not know the significance, purpose or value of a material from the nomenclature that is used to identify the material in the MTA. Very few are likely to go back to their investigators to ask additional questions about the material being transferred, its significance to the larger intellectual property (IP) portfolio of the lab and institution, and the requester's need for it. This is probably one of the more important pieces of information in an MTA but is often ignored in favor of the legal terms.

---

[22] Principles and Guidelines for Recipients of NIH Research Grants and Contracts on Obtaining and Disseminating Biomedical Research Resources, 64 Fed. Reg. 72090 (Dec. 23, 1999). *See* www.govinfo .gov/content/pkg/FR-1999-12-23/pdf/99-33292.pdf.

The NIH working group summarized the problems with MTAs into the following four categories:

1. The transaction costs for the majority of MTAs where it is not clear if the materials have any commercial value
2. Heterogeneity in the types of institutions engaged in biomedical research, that is Biotech firms, Academic institutions and Pharma
3. Differing perspectives and objectives between the scientists and the legal, corporate, TTO staff, and
4. Estimating the value or commercial importance of materials is not easy.[23]

10.1 PERSPECTIVE MATTERS

One of the themes that emerges from the NIH working group, the National Research Council Report study and some of other studies on this subject, is that each sector views the other as the cause of the delays and unreasonableness. Academic TTOs believe the problem lies with corporate partners while the latter believe it lies with universities; each believes the other has unrealistic expectations about the value of their materials. In our practice, we have seen onerous terms from all sides that are not limited to corporate, nonprofit, government or academia. Within each sector we have found substantial differences in the practices and policies of individual players. These are variable enough for us to avoid generalizations about a particular sector with whom it is easier or more difficult to work.

Furthermore, one's view can be quite different depending on whether you are a provider or the recipient of materials. Eisenberg summarizes it this way: "Institutions tend to be high-minded about the importance of unfettered access to the research tools that they want to acquire from others, but no institution is willing to share freely the materials and discoveries from which they derive significant competitive advantage."[24]

The issues that are negotiated within the academy–industry interactions may be different and less acceptable to each side than those in academy–academy or industry–industry transfers, and the emphasis placed on the ability to publish, on intellectual property, valuation or liability may indeed differ when viewed from outside each sector. Thus, each group has a set of shared understandings that are reinforced in interactions within the group but can create tension when interacting outside that group.

In addition to the differing priorities and values described above, there is a difference in the kinds of science done in different sectors. For example, research institutes and universities often generate many more materials because they are

---

[23] MEETING MINUTES OF THE NAT'L INST. HEALTH, WORKING GROUP ON RESEARCH TOOLS (June 4, 1998). *See* https://acd.od.nih.gov/documents/minutes/06041998minutes.html; Eisenberg, *supra* note 10.

[24] Eisenberg, *supra* note 10.

involved in basic research in a broad range of subjects. For example, in the biological sciences these may include environmental science, plant science, genetics, marine and aquatic biology, wildlife biology, virology and microbiology, cell and molecular biology, climate change science, forestry, natural resources among others. The existence of these materials is better known to the larger scientific community because academic scientists publish and present their data more than corporate scientists. Academic scientists can do this because they are less restricted by confidentiality than corporate scientists who are careful in what they can and cannot disclose. Consequently, noncorporate research possesses a wider range of known materials, many of which may not have a high perceived commercial value.

Furthermore, many academic institutions do not provide as much scrutiny to outgoing MTAs, and investigators may have wider latitude to distribute these without much negotiation using standard MTAs. In contrast, the amount of diversity in materials from corporations may not be readily known to most academic investigators. The materials that are known and requested from corporations tend to be proprietary drugs or other high value materials that many companies are hesitant to send out due to associated risks to products in development or already on the market.

From an industry perspective, many universities began to be viewed as commercial competitors after they acquired rights to their own intellectual property and materials and benefited from the financial incentives provided by the Bayh-Dole Act. One of the most common fears among industry providers is that materials provided to academic researchers may end up in the hands of business competitors because universities will collaborate with multiple companies and are often not diligent in keeping a firewall between projects. Another fear expressed by industry, especially if the material is patented and on the market, is that the recipient may patent an aspect of their material (e.g., a new use) that will block the provider and require them to obtain a license for their own material from the recipient. Finally, industry often fears that research on its material may reveal unfavorable properties that could jeopardize its ongoing development and commercialization efforts.

10.2 PRIOR STUDIES ON MTAS

Because they are among the simplest agreements and conceptually easy to understand, MTAs are often the subject of choice for science administrators, economists, legal scholars or social scientists to quantify and analyze. Thus, the literature includes several studies that consider MTAs from a policy, legal or technology transfer perspective.

A word of caution in this regard: While MTAs may appear simple, they can have complexity both within the contractual terms themselves or in their relationship to the overall scientific assets wielded by either academic or commercial institutions. In actual practice, MTAs are one among a networked series of agreements that are often linked and used to manage the complete portfolio of assets for a particular innovation. The portfolio or relevant parts of it are examined when licensing or collaborating. The materials transferred may have little or no commercial potential or they may be the cornerstone of a new therapeutic, diagnostic or platform technology. MTAs can, therefore, be simple contracts with few terms other than non-transfer and liability, or complex license agreements that specify funding, control of results and data as well as the disposition of future intellectual property rights. Analyses that view all MTAs as falling into one category necessarily struggle to make sense of the overall situation.

We will not discuss here the many studies that have described the changing environment of sharing materials and data since they have been reviewed elsewhere.[25] From the various studies and committee reports as well as views of seasoned technology transfer professionals two major strategies have been proposed to make material transfers more efficient: (1) Using standardized templates and (2) using repositories.

10.3 SOLUTIONS: STANDARDIZED AGREEMENTS

One of the early proposed solutions to the problem of delays was to use standardized MTAs with an agreed upon set of terms that would decrease negotiation time. As noted above the UBMTA, developed by the NIH and AUTM, was among the first such effort. The final version was published in the Federal Register on March 8, 1995, and AUTM agreed to be the official repository of signed agreements and manage the official list of signatories.[26]

Joyce Brinton, Harvard's former director of technology transfer, provided a concise history of the process leading to the 1995 UBMTA:

In the late1980s, there was a rising tide of concern about the impact of material transfer agreements (MTAs) on the research enterprise. A number of articles were written about the problem, faculty members were complaining, and technology transfer offices were feeling the heat. The NIH Office of Technology Transfer was receiving so many complaints that it convened a meeting in 1990 to discuss possible solutions. That meeting was held on the NIH campus and drew a considerable number of concerned technology transfer professionals and AUTM leaders. That

[25] Patrick L. Taylor, *Research Sharing, Ethics and Public Benefit*, 25 NATURE 398–401 (2007); Philip Mirowski, *Livin' with the MTA*, 46 MINERVA 317 (2008); Jane Nielsen et al., *Material Transfer Agreements and Institutional Processes*, in AUSTRALIAN BIOMEDICAL RESEARCH: MUST "MTA" EQUATE WITH "DELAY"?. Copy on file with authors.
[26] Uniform Biological Material Transfer Agreement: Discussion of Public Comments Received; Publication of the Final Format of the Agreement, 60 Fed. Reg., 12771 (Mar. 8, 1995). *See* www .govinfo.gov/content/pkg/FR-1995-03-08/pdf/95-5644.pdf.

was the beginning of the effort that resulted in the UBMTA. The goals of the participants in the effort were lofty – to develop an agreement or agreements that would simplify exchanges of biological materials among nonprofit institutions and, perhaps, even transfers from the for-profit sector to nonprofits.[27]

As of August 2019, 676 institutions (signatories) have agreed to the terms of the UBMTA. This means, in theory, that transfers of materials among these institutions could be accomplished under its terms. However, we and others have observed that, while the signatories may wish to use this as a first resort, not infrequently, as providers, some signatories offer MTAs that are not the UBMTA. Eisenberg mentioned this in 1999: "But although many universities have agreed in principle to the terms of this standard agreement, few seem.to use it when they send out their own research tools to other institutions." More recently, a survey of Australian universities notes that US universities do not want to use the UBMTA.[28]

In 1999, after the conclusion of the Working Group on Research Tools, the NIH Office of Technology Transfer proposed a simpler MTA template for use by its grantees and the research community. This was published in the Federal Register along with the Principles and Guidelines for Sharing Biomedical Research Resources.[29] The Simple Letter Agreement (SLA) for Transfer of Non-Proprietary Biological Material, is a one-page template that initially was proposed as nonnegotiable template for use by research institutions throughout the US. This agreement is now the default MTA for NIH intramural laboratories.

Some research consortia, recognizing the need for rapid sharing of materials to meet their goals, have implemented their own versions of a standardized MTA to reduce transaction costs. Among these are the Collaboration for AIDS Vaccine Discovery (CAVD; Bill and Melinda Gates Foundation) and the TB Drug Accelerator. Use of these agreements is limited to the respective consortia.

Even as these standardized MTAs were being implemented, there was a realization among some seasoned technology transfer professionals that this would not solve the problem. Indeed, after many working groups and recommendations, guidelines and templates, the problems associated with transfer of materials and research tools have not been solved and MTA numbers continue to grow. We and others have observed that today academic scientists are more accepting of MTAs than when they were first introduced, and TTOs have evolved strategies for handling this volume.[30]

[27] Joyce Brinton, *The Uniform Biological Material Transfer Agreement: Origin and Evolution*, www.autm.net/AUTMMain/media/ThirdEditionPDFs/V3/TTP_V3_P3_UBMTA_ex.pdf.
[28] Nielsen et al., *supra* note 25.
[29] Principles and Guidelines for Recipients of NIH Research Grants and Contracts on Obtaining and Disseminating Biomedical Research Resources, 64 Fed. Reg. 72090 (Dec. 23, 1999). See www.govinfo.gov/content/pkg/FR-1999-12-23/pdf/99-33292.pdf.
[30] Nielsen et al., *supra* note 25.

10.4 SOLUTION: REPOSITORIES

As discussed above, the standardization of MTA terms provides one avenue to address the transaction costs associated with MTAs. Repositories or biobanks provide another. The terms "biobank," "biorepository," "biospecimen resource" and "biological resource center" all refer to the facilities and related processes that govern the collection, processing and storage of materials.

Repositories can alleviate the pressure from MTAs for the following reasons: Materials can be deposited in a repository, relieving the burden of negotiating outgoing MTAs from the TTO and, often, the cost of producing and shipping the materials from the provider scientist. Because most repositories use standard MTAs for both depositing and requesting materials, they offer the potential to reduce or eliminate negotiations. Repositories provide an efficiency overall because those contributing to them and drawing from them agree to do so through material transfer agreements that for the most part permit no further negotiation.

MTAs play an important role in repositories because they govern both the taking in of materials by the repositories (incoming MTAs) and the shipping out of materials to recipients (outgoing MTAs). Repositories prefer to use a single non-negotiable MTA for each of these transactions but often feel pressure to modify them. Consequently there is an art to managing modifications to these agreements and a challenge to ensuring consistency between the incoming and outgoing MTAs for each material. If depositors wish to attach nonstandard conditions to their materials and the repository accepts these because they view the materials as critical for their users, these nonstandard terms will have to be reelected in the outgoing MTA for that particular material. As a repository grows it may accumulate restrictions on many materials, leading to many varieties of outgoing MTAs and detracting from the intended value of the repository. Some repositories that were working in a highly commercial research area such as that for AIDS drug development decided early on to allow depositors to provide materials under a limited number of options with controls over what can be done commercially with their materials; these fixed categories were reflected in their standard outgoing MTA.

As a world leader in biomedical research funding NIH recognized this need early on, and responded by establishing many repositories for the research community. The National Institute of Allergy and Infectious Disease (NIAID) at NIH manages twenty-three repositories that provide materials free of cost to scientists around the world. The National Cancer Institute (NCI) manages a set of repositories, many of which are tailored to meet the need of cancer researchers; these include repositories for Tumors and Tumor Cell Lines, Patient-Derived Bio-Models, Chemical Agents, Natural Products, Biologicals, mouse cancer models. Other institutes and centers of the NIH maintain many more repositories such as the Mutant Mouse Resource & Research Centers, one of the largest collections of spontaneous and induced mutant mouse strains and ES cell lines, the Drosophila Genomics Resource Center, National Natural Toxins Research Center, and Protein Structure Initiative Material Repository. Globally there are so many repositories that most scientists only know the ones in their area of specialization. The growth in number of repositories is reflected in the fact that NCI has created a specimen locator that will locate a specific specimen in global list of repositories (www.specimens.cancer.gov/).

Beyond NIH, the World Federation for Culture Collections (WFCC) is a Multidisciplinary Commission of the International Union of Biological Sciences (IUBS) and a Federation within the International Union of Microbiological Societies (IUMS). The WFCC is concerned with the collection, authentication, maintenance and distribution of cultures of microorganisms and cultured cells and operates as a clearing house for information on collections of microbiological specimens (www.wfcc.info/). An informal collection of global biobanks can be found at the Global Biobank Directory managed by volunteers (https://specimen central.com/biobank-directory/). Because there are so many repositories of varying sizes and with differing levels of expertise, organizations such as the International Society for Biosafety Research (ISBER) have arisen to addresses harmonization of scientific, technical, legal and ethical issues relevant to repositories of biological and environmental specimens (www.isber.org/).

To illustrate the genesis of repositories and how they function, we describe here several repositories established by NIAID. The NIH AIDS Reagent Program evolved from a small bank of HIV research materials into a unique worldwide resource of state-of-the art reagents to accelerate the study of HIV and other pathogens. Many of these reagents are not commercially available. Since the publication of the first catalog in 1988, listing sixty-two reagents from twenty contributors, the AIDS Reagent Program has grown significantly. It currently offers over 2,000 reagents from hundreds of contributors. Reagents are shipped to scientists all over the world. The value of the AIDS Reagent Program is evident from the diversity of registered users; close to 3,800 scientists from 65 countries are currently actively registered to receive reagents. Although the majority of registrants are scientists at academic institutions, many are also from private industry and the US Government. Since 1988, over 8,500 unique materials have been contributed, over 15,000 requests have been received, resulting in approximately 365 publications a year. The AIDS Reagent Program MTA allows depositors to submit materials with five options regarding commercial rights that range from no restrictions on commercial exploitation to prohibition of commercial use.

The Malaria Research and Reference Reagent Resource Center (MR4) facilitates malaria research by improving availability of parasite, vector and human reagents and standardized assays. The need for a centralized malaria research reagent source was identified at the International Conference on Malaria in Africa, Dakar, Senegal

TABLE 10.1 *NIH repositories (data as of 2017)*

Repository	AIDS Reagent Program	MR4	BEI Resources
Inception	1988	1998	2003
Unique materials contributed	>8,500	>1,200	>10,000
Requests in 2017	>15,000	1,600	6,700
Publications/yr	325	100	20
Countries of requesters	65	66	30
Registrants	>3,800	650	677

in 1997. MR4 was established by NIAID in 1998 via contract with the American Type Culture Collection. Malaria researchers have access to a centralized resource in MR4 that provides parasites, proteins, reagents and mosquitos for reference standards or to generate new renewable reagents. Over 600 labs worldwide have deposited or withdrawn from the repository for purposes of malaria research. MR4 is now part of the larger NIAID operated Biological and Emerging Infections Resources Program (BEI Resources Repository), which is a central repository that supplies organisms and reagents to the broad community of microbiology and infectious diseases researchers. It was most recently used to facilitate the sharing of scarce Zika virus samples across the global research community. This was crucial to support the development of vaccines and other medical counter measures, as well as diagnostic tests during the outbreak.

Some repositories such as Addgene have been very successful at sharing research materials such as plasmids via an efficient unmodified electronic MTA system.

10.5 TTO PERSPECTIVES AND TRANSACTION COSTS

As noted above, the adoption of MTAs and their increased use created concerns and complaints among the members of the research community. But the scientists were not alone: Technology transfer staff were unprepared and also struggling with the avalanche of MTAs. "University technology transfer professionals report that agreements presented for the transfer of research tools impose increasingly onerous terms. They say that the burden of reviewing and renegotiating each of a rapidly growing number of agreements for what used to be routine exchanges among scientists is overwhelming their limited resources."[31]

When an MTA is first received by an institution, it must be reviewed to determine whether it contains any clauses that conflict with the legal and policy guidelines for that institution. As discussed above these can differ widely depending on the institution or sector. If there is conflicting language, the terms must be negotiated, triggering exchanges between the negotiators that typically entail multiple iterations.

---

[31] Eisenberg, *supra* note 10.

Often the MTA is received by the scientist and forwarded to the TTO, and in these cases additional effort must be expended to locate a technology transfer counterpart at the other organization who has the authority to negotiate. A process of negotiation begins that may be prolonged if the other side does not want to make the changes, takes a long time to respond or there is a change in personnel during negotiation. If an impasse arises and there is a great need for the material, a TTO may need to obtain institutional approval for a policy deviation which can take time. Other times a TTO may need clarification on legal interpretation from its general counsel.

When the parties agree on terms, one of the two will generate a finalized original, often by printing and signing a paper version of the document. On receipt of the partially executed original, the second party must visually check to see if it has all the changes agreed upon and no new changes have been inadvertently introduced. Following this the document is signed by the other party. Depending on who signs for each party, that is, how high in the organization it needs to go, further delays may be added to the process.

Use of a standard MTA that is familiar to both parties obviates many of these steps and accelerates the process. It is worth reiterating that most organizations assign a low priority to MTAs, so these negotiations may be at the bottom of the list for a provider. Many private sector companies have a "take it or leave it" attitude, because they cannot justify the expenditure of costly legal time on MTA modifications. If these do not work out, then negotiations will have failed.

Another factor that contributes to varying times in agreement processing is the structure of the office handling these. TTOs are diverse in size, in staff expertise, responsibilities assigned and organizational structure. It should come as no surprise, therefore, that the way MTAs, or other technology transfer processes, are handled varies from office to office. A recent survey points out that even "a small jurisdiction such as Australia, reveals different hierarchical structures through which contracts must progress to execution," and that "Australian institutions have varying capacities to deal with MTAs promptly and efficiently, based on resourcing issues but also organizational makeup and levels of delegation."[32] Some offices have a single person assigned to handle MTAs, others have large numbers if not all of them handled by junior staff or trainees. Other TTOs, like ours, can have them distributed across their staff, to be handled along with the rest of the portfolio for a research laboratory.

Those TTOs that have a single person assigned to MTA processing may achieve faster processing because that individual is very familiar with the terms of MTAs in both their own as well as those of outside entities because they see more of them than if this was only one of their technology transfer activities. On the other hand, this person may also miss the significance and value of a material being transferred

---

[32] J. L. Nielsen, T. Whitton, and D. Nicol, *Material Transfer Agreements and Institutional Processes in Australian Biomedical Research: Must "MTA" Equate with "Delay"?* In preparation, copy on file with authors.

because there is a lack of context for the scientific and IP portfolios related to the activities of the providing laboratory.

Because a majority of MTAs can often be simple and follow standard language, TTOs often view MTAs as less complex agreements that are assigned to the most junior employees or trainees before they can move on to more complex agreements. However, as described previously, MTAs can be complex contracts and important tools for managing intellectual property assets to collaborate or commercialize technology. Seasoned TTOs recognize that MTAs could be the first step towards a larger collaboration between two organizations and that sometimes MTA discussions lead to the use, in the end, of an entirely different agreement. Our office works under the understanding that they need to be viewed in the context of the entire portfolio of an investigator and are managed by each portfolio manager along with the patents, licenses and other collaboration agreements.

Today, technology transfer officers negotiate more MTAs than ever and have better tools to track them, but they are still a significant resource sink. However, the negotiations are not as challenging as they once were, for at least two reasons: First, TTOs now see many standard agreements, and second, because in the past few decades TTOs and their partners have seen almost every variety of clause that can be in an MTA. Nonetheless, MTAs must be reviewed, and their terms often negotiated because there may always be language that is not acceptable.

In our view, MTAs will be a feature of the scientific process for the foreseeable future, and standard templates may alleviate the burden MTAs impose to a limited extent. MTAs must be reviewed carefully because they may create obligations for materials that are useful or critical for other larger projects. While it is often heard that the majority of MTAs are not important in practice, this determination is almost impossible to make without knowing much more about the material, its usefulness in that particular area of study and expertise at predicting its commercial future. These are labor-intensive activities, creating a tax on TTO resources that are already stretched. One of the most critical aspects of an MTA, understanding the value of and describing accurately the material to be shared, is underappreciated at this time.

There are other logistical challenges that TTOs face regarding the large numbers of these agreements; MTAs once executed are often forgotten. Katherine Ku noted more than a decade ago, "The biggest irony of all is that when there is a dispute about materials, often neither party can find the MTA because the dispute occurs many years later. The sheer burden of tracking, storage and retrieval is huge for everyone."[33] Mirowski also found that, "I have had some TTO officers in a reflective mood concede that they may have file cabinets full of ticking time bombs; but their tone has been that ignorance is bliss. No one has informed me that all their MTAs are neatly archived in an easy to retrieve electronic database somewhere."[34]

---

[33]   Katherine Ku and James Henderson, *The MTA—Rip It up and Start Again?*, 25 NATURE 721–22 (2007).
[34]   Mirowski, *supra* note 25.

TABLE 10.2 *NIAID MTAs by year*

Start Year	2016	2017	2018
Executed	784	793	815
Failed	61	58	62
Pending	10	25	48
Total	**855**	**876**	**925**

In the TTO office of the National Institute for Allergy and Infectious Diseases, out of approximately 900 MTA requests per year, about 90 percent are successfully negotiated and executed. Most are completed within the year while a few may drag out for a number of different reasons such as lack of response, inability to agree on terms, change in staff at either TTO and so forth. About half of the MTAs that come through this office are for incoming materials, but it is worth noting that a substantial portion of outgoing unmodified MTAs are not reviewed because the heads of various laboratories at NIAID are authorized to sign these. We can use NIH templates for approximately 70 percent of these transfers and a majority (~85 percent) of the exchanges are with US institutions.

Even today, after the implementation of standard MTAs and the realization of other efficiencies, they remain a significant part of the NIAID TTO workload.[35] Like other TTOs this office is charged with many responsibilities and limited resources and like other TTOs, we would rather allocate time and effort to areas that have a more significant scientific, public health or financial impact.

10.6 CONCLUSIONS

This chapter has described some of the components of the MTA negotiation process and the role of standard MTAs and repositories, and provided insights from a nationally and internationally significant TTO office into how they play out in practice.

MTAs will be part of the scientific research and development process for the foreseeable future and their number is only set to increase in that time. It is possible to speed up material transfers by using standard templates, repositories, delegation and other process engineering steps, but there will be a subset of agreements that are not amenable to these. It is important to keep in mind that some materials will have commercial value and may be linked to other intellectual property.

---

[35] John P. Walsh, Wesley M. Cohen, and Charlene Cho, *When Exclusivity Matters: Material versus Intellectual Property in Academic Biomedical Research*, 36 RES. POL'Y 1184, 1194 (2007).

The Pandemic Influenza Preparedness Framework as an Access and Benefit Sharing Mechanism

Anne Huvos, Steven A. Solomon, and Claudia Nannini[*]

11.1 INTRODUCTION

Infectious diseases have the ability to change over time due to pathogen mutation, making the need to have access to biological samples and associated data imperative for assessing the risk posed by the infectious agent and formulating effective diagnostics, medicines, and vaccines.[1] Influenza is a virus that causes disease in humans ranging from mild to lethal. It has a history of mutating quickly and unpredictably, in ways which may evade existing human immunities, and as such, a network of researchers is necessary to share knowledge between countries as to mutations, treatments, and preparedness. Since 1952, this network – known today as the Global Influenza Surveillance and Response System (GISRS) – has been coordinated by WHO.[2] The 153 laboratories in the system conduct year-round surveillance, monitor the evolution of viruses and provide recommendations as to which influenza viruses should be included in vaccines.[3] The system is structured around six WHO collaborating centers located in Australia, China, Japan, the UK and the US, four WHO Essential Regulatory Laboratories, 143 institutions recognized by WHO as national influenza centers (NICs) located in 115 countries as well as six H5 Reference Laboratories (some laboratories serve in several capacities). NICs are the backbone of the system as they collect specimens for the detection of influenza viruses through national surveillance networks. This system has been instrumental in keeping the world prepared for influenza pandemics as well as generating important medicines and non-pandemic or seasonal vaccines.

In 2011, an important adaptation was made to this system: the Pandemic Influenza Preparedness for the sharing of influenza viruses and access to vaccines and other benefits (PIP Framework). It is a landmark, innovative public health arrangement to

[*] The authors are staff members of the World Health Organization. The authors alone are responsible for the views expressed in this publication and they do not necessarily represent the decisions, policies or views of the World Health Organization.

[1] www.who.int/genomics/public/geneticdiseases/en/.
[2] WORLD HEALTH ORG., *Global Influenza Surveillance and Response System (GISRS)*, www.who.int /influenza/gisrs_laboratory/en/.
[3] www.who.int/influenza/pip/virus_sharing/gisrs_self_assessment.pdf.

increase global preparedness to respond to pandemic influenza and it brings together the 194 Member States of the World Health Organization, manufacturers involved in the influenza preparedness and response system, civil society organizations, other stakeholders, and, of course, the World Health Organization itself. Its guiding principles include transparency, partnership, and equity. WHO Member States negotiated the PIP Framework in response to two global needs: The need to ensure the timely and systematic sharing with GISRS of influenza viruses with pandemic potential to safeguard global public health on the one hand, and the need to ensure that benefits arising from such virus sharing were equitably shared with all countries, on the other.

The purpose of this chapter is to understand the PIP Framework as an "access and benefit sharing" mechanism as that concept has been understood in the context of international law. With the entry into force of the 2010 Nagoya Protocol on Access to Genetic Resources and the Fair and Equitable Sharing of Benefits Arising from their Utilization to the Convention on Biological Diversity (Nagoya Protocol) in 2014, the global community is now exploring the many ways that the Nagoya Protocol's mandates might be fulfilled. The PIP Framework provides rich experience from which to draw lessons. This chapter will outline the histories of both the PIP Framework and the Nagoya Protocol as they are relevant to human pathogens, explain the World Health Organization's analysis of the Nagoya Protocol's application to matters relevant to human health, and conclude with some observations relevant to the increasing relevance of digital sequence information (DSI) or genetic sequence data (GSD) which increasingly affects both the Nagoya Protocol's and the World Health Organization's legal mandates.

11.2 PANDEMIC INFLUENZA PREPAREDNESS FRAMEWORK

The GISRS facilitated virus sharing continuously between 1952 and late 2006. In that year, however, several countries affected by the highly pathogenic influenza virus A(H5N1), started to question the fairness of the system: While viruses were shared by countries, countries did not have access to resulting, life-saving vaccines at an affordable price. One country, Indonesia, suspended sharing its A(H5N1) viruses with the system.

The legal foundation for this critical move was the 1993 Convention on Biological Diversity (CBD), which provides that "the authority to determine access to genetic resources rests with the national governments and is subject to national legislation" (Article 15.1). In addition, the CBD provides that "access to genetic resources shall be subject to prior informed consent of the Contracting Party providing such resources" (Article 15.5). And finally, a key article of the Convention provides that any access granted "shall be on mutually agreed terms" (Article 15.4). Based on these core CBD principles, Indonesia asserted that it controlled access to samples collected in its territory, that no use of such samples by other parties (notably manufacturers) could occur without its prior informed consent, and that any use of such samples should produce benefits for Indonesia. Indonesia's Minister of Health, Dr Siti Fadilah Supari, called GISRS "unfair," drawing the world's attention to the issue.[4] WHO leaders met with Supari to discuss what to do about the issues raised in early 2007. "Indonesia's leadership alerted the international community to the needs of developing countries to benefit from sharing virus samples, including access to quality pandemic vaccines at affordable prices."[5] The PIP Framework was one of the long-term solutions developed to address the issue. It was adopted by the Sixty-fourth World Health Assembly in May 2011.[6]

The PIP Framework is structured around the two key issues at the heart of pandemic influenza preparedness and response: Virus sharing, which enables GISRS laboratories to assess the risk posed by specific viruses and develop candidate vaccine viruses, on the one hand, and benefit sharing, which ensures that vaccines and other critical pandemic response products will be available equitably among all countries in need when the next pandemic strikes. A set of standard material transfer agreements, known by their acronyms as "SMTA-1" and "SMTA-2" supports this structure.

As already mentioned, a key function of GISRS[7] is to assess the risk posed by influenza viruses with pandemic potential as well as assisting in the development of preparedness measures that result in the production of influenza vaccines.[8] In order to carry out these functions, GISRS laboratories regularly share viruses among themselves as different laboratories provide different analyses and expertise. The sharing of influenza viruses with pandemic potential among laboratories *within* GISRS is done under SMTA-1.[9]

If materials are sent to laboratories or entities *outside* GISRS, the SMTA-2 is used.[10] SMTA-2s are legally binding agreements concluded by the WHO with three different categories of entities: Influenza vaccine and antiviral manufacturers; manufacturers of other pandemic related products; and all other recipients of PIP biological materials (BM), including universities, research institutions, and biotech companies.[11] SMTA-2 are intended to save time when the next influenza

---

[4]   Indonesia to Resume Sharing H5N1 Avian Influenza Virus Samples Following a WHO Meeting in Jakarta, WORLD HEALTH ORG., www.who.int/mediacentre/news/releases/2007/pr09/en/.

[5]   Joint Statement from the Ministry of Health, Indonesia and the World Health Organization, *Sharing of Avian Influenza Viruses and Pandemic Vaccine Production*, WORLD HEALTH ORG., www.who.int /mediacentre/news/statements/2007/s02/en/.

[6]   Resolution WHA64.5 Pandemic Influenza Preparedness: Sharing of Influenza Viruses and Access to Vaccines and Other Benefits.

[7]   WORLD HEALTH ORG., *Global Influenza Surveillance and Response System (GISRS)*, www.who.int /influenza/gisrs_laboratory/en/.

[8]   *Virus Sharing*, WORLD HEALTH ORG., www.who.int/influenza/pip/virus_sharing/en/.

[9]   Pursuant to section 5.4.1 of the PIP Framework.

[10] Pursuant to section 5.4.2 of the PIP Framework.

[11] *Standard Material Transfer Agreements (SMTA 2)*, WORLD HEALTH ORG., www.who.int/influenza/pip/ benefit_sharing/smta2/en/. A list of all SMTA-2s concluded to date is available at www.who.int /influenza/pip/benefit_sharing/smta2_signed/en/.

pandemic occurs because each agreement conforms to the standard terms negotiated and adopted by 194 countries, and annexed to the PIP Framework itself. In the
case of manufacturers, those agreements provide options to provide to the WHO real
time access to pandemic products at the time of a pandemic (e.g. vaccines, antivirals, diagnostics) as well as the possibility of licensing intellectual property and
technology.[12] Manufacturers select benefit sharing options based on their nature and
capacities. As an example, influenza vaccine manufacturers are expected to commit
to provide to the WHO at least 10 percent of their future pandemic vaccine
production.

As well, the PIP Framework provides for a "partnership contribution," that is annual
payments to the WHO from influenza vaccine, diagnostic, and pharmaceutical
manufacturers that use GISRS.[13] The funds are used by the WHO to support work
to increase preparedness and response capacities in countries that require such
support. The partnership contribution is based on trust and use of GISRS. The current
annual amount contributed is US$ 28 million and as of September 2019, US$
191 million have been collected by the WHO.

The Pandemic Influenza Preparedness Framework is therefore a unique and
innovative partnership that involves Member States, GISRS, industry, civil society,
and the WHO in a system that provides broad access to necessary research inputs
while also ensuring the equitable sharing of benefits resulting therefrom, both
through SMTA-2s and through the partnership contribution.

There are certain unique characteristics related to influenza that may limit the
applicability of the PIP Framework model in other areas where pathogen sharing is
not directly related to commercial revenue from a medical countermeasure such as
vaccines. Influenza is a vaccine preventable disease that affects all countries,
every year. The virus's high volatility requires yearly development of a vaccine that
is specific to the hemisphere in which a season is occurring. Thus, manufacturers
produce two different vaccines every year: One to respond to epidemics in the
northern hemisphere, and another for the southern hemisphere. These vaccines
are then used by the public health sectors of countries as part of their influenza
prevention and control strategies.

11.3 THE CONVENTION ON BIOLOGICAL DIVERSITY AND THE NAGOYA PROTOCOL

The basis in international law for countries to claim sovereignty over viruses (and
other genetic resources) is located in the Convention on Biological Diversity,
a treaty that resulted from several decades of international concern with the environment. In 1972, the UN held the first of many global conferences, on the Human

---

[12]   *Id.* at 15.
[13]   Pursuant to section 6.14.3 of the PIP Framework.

Environment at Stockholm, Sweden.[14] In the decade after the 1972 conference, scientists and nongovernmental organizations had elevated the issue of biodiversity preservation.[15] In 1987, the governing council of the United Nations Environmental Programme created a working group to explore the possibility of developing a legally binding treaty to protect biological resources.[16] In 1991, formal multilateral negotiations began on a Convention for Biological Diversity.

Eventually these preparatory meetings culminated in the 1992 UN Conference on Environmental and Development (or Earth Summit) held in June 1992 in Rio De Janeiro, the result of which included the Rio Declaration, the Convention on Biological Diversity, the UN Framework Convention on Climate Change, and the UN Convention to Combat Desertification. Article 15 of the CBD required states parties to take the necessary measures "with the aim of sharing in a fair and equitable way the results of research and development and the benefits arising from the commercial and other utilization of genetic resources with the Contracting Party providing such resources," a phrase that gave rise to a great deal of uncertainty even as it shaped national laws.[17] Before 2010, CBD Article 15 had been largely guided by the nonbinding Bonn Guidelines on Access to Genetic Resources and Fair and Equitable Sharing of the Benefits Arising Out of Their Utilization. Beginning with the seventh meeting of the Conference of the Parties to the CBD in 2004, parties to the treaty began the process of establishing a voluntary, but binding, protocol to give effect to CBD Article 15. The result was the 2010 Nagoya Protocol, which entered into force 12 October, 2014.

As an implementing treaty of the CBD, the Nagoya Protocol clarifies the CBD's access and benefit sharing provisions (ABS). The Nagoya Protocol clarified that parties seeking to acquire and use genetic resources from states parties are expected to obtain prior informed consent (PIC) for access to those resources, and also reach mutually agreed terms (MAT) for their use and sharing of benefits.[18] The stated objectives of the Nagoya Protocol – "the fair and equitable sharing of the benefits arising from the utilization of genetic resources, including by the appropriate access to genetic resources ... " – aligns in significant part with the objectives of the PIP Framework:

> The objective of the Pandemic Influenza Preparedness Framework is to improve pandemic influenza preparedness and response, and strengthen the protection against the pandemic influenza by improving and strengthening the WHO global influenza surveillance and response system ("WHO GISRS"), with the objective of a fair, transparent, equitable, efficient, effective system for, on an equal footing: (i)

[14] http://legal.un.org/avl/ha/dunche/dunche.html.
[15] Id.
[16] UNEP Resolution 14/26, adopted in 1987.
[17] CBD Article 15.
[18] *Information Provided by Parties to the Nagoya Protocol on the National Implementation of Article 8(b) and Other Relevant Provisions of the Protocol*, CONVENTION ON BIOLOGICAL DIVERSITY, 2018 at 2 www .who.int/influenza/pip/NoteES_Implementation_NP_8b.pdf.

the *sharing* of H5N1 and other influenza *viruses with human pandemic potential*; and (ii) *access to* vaccines and sharing of other *benefits*.[19]

The Nagoya Protocol provides a framework through which states parties adopt their own implementing legislation as to prior informed consent (PIC) and mutually agreed terms (MAT).[20] While these principles are binding and broad, the details of implementing them are left to domestic legislation.[21] Therefore, unless one of the Nagoya Protocol's mechanisms addressed to special international instruments or international cooperation (more fully addressed below in Section 11.4) is used, the default mechanism is a bilateral negotiation between a genetic resources user and a provider country under the law of the latter.

11.4 THE NAGOYA PROTOCOL AND PIP FRAMEWORK: THE WHO'S ANALYSIS

In light of the potential relevance of the Nagoya Protocol for activities undertaken by the World Health Organization, the Executive Board at its 138th session in January 2016 considered the report of the First Meeting of the Review Committee on the Role of the International Health Regulations (2005).[22] During the discussions, it was agreed that the Secretariat would prepare a study, for presentation to the Board at its 140th session, in order to analyze how implementation of the Nagoya Protocol might affect the sharing of pathogens, and the potential public health implications.[23]

A central conclusion of the study was that the Nagoya Protocol has implications for the public health response to infectious diseases, including influenza; and that these implications include opportunities to advance both public health and principles of fair and equitable sharing of benefits.[24] However, implementation of the Protocol generates potential legal uncertainty which has the potential for slowing or limiting the sharing of human pathogens, which in turn could delay public health risk assessment and the development of medical countermeasures, such as vaccines, diagnostics, and antivirals.[25] Thus implications may be positive, negative, or mixed depending on how the Protocol's provisions are implemented by each country.

The WHO study concluded that access to pathogens should be governed by approaches that (1) promote the timely sharing of pathogens and associated data for

---

[19] *Pandemic Influenza Preparedness Framework for the Sharing of Influenza Viruses and Access to Vaccines and Other Benefits*, WORLD HEALTH ORGANIZATION, SECTION 2 at 6. https://apps.who.int/iris/bitstream/ handle/10665/44796/9789241503082_eng.pdf;jsessionid=55DAD544F83899B8F21EF7E638D842D9? sequence=1. Emphasis added.

[20] *Implementation of the Nagoya Protocol and Pathogen Sharing: Public Health Implications*, WORLD HEALTH ORG. SECRETARIAT (2016) at 14.

[21] *Id.*

[22] *Id.* at 5.

[23] www.who.int/influenza/pip/2016-review/NagoyaStudyAdvanceCopy_full.pdf?ua=1.

[24] Document EB140/15, paragraph 13.

[25] www.who.int/influenza/pip/2016-review/NagoyaStudyAdvanceCopy_full.pdf?ua=1.

global health purposes and (2) promote the fair and equitable sharing of resulting benefits (both monetary and non-monetary). These conclusions are consistent with the PIP Framework and they are enabled by several provisions of the Nagoya Protocol including Article 4.4's provision for specialized international instruments, Article 8's provisions regarding health emergencies, and Article 19 and 20's provisions for international collaboration.

Article 4 of the Nagoya Protocol covers the relationship between the protocol and other international agreements and instruments.[26] Article 4 provides that the Protocol will not apply to certain specific genetic resources if they are "covered by another specialized international instrument that is consistent with, and does not run counter to, the objectives of the CBD and Nagoya Protocol."[27] Article 4 of the Nagoya Protocol provides in pertinent part:

> 4.3. This Protocol shall be implemented in a mutually supportive manner with other international instruments relevant to this Protocol. Due regard should be paid to useful and relevant ongoing work or practices under such international instruments and relevant international organizations, provided that they are supportive of and do not run counter to the objectives of the Convention and this Protocol.
>
> 4.4. This Protocol is the instrument for the implementation of the access and benefit-sharing provisions of the Convention. Where a specialized international access and benefit-sharing instrument applies that is consistent with, and does not run counter to the objectives of the Convention and this Protocol, this Protocol does not apply for the Party or Parties to the specialized instrument in respect of the specific genetic resource covered by and for the purpose of the specialized instrument.[28]

The foundational principles of fairness and equity that are at the heart of the PIP Framework[29] closely align with those that underpin the CBD and the Nagoya Protocol, and in this manner the PIP Framework appears to provide a possible model for how such a specialized international instrument might work. Indeed, it is worth noting that, within the European Union, the PIP Framework was recognized as a specialized international access and benefit sharing instrument for influenza viruses with pandemic potential, within the meaning of Article 4.4 of the Nagoya Protocol.[30] That said, as mentioned above, the replicability of the PIP Framework for pathogens other than influenza, would need careful consideration due to the unique nature of influenza in public health.

---

[26] *Implementation of the Nagoya Protocol and Pathogen Sharing: Public Health Implications*, WORLD HEALTH ORG. SECRETARIAT (2016) at 24.

[27] *Id.*

[28] http://www.cbd.int/abs/text/articles/default.shtml?sec=abs-04.

[29] See PIP Framework section 1.

[30] Regulation (EU) No 511/2014 of the European Parliament and of the Council of 16 April 2014, preambular paragraph 16.

Article 8(b) of the Nagoya Protocol provides that in the development and implementation of its access and benefit sharing legislation or regulatory requirements, each Party shall:

> pay due regard to cases of present or imminent emergencies that threaten or damage human, animal or plant health, as determined nationally or internationally. Parties may take into consideration the need for expeditious access to genetic resources and expeditious fair and equitable sharing of benefits arising out of the use of such genetic resources, including access to affordable treatments by those in need, especially in developing countries.[31]

Some Parties to the Nagoya Protocol appear to be attentive to Article 8's objectives. In a recent survey conducted by the CBD, out of the seventy-five countries that submitted a report, thirty-nine parties and three non-parties reported having paid due regard to cases of present or imminent emergencies that threaten or damage human, animal or plant health, while thirty parties and three non-parties reported not having done so.[32] It is of high priority to the WHO that all parties address the need for rapid pathogen sharing during public health emergencies to facilitate and accelerate development of critical response products such as diagnostics, medicines, and vaccines. Concomitantly, measures to ensure the fair and equitable access to such response products by all countries in need, must also be developed.

By its nature, the Nagoya Protocol seeks to facilitate international cooperation and to promote measures which facilitate the realization of PIC and MAT objectives. Article 19 provides that:

1. Each Party shall encourage, as appropriate, the development, update and use of sectoral and cross-sectoral model contractual clauses for mutually agreed terms.
2. The Conference of the Parties serving as the meeting of the Parties to this Protocol shall periodically take stock of the use of sectoral and cross-sectoral model contractual clauses.

Article 20 provides that:

1. Each Party shall encourage, as appropriate, the development, update and use of voluntary codes of conduct, guidelines and best practices and/or standards in relation to access and benefit-sharing.
2. The Conference of the Parties serving as the meeting of the Parties to this Protocol shall periodically take stock of the use of voluntary codes of conduct, guidelines and best practices and/or standards and consider the adoption of specific codes of conduct, guidelines and best practices and/or standards.

---

[31] *Implementation of the Nagoya Protocol and Pathogen Sharing: Public Health Implications*, WORLD HEALTH ORG. SECRETARIAT (2016) at 21.

[32] www.cbd.int/doc/c/d59c/1f59/360a556de30e9e7026b82bae/np-mop-03-inf-04-en.pdf.

The Nagoya Protocol thus aims to facilitate prior informed consent and mutually agreed terms through model contract clauses and through codes of conduct, guidelines, and best practices, many of which may incorporate public health protection priorities.[33] Parties to the agreement are required to monitor the implementation of obligations and report to the governing body, the Conference of the Parties to the Convention of Biological Diversity (COP-MOP).[34]

The study ultimately concludes that the Protocol's goals are well drafted and thought through, with a balance between expeditious and fair sharing of genetic material and the resulting products. However, this is based on the actual wording of the provisions and review and discussions with respondents that have utilized the Protocol, not from studies of the effects of implementation of the Protocol itself. For now, much is still uncertain and it is unclear what can and cannot be covered.[35]

11.5 DIGITAL SEQUENCE INFORMATION (DSI) OR GENETIC SEQUENCE DATA (GSD)

One of the technological advances that has complicated implementation of the PIP Framework and the Nagoya Protocol is the increasing use of genetic sequence data (GSD) or digital sequence information (DSI)[36] to achieve many of the purposes that use of tangible genetic resources formerly achieved. Through this process, viral samples can be analyzed as DNA and RNA sequences, and shared as information, rather than material.[37] GSD enables researchers to access the "instructions" of the virus by breaking down its components to the correct sequence, allowing to reassemble these components for digital testing of the DNA and RNA viral strains without the need for the physical viral sample at all.[38] In this connection, databases such as Genbank, the Global Initiative on Sharing All Influenza Data (GISAID), and similar databases play a key role in enabling and promoting the international sharing of all influenza virus sequences.[39]

The PIP Framework was developed during a time when the sharing of GSD was important but not sufficiently understood at a systematic level to be incorporated

---

[33] Worku Yifru, *Nagoya Protocol and Public Health*, SECRETARIAT OF THE CONVENTION ON BIOLOGICAL DIVERSITY, 2018 at 6, www.who.int/influenza/CBD_NP_PH.pdf.

[34] Facilitating Access and Benefitsharing (ABS) for Pathogens to Support Public Health, World Health Org., 2018www.who.int/influenza/ABS_Workshop_Report_7Sep_hyperlinks.pdf at 5.

[35] *See generally, Implementation of the Nagoya Protocol and Pathogen Sharing: Public Health Implications*, WORLD HEALTH ORG. SECRETARIAT (2016).

[36] While in this chapter the terms GSD and DSI are used interchangeably, there is no consensus on what DSI covers and there are many discussions on this matter in the CBD context.

[37] See generally https://jvi.asm.org/content/jvi/84/5/2245.full.pdf Vol. 84 No. 5, 2245 at 2252.

[38] Se *Implementation of the Nagoya Protocol and Pathogen Sharing: Public Health Implications*, WORLD HEALTH ORG. SECRETARIAT (2016) at 13.

[39] The PIP Framework itself recognizes "that greater transparency and access concerning influenza virus genetic sequence data us important to public health and there is a movement towards the use of public-domain or public-access databases such as Genbank and GISAID respectively" (Section 5.2.2 of the PIP Framework).

TABLE 11.1

Type of Pathogen	Falls within the PIP Framework ABS?	Is it a genetic resource under the Nagoya Protocol?	Is there an existing multilateral mechanism to "fulfill" Nagoya Protocol requirements/ objectives?
IVPP (Influenza Viruses with human pandemic potential)	Yes	Yes	Yes, PIP, in the EU which recognized PIP as a "specialized international instrument" under Article 4.4.
GSD IVPP	Yes and No	TBD	Yes and No
Seasonal Influenza	No	Yes	No
GSD Seasonal Influenza	No	TBD	No
Other pathogens	No	Yes	No
GSD Other pathogens	No	TBD	No

into the agreement. The PIP Framework suggested that Member States share GSD in a timely manner, stressing the interests in protecting public health.[40] Now, GSD has become a far more central aspect of research facilitated by the PIP Framework.[41] As Table 11.1 below illustrates, this same phenomenon may be true for many genetic resources that are digitally analyzed and the resulting information shared.

The World Health Organization's position with respect to DSI mirrors that for pathogen sharing generally:

> WHO believes that DSI from pathogens is a global public health good that should be widely available to all; in addition, benefits derived from use of DSI should be shared equitably with all, without impeding the rapid, timely and broad sharing of sequences for disease control, prevention and preparedness.[42]

11.6 CONCLUSION

This chapter has endeavored to analyze the PIP Framework as a unique, international, normative instrument with relevance to the Nagoya Protocol,

---

[40] *Pandemic Influenza Preparedness Framework for the Sharing of Influenza Viruses and Access to Vaccines and Other Benefits*, WORLD HEALTH ORG., 2011 at 12 and 13.

[41] www.cbd.int/abs/nagoya-protocol/signatories/default.shtml.

[42] *Comments by the World Health Organization on the Draft Factfinding and Scoping Study "The Emergence and Growth of Digital Sequence Information in Research And Development : Implications for the Conservation and Sustainable Use of Biodiversity, and Fair and Equitable Benefit Sharing,"* WORLD HEALTH ORG., 2017.

including its legally binding standard material transfer agreements, its approach to GSD, and its balance between virus sharing and benefit sharing. Article 4 of the Nagoya Protocol obviously provides the possibility of many specialized international instruments, and many of the PIP Framework components may be relevant.[43]

In the context of human pathogens, bilateral negotiations between users and provider countries allow flexibility in the formation of the terms and contracts created between the two; they also allow for more negotiation and the time, money, and resources expended in doing so. This bilateral approach, however, is not supportive of a common, multilateral approach that is needed to efficiently and equitably address a public health threat.[44] It is time-consuming to find time for parties to meet, discuss, negotiate, agree on terms, and execute an agreement acceptable to both parties, all under stringent time considerations that exist when there is a public health emergency. For influenza vaccine production, for example, there is a six-month cycle for the manufacture of seasonal influenza vaccine, suggesting that if bilateral agreements between users and provider countries for access to viruses were to be required, there would be significant delays in availability of the vaccine with concomitant increases in morbidity and mortality.[45] Those delays are also likely to mean lower rates of immunization.[46]

Bilateral agreements are not necessarily scalable as different users and provider countries may have significantly different interests. As well, such agreements may not build the trust necessary for a broader response to disease threats. By their nature they are exclusive rather than inclusive.

As for the World Health Organization, it remains committed to studying the intersection of its work and the Nagoya Protocol, and to implementing partnerships that work in both contexts. In May 2019, the World Health Assembly met to discuss these and many other issues that arise at the junction between implementation of the Nagoya Protocol and the work undertaken by the World Health Organization. Following the Secretariat's report in 2016, the Director-General urged those implementing the Nagoya Protocol such as member states, international organizations and the CBD Secretariat to maintain a transparent dialogue with Nagoya Protocol stakeholders.

---

[43] *Implementation of the Nagoya Protocol and Pathogen Sharing: Public Health Implications*, WORLD HEALTH ORG. SECRETARIAT (2016) at 19.

[44] Implementation of the Nagoya Protocol and Pathogen Sharing: Public Health Implications, CONVENTION ON BIOLOGICAL DIVERSITY, Nov 2016. www.cbd.int/doc/meetings/abs/np-mop-02/informa tion/np-mop-02-inf-12-en.pdf.

[45] *Id* at 19.

[46] Facilitating Access and Benefitsharing (ABS) for Pathogens to Support Public Health, World Health Org., 2018 www.who.int/influenza/ABS_Workshop_Report_7Sep_hyperlinks.pdf at 6 and 7.

The Health Assembly requested the Director-General to broaden engagement with Member States, the Secretariat of the Convention on Biological Diversity, relevant international organizations and relevant stakeholders, to provide information on current pathogen-sharing practices and arrangements, the implementation of access and benefit-sharing measures, as well as the potential public health outcomes and other implications.[47]

---

[47] *World Health Assembly Update, 28 May 2019*, WORLD HEALTH ORG., www.who.int/news-room/detail/28-05-2019-world-health-update-28-may-2019.

Conclusion

Gian Luca Burci

The contributions in this volume represent an effort to outline a specific problem that is relatively new in international infectious disease research: How to balance the rights that written agreements for sharing pathogens and data allocate to parties (including allocations imposed by law), and how to minimize the burden that the agreement formation process itself imposes upon research, especially during public health emergencies. That outline is necessarily filled in with substance drawn from incredibly diverse legal regimes: International documents and agreements, national legislation, EU-level and regional frameworks and regulations, contracts that are expressed in MTAs, and soft norms.[1] Researchers and institutions also tend to adopt their own norms and practices. Still, this volume covers the most relevant trends and aspects concerning the infectious disease research field as it has evolved since the Convention on Biological Diversity.

Where do the foregoing chapters leave us in terms of the variables and factors affecting the transfer of samples and data for purposes of infectious disease research? And, as urgently, where are the critical gaps and what do the current problems and solutions posed herein suggest in terms of future directions of infectious disease research and accompanying legal management of those directions? In this concluding chapter, I will reach some general conclusions on the intersection between pathogen and data sharing on the one hand, and the equitable concerns of various parties on the other.

The preceding chapters confirm the analysis by Sam Halabi and Rebecca Katz in the introduction about the content and state of pathogen sharing and the challenges the old system now faces. The international sharing of pathogens has been relatively unregulated until the last three or so decades. As Michelle Rourke, Michael Mowatt, and Mukul Ranjan detail, it was previously based on informal collaboration among scientists, who shared out of a sense of integrity for the scientific process.

The 1992 UN Biodiversity Convention (CBD) provided for sovereign control over genetic resources and aimed at preserving biodiversity, regulating access, and ensuring the sharing of benefits with source countries. The biodiversity regime

---

[1] Gian Luca Burci, *Global Health Law: Present and Future*, in Gian Luca Burci and Brigit Toebes (eds.), RESEARCH HANDBOOK ON GLOBAL HEALTH LAW (2018).

was not as a general matter forged with public health foremost in mind; the two systems ignored each other until developing countries invoked the CBD during the 2005 global avian influenza pandemic as the legal basis to stop sharing viruses without a clear guarantee of benefits.[2] In Ben Krohmal's chapter, he shows with one of the most important early surveys done on the issue, that the sentiment expressed by governments during the avian influenza episode was broadly shared by researchers in developing countries as well. This episode led to the adoption in 2011 of a multilateral framework coordinated by WHO for sharing pandemic flu viruses and benefits (PIP Framework). As Anne Huvos, Steve Solomon, and Claudia Nannini argue, this approach may offer valuable experiences for other pathogens beyond influenza.

The 2010 Nagoya Protocol to the CBD regulates, in detail, the sharing of benefits arising from the utilization of genetic resources and adopts a bilateral approach in contrast with the multilateral cooperative approach required for public health. The Protocol has 118 parties and there is evidence that it is affecting virus sharing, most disquietingly for seasonal influenza. Brian Bird's chapter provides some sense of how expansive the research is that may be governed by laws adopted pursuant to the Nagoya Protocol or even the determinations by sovereign governments that research activities should be informed by its spirit, even if no national law yet applies. Even though the Protocol sets clear default rules and has a number of safeguards that could address health concerns, like special considerations for health under Article 8 or a specialized international instrument under Article 4.4, there is still considerable uncertainty with respect to its implementation.

A separate issue concerns genetic sequence technology that turns biological samples into computer files that can be freely accessed in public databases and turned back into a real virus in a lab. This technology is spreading rapidly and can sideline the PIP Framework and the Nagoya Protocol, both grounded on accessing physical biological material. The chapters by Ben Berkman, Haley Sullivan, Sam Halabi, Rebecca Katz and Joshua Teperowski Monrad carry the implications of expanded genetic research further, highlighting the ethical and biosecurity risks that accompany increased research efforts in low- and middle-income countries.

While much needs to be clarified, both WHO and the CBD/Nagoya governance are working and collaborating to reconcile two very different mechanisms and address uncertainties, in particular the treatment of genetic sequencing, how public health priorities can be safeguarded within the CBD/Nagoya framework, and whether the PIP Framework model is feasible beyond pandemic influenza. However, political consensus is elusive for the moment and the two communities involved do not always speak the same language.

---

[2]   Gian Luca Burci, *Sharing Pathogens and Medicines: Keys to Global Health Security*, May 22, 2019, available at https://graduateinstitute.ch/communications/news/sharing-pathogens-and-medicines-keys-global-health-security.

For example, in 2018, the WHA, the governing body of the World Health Organization, considered a five-year global strategic plan (2018–23) to "improve public health preparedness and response on the international spread of disease, following its annual debate on the implementation of the International Health Regulations (2005)."[3] The plan and its implementation are going to be essential for the achievement of the WHO's strategic priority, reflected in the WHO's Thirteenth General Programme of Work. That Programme aims to better protect one billion people from health emergencies by 2023 and, together with the implementation of other relevant instruments negotiated under UN auspices, work towards achieving Sustainable Development Goal Three ("Ensure healthy lives and promote well-being for all at all ages").

At the end of an intense debate, the Health Assembly adopted decision WHA71 (15) on May 26, 2018. That plan does not specifically address the recommendation from elsewhere in the WHO that it should champion the open and equitable sharing of information on public health risks, including the sharing of biological samples and gene sequence data during public health emergencies. This is an issue of urgent importance for the timely development of medicines, vaccines, and diagnostics in light of the Nagoya Protocol. Because the Protocol advises users who wish to access genetic resources to obtain the prior informed consent (PIC) of the provider country and negotiate and agree on the terms and conditions of access and utilization of this resource through the establishment of mutually agreed terms (MAT), the objective of the Plan and the Protocol are thus in tension.

There is no visible momentum for a new dedicated treaty on this issue, thus the priority will be to coordinate the existing regimes with full consideration for the need to ensure both equity and global health security and the considerable potential for synergy between them. The possible channels for this coordination are identified in Part III of the book. Sherry Brett-Major carefully dissects material transfer agreements and identifies where disputes are likely to arise and how to avoid them. Mukul Ranjan and Michael Mowatt outline successful uses of standardized agreements and repositories that facilitate transfers of research inputs, especially in specific contexts like emergencies or for specific diseases like malaria. Writing from the perspective of official government responders in the context of infectious disease emergencies, Maria Julia Marinissen (US), Ruvani Chandrasekera (US), John Simpson (UK), Theodore Kuschak (Canada), and Lauren Barna (US) analyze how existing international health security partnerships like the Global Health Security Initiative may be used to facilitate transfers of pathogens and related information. Anne Huvos, Steven Solomon, and Claudia Nannini analyze the lessons that may be taken from the PIP Framework, as well as the potential importance of genetic sequence data or

---

[3] Gian Luca Burci and Jakob Quirin, *Implementation of the International Health Regulations (2005): Recent Developments at the World Health Organization*, 22 ASIL INSIGHTS available at www.asil.org/insights/volume/22/issue/13/implementation-international-health-regulations-2005-recent-developments.

digital sequence data, which raise novel questions for current law, both national and international.

Together, these contributions effectively outline the most important issues facing the public health priority for sharing pathogens and data. Standard agreements, repositories, the appropriate expansion of the PIP Framework, more informed negotiators and scientists, and current networks for global health security may certainly serve as part of constructing the balance between the need for sharing on the one hand, and the demands for equitable distribution of benefits on the other.[4] As Alexandra Phelan reminds us, what is at stake is fundamentally a matter of human rights, and should be understood as such. It would be sadly ironic if an international legal regime aiming at the conservation and equitable management of a shrinking pool of genetic resources compromised international scientific collaboration, the benefits resulting from that collaboration, and ultimately the protection of the health of humankind.

---

[4] Eric W. Welch, Federica Fusi, Sélim Louafi, and Michael Siciliano, *Genetic Resource Policies in International Collaborative Research for Food and Agriculture: A Study of USAID-Funded Innovation Labs*, 15 GLOBAL FOOD SECURITY 33–42 (2017); Gurdial Singh Nijar, Sélim Louafi, and Eric W. Welch, *The Implementation of the Nagoya ABS Protocol for the Research Sector: Experience and Challenges*, 17 INTERNATIONAL ENVIRONMENTAL AGREEMENTS: POLITICS, LAW AND ECONOMICS 607–21 (2017); Claire Lajaunie and Calvin Wai-Loon Ho, *Pathogens Collections, Biobanks and Related-Data in a One Health Legal and Ethical Perspective*, 1 PARASITOLOGY 2 (2017).

Index

Access and Benefit Sharing (ABS), xvii, xxi, 9, 11, 14, 19, 22, 23, 26, 28, 156, 164
actionability
and the return of incidental findings during genetic research, 78, 79–81, 82, 83, 84, 89
actionability at the participant's research setting level" (ASPRL)
and the return of incidental findings in genetic research, 80
Africa Centres for Disease Control and Prevention (Africa CDC), 109
African Charter on Human and Peoples' Rights, 124
Agreement on Trade Related Aspects of Intellectual Property (TRIPS), xix, 9, 14, 34, 35
Alphamed Pharmaceuticals v. Arriva Pharmaceuticals, 152
American Type Culture Collection v. Coleman, 152
annexed research sites, 4
antivirals, 6, 11, 16, 17, 128
Arizona Board of Regents v. Seattle Genetics, 149
Ass'n for Molecular Pathology v. Myriad Genetics Inc., 569 U.S. 576 (2013), 34, 35, 43
Association of University Technology Managers (AUTM), 178
authorship
of scientific publications, 48, 49, 50, 51, 154

Bacillus anthracis
anthrax, 100
bats
and emerging infectious diseases, 52, 57, 62, 63, 64, 68, 69
and sample collection, 69
Bavarian Nordic v. Acambis, 149
Bayh-Dole Act, 176, 177, 184
biobank, 5, 19, 102, 110, 165, 166, 187, 188

Biological and Toxin Weapons Convention (BWC), 103, 105, 106
biological sciences
subdisciplines of, 184
biopiracy, 5, 10, 21, 23, 27, 41
bioprospecting, 14, 34
BioZulua
Venezuela biodiversity project, 15
Bonn Guidelines on Access to Genetic Resources and Fair and Equitable Sharing of the Benefits Arising Out of Their Utilization, 10
Brazil, 5, 9, 14, 16, 18, 91, 92, 168, 169, 180
BRCA 1, 78, 80
genetic predisposition for breast cancer, 80, 84–87
bushmeat
and emerging infectious diseases, 59

Cancer Genetics v. Kreatech Technology, 149
Cech Report, 179
Chan, Margaret, 42, 162
Charter of Economic Rights and Duties of States, 7
Chatham House Centre on Global Health Security, 111
Christison v. Biogen Idec, 149
Cold Spring Harbor
and open scientific sharing, 175
commodities, 7, 38
common heritage, 4, 23, 35, 37, 43
Convention for Biological Diversity, 8
Convention on Biological Diversity
and inclusion of viruses, 37
and U.S. support during negotiations, 35
Article 15, xviii, xxi, 10, 121
Article 16, xviii, xxi, 14
Article 2, xxi, 8, 9, 10, 35–36, 205, 206
history of, 22, 35–36
cooperative research agreements, 139

CPSIA information can be obtained
at www.ICGtesting.com
Printed in the USA
LVHW012333020820
662197LV00005B/86